IB Economics Answer Book (tried & tested)

Standard & Higher Level

by Dipak Khimji & John Evans-Klock

ISBN: 1523706376
ISBN-13: 978-1523706372

–1 ACKNOWLEDGMENTS

This workbook and the accompanying answer book are dedicated to all the students that we have served over the last 30 years and to our better halves Christine Evans-Klock and Bina Khimji as well as Esha Khimji who have continuously supported us during the writing of these books. A big thank you goes out to Samarth Agarwal for his invaluable help in sorting out the graphics and layout.

In addition, Mani Amini (house), Chrystina Angeline (factory) and the Swiss Confederation (bus) are thanked for letting us use their symbols to make the diagrams prettier. Delve Fonts are thanked for allowing the use of their very-readable font family *Overpass* in the diagrams.

CONTENTS

NOTE: Asterisks *, **, denote progressively challenging questions.
'h' denotes higher level questions only

0 AIMS

For the student the workbook provides an opportunity to put in practice material covered in class by the teacher. It is meant to be a proactive tool to help consolidate detailed knowledge of the IB economics course and can help in preparation for class tests as well as the final IB exam. Students are encouraged to write in the margins, add notes and doodle to customise the workbook. Students at the International School of Geneva have worked through the exercises and have helped to refine the material.

For the teacher this answer book carries all the answers to the questions as well as detailed explanations to the evaluation questions. The evaluation questions can be set as mini essays in class and for homework to enhance the students' essay writing skills specifically for the IB examination. The other questions provide a way of ensuring students have adequate knowledge, analysis and evaluation skills to approach IB questions. The workbook can act as a record of student progress in class and at home. Each chapter is designed to develop knowledge, analysis and evaluation skills. It is important to note that the aim of this workbook was not to address specifically any single IB paper but rather to fully develop the necessary skills required in IB economics. The questions set, vary in difficulty and cater to the needs of students of all abilities. Asterisks, * and ** are used to point out challenging questions. Questions for Higher level only are marked by 'h'. All the other non-marked questions are part of the core syllabus.

For parents the workbook is aimed to close the gap between what is being taught in class and the work being done by the student.

1 THE FOUNDATIONS OF ECONOMICS.

1.   List the four factors of production and their corresponding rewards:

Factors of Production		Reward
I	*Land*	*Rent*
II	*Labour*	*Wage*
III	*Capital*	*Interest*
IV	*Entrepreneurship*	*Profit*

2.   Why is money not considered by economists as a factor of production?

It is a representation of the value of the factors of production

3.   In economics the three basic questions are:

I *What to produce?*   **II** *How to produce?*   **III** *For whom to produce?*

4.   Statements containing phrases such as 'poor people should buy the essentials and not waste their incomes on branded products' or 'governments ought to spend more on healthcare and less on defence' or 'keeping inflation under control is more important than lowering unemployment' are: Choose

I Positive Economic Statements or **II** **Normative Economic Statements**

Explain *Normative because the statement gives an opinion and, since it concerns what should be rather that what is factual, it cannot be verified.*

5.   Which of the following is a positive economic statement?

A   Companies focused on maximising profits should be encouraged.

B   Unemployment has been rising over the last five years.

C   The government needs to reduce its influence in the free market.

D   Economic growth should be encouraged if more jobs are to be created.

Explain B   *change in unemployment rate can be verified using evidence*

6. Each country is faced with dealing with the basic economic problem of:

A Producing products as cheaply as possible.

B Satisfying consumers' limited desires with unlimited resources.

C Reducing taxes and allowing workers to make higher incomes.

D Allocating limited resources to satisfy unlimited wants.

Explain D *Sentence D is an alternative explanation of the problem of scarcity each individual faces.*

7. In economic sense, an example of an investment is as:

A. Purchasing an old house.

B. Buying gold.

C. Saving money in a fixed deposit account.

D. Building a new factory.

Explain D *It is an increase in physical capital, which can be used in production.*

8. In economics a free good is defined as one which

A Is given away at zero price in shops.

B Is a free download from the internet.

C Does not use scarce resources when being produced.

D The government provides to its citizens.

Explain C *A free good is supply > demand at price 0 (no opportunity cost) eg. Water but not clean water*

9. Explain why air is considered to be a free good but air-conditioned air is not a free good. *Air does not use scarce resources but clean air does.*

10. Using a real world example explain what is opportunity cost. **Explain**

A government using funds to build an airport has an opportunity cost of building a new hospital

11.   Is there an opportunity cost involved in the government subsidising the bus system in the cities?

Explain *Yes, the funds could be used for the next best alternative*

12.   From a given amount of flour if a baker can bake five loaves of bread or 15 croissants, then what is the opportunity cost of producing one croissant? **Explain** *1 croissant = 1/3 loaf*

13.   Define accurately the production possibility frontier (ppf).

This is the series of combinations of 2 goods and services (x and y) that an economy can produce, with each y the most that can be produced given x, using all of its factors of production fully and efficiently, at the current level of technology.

The production possibility frontier for Country A is shown below. Country A produces only two goods rice and houses. Use the diagram to answer Questions 14 to 18.

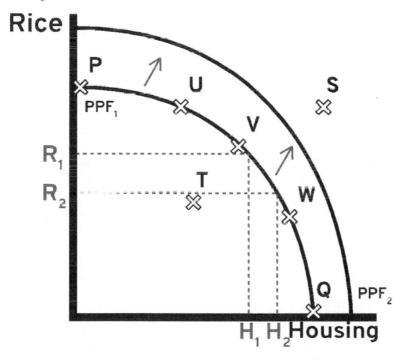

14.   Which letter(s) signify the following: (Note: answers can have more than one letter)

a) Country A is using all its factors of production in only building houses *P.*

b) Country A is employing all its resources in growing rice *Q.*

c) Unemployed or unused factors of production *T.*

d) Currently unattainable production *S.*

e) Country A is using all it factors of production fully and efficiently *U, V, W, P and Q* .

15.   If Country A wishes to increase the number of houses built from **H1** to **H2** then the opportunity cost of this move is *R_1 to R_2*

16.   If over time there is technological progress in the harvesting of rice, explain how could this be shown in the diagram above?

PPF1 curve will shift to PPF2 curve with a bias towards rice. Max housing P stays the same.

17.   List and explain three factors that could shift the production possibility frontier (ppf) inwards.

War destroys factors of production. Natural disasters destroy houses, Climate change can hurt rice production.

18.   Rice is considered as a consumer good whereas a house is considered as a capital good. Explain the difference between the two and give another example to illustrate the difference between a consumer and a capital good.

Capital goods enable production of consumer goods or services, car factory is considered as a capital good and cars are consumer goods.

19.   Explain what a convex (bowed outward) ppf curve imply in terms of opportunity cost.

It implies rising marginal opportunity cost. Society has to sacrifice ever increasing amounts of the other good to squeeze out more output.

20. Opportunity cost occurs when:

A   Demand is less than supply.

B   A government wants to impose a sales tax.

C   Supply is infinite.

D   Price is greater than zero implying resources are scarce.

Explain. D   *If resources are scarce, there is an opportunity cost as the resource used in one industry cannot be used in another area.*

EVALUATION QUESTIONS   **(Foundations of economics)**

Economics textbooks often use the phrase **'ceteris paribus'** when describing the workings of a theory.

21. Explain, what is meant by **'ceteris paribus'**. *All other factors held constant except one variable.*

22. Evaluate the importance of using '**ceteris paribus**' in theoretical and applied economics.

The phrase ceteris paribus allows us to focus the effect of one particular variable on society in theoretical economics. It enables us to study and determine cause and effect. In the real world cause and effects are often blurred and it is difficult to determine whether the change in behaviour is solely due to a change in one particular variable. Time lags make predictions even more difficult.

23.   Economists are often interested in using marginal analysis when studying behaviour.

Briefly explain using examples what is marginal analysis and comment on its usefulness to the individual (when shopping), to firms (when introducing an additional feature on their product) and to the local government (when contemplating raising parking fees)

Marginal analysis a change in behaviour as a result of change in a unit of variable. It calculates extra satisfaction from spending one more franc. Starbucks charges for adding whipped cream. If parking fees are too high, the parking lot will be unused, hence, inefficient.

2 DEMAND AND SUPPLY I

1.   State the Law of Demand: *As price rises quantity demanded decreases (ceteris paribus)*

2.   What do economists mean by effective demand: *Desire to buy and income*

3.   Explain the law of demand using income and substitution effects:

Income effect: As price x rises (ceteris paribus), buying power of income falls and hence less is demanded (increase in $P_x \rightarrow$ fall in Q_{Dx}).

Substitution effect: relative price of other goods fall and hence demand for x falls (rise in price x = fall in QDx)

4.   List 5 major factors which affect the demand for a normal good:

Price of good, income, price of substitutes, price of complements, taste/preference, level of advertising, price expectation, religion, demography etc

5.   The demand for *normal/luxury* goods rise and the demand for *inferior* goods fall as consumers' incomes rise.

6.   Two goods X and Y are *complements* (e.g. *printer and ink*) if when the price of good X falls the demand for good Y rises.

7.   Good X and Y are *substitutes* (e.g. *Pepsi and coca cola*) if when the price of good X rises the demand for good Y rises.

8.   State the Law of Supply: *Ceteris paribus, as price x rises QSx rises.*

9.   Explain the possible reasons behind the law of supply:

As Px rises (ceteris paribus), profit margin rises, greater incentive to supply and Law of Diminishing Returns.

10.   List 5 major factors which affect the supply of a good:

Price of good, cost of production (FoPs), taxes/subsidies, profitability of alternative use of FoPs, supply shock (natural disasters).

11. Supply and demand may be affected by events. For the following (independent) events:

(1) Circle **rise** or **fall** and **demand** or **supply** for good X.
(2) Then show the effects of the shifts on the equilibrium price and quantity. Make sure diagrams are fully labelled and arrows are used to show direction of changes.

a) Price of complementary good rises	b) Sales tax of $1 per packet imposed	c) Sales tax of 10 % is imposed
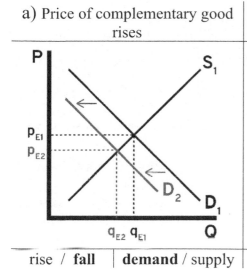	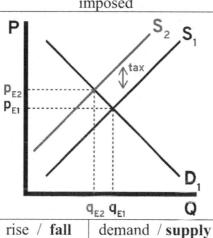	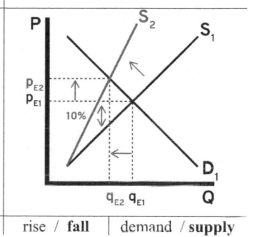
rise / **fall** | **demand** / supply	rise / **fall** | demand / **supply**	rise / **fall** | demand / **supply**

d) Sales tax falls from 10 % to 3 %	e) Raw material prices rise	f) Consumer incomes fall (normal good)
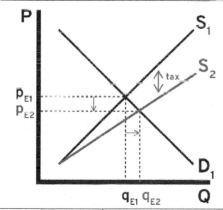	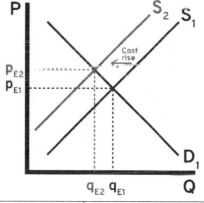	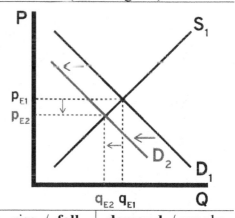
rise / fall | demand / **supply**	rise / **fall** | demand / **supply**	rise / **fall** | **demand** / supply

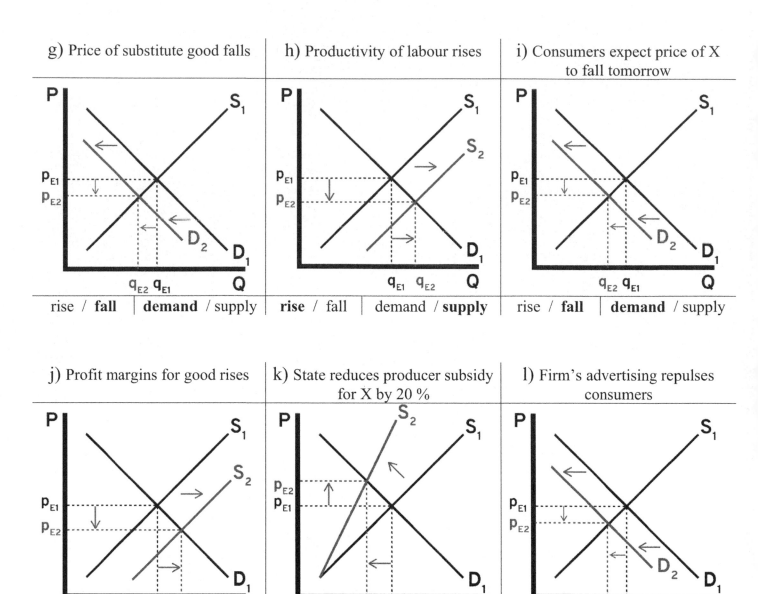

g) Price of substitute good falls

rise / **fall** | **demand** / supply

h) Productivity of labour rises

rise / fall | demand / **supply**

i) Consumers expect price of X to fall tomorrow

rise / **fall** | **demand** / supply

j) Profit margins for good rises

rise / fall | demand / **supply**

k) State reduces producer subsidy for X by 20 %

rise / **fall** | demand / **supply**

l) Firm's advertising repulses consumers

rise / **fall** | **demand** / supply

12. Assuming a free market for coffee, if the current price is P₁, then it is likely that:

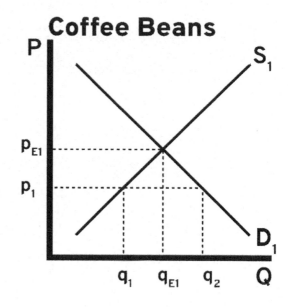

Coffee Beans

A   the demand curve for coffee will shift to the left.

B   the supply curve of coffee beans will shift to the right.

C   the price of coffee beans will rise.

D   the price of coffee beans will remain at P₁.

Explain_C   *There is an excess in demand*

13.   A fall in demand for petrol from motorists is probably a result of

A   a fall in the costs of aluminium inputs in cars.

B   a fall in car insurance premiums.

C   a significant fall in price of a monthly pass for buses and trams.

D   a fall in the price of second hand cars.

Explain_C   *Prices of substitutes have fallen*

14.   Products S, T, and U are normal goods and related in the following way. Product S is a complement to product U. Product S is a substitute to product T.

What will happen to the sales of S, when the price of product T falls and the price of product U rises while the price of product S stays the same?

A   Sales of S will be indeterminate give the above information.

B   Sales of S will rise.

C   Sales of product S will remain unchanged.

D   Sales of product S will fall.

Explain_D   *Demand for S falls, as price U rises, and as price of T falls, Qd for u falls as S and U are complements, substitute less expensive reinforces.*

15.   One of the following will not shift the demand curve for good X.

   A   a change in the income of the buyer.

   B   a rise in the indirect tax imposed by the government on good X.

   C   a fall in the price of a substitute product.

   D   a fall in the price of a complementary product.

Explain_B   *indirect tax shifts the supply line which implies movement along the demand line.*

16.   One of the following will not shift the supply line for a good.

   A   a fall in the price of an extensively used input.

   B   a rise in the consumers' real incomes

   C   a rise in the sales tax from 5% to 8%.

   D   none of the above.

Explain_B *As income rises, demand rises, supply line accommodates the shift in demand.*

17.   Which of the following is not held constant for a demand line?

   A   tastes of buyers.

   B   prices of competing products.

   C   the level of advertising.

   D   the price of the good itself.

Explain_D   *Along the single demand line, price is the only variable.*

EVALUATION QUESTIONS   (Demand & Supply I)

18.   Examine the logic behind the statement, 'a rise in demand for rice will cause an increase in the price of rice. The price rise will then cause a fall in demand until its falls back to its original level.

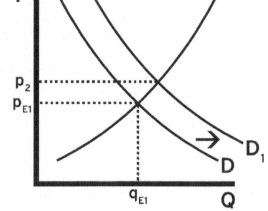

- *Overall fallacy, confusion between shift and movement along same demand line*
- *First statement implies shift in demand curve*
- *Second statement is a movement along the demand line*
- *No logical reason to believe price falls back to P_{E1}*

19.   Evaluate the effects of a significant and sustained rise in the supply of oil on the market for oil, for coal and natural gas, for cars, for solar panel installation, for pedal bikes, for electric bikes and for public transport.

Supply oil rises, price of oil falls.

- *If coal and natural gas are substitutes for oil*
  Demand for coal + gas falls, Price of coal and gas falls

- *Cars and oil are complements.*
  Price of oil falls, Demand for oil rises, Demand for cars rise

- *Solar and oil are weak substitutes*
  Price of oil falls, Demand for oil rises, Demand for solar installations fall

- *Pedal bikes and cars are weak substitutes*
  Price of oil falls. Demand for cars rises, demand pedal bikes falls.

- *Electric bikes and oil are complementary if electricity is generated from oil though the substitute relation may not as strong.*
  Price of oil falls, price of electricity may fall raising demand for electric bikes or demand for electric bikes may fall if cost of running a car fall.

- *Oil is an input in public transport, but public transport is also a substitute.*
  Price of oil falls, cost of production of public transport falls (ceteris paribus), Supply of public transport rise and demand will accommodate this. However, demand for public transport falls as a result of driving being a substitute. Net effect on price is a fall, but on quantity depends which is stronger.

20.   Apart from a few years, most of the time it is observed that the average price of housing is rising even when more and more spaces are being converted to apartments. Analyse using determinants of demand and supply how this is possible. Evaluate the long-term implications of house prices rising faster than incomes on average.

- *price of housing determined by forces of D&S*
- *Increase in Price of house due to increase in Demand for house*
- *Rise in price of houses may lead to rise in demand and subsequently rise in supply of apartments.*
- *Overall rate of demand for housing is rising faster than supply of housing = higher prices (Diagram, D shifting out more than S shifting out)*
- *Housing will take up more of income. This will also result in more and more renters being taken up by housing. There are limits (cannot have 100% income going into housing) More migration only. Greater pressure on Govt to intervene.*

21. A small fast food kebab shop finds that demand for kebabs vary during the day. At lunchtimes and on late nights on Fridays and Saturdays the queues are very long and out of the shop. The waiting period is 23 minutes on average at these times. Evaluate the options available to the shop including differential pricing.

- *Off peak lower price + special offers*
- *On peak higher price*
- *Expand business, introduce ordering food whilst in the queue.*
- *Sell additional services during 25 minutes waiting time*
- *Pre-prepared. (microwave it)*
- *Not clear which is more profitable without further information.*

22.   Evaluate with the help of diagrams:

a)   the possible effects of a fall in the price of music downloads on the demand for live concert attendance. *Music download can be substitutes for some consumers and complements for others.*

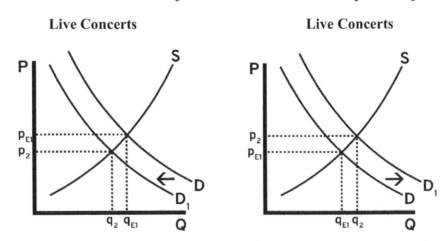

b)   the probable effects on the demand for music downloads of a rock band when the price of concerts tickets for the rock band falls. Are the above symmetrical?

Fall in price of concert tickets could cause fall in D(downloads) (substitutes) or rise in D(downloads) (complement)

3 DEMAND AND SUPPLY II

1.   An effective price ceiling requires the price of a good to be set above / *below* the market equilibrium level. *below*

2.   An effective minimum wage rate is set *above* / below the equilibrium wage rate for labour.

   above

3.   Show an effective price ceiling and a price floor on the diagram below.

4.   State 2 reasons why a government may be interested in setting a price floor in some sectors and 2 reasons for setting a price ceiling in other sectors.

Price floor or minimum wage protects low income workers and low income producers.

Price ceiling protects low income consumers below poverty line and rent controls in large cities.

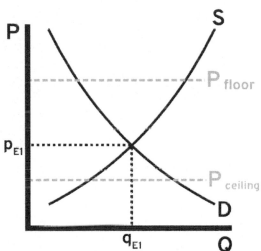

5.   A shortage occurs when *demand* / supply is greater than demand / *supply*, while a surplus exists when demand / *supply* is greater than *demand* / supply.

6.   Define consumer surplus: *The difference between the price the consumer is willing to pay and what the consumer actually pays, summed over all units of output.*

7.   Define producer surplus: *The difference between what the producer receives and the minimum price the producer is willing to accept, summed over all units of output.*

8. Show consumer and producer surplus in the demand/supply diagram below.

Community Surplus = Consumer surplus + Producer surplus

9.   Define efficiency in allocation:

There is no dead weight loss and the community surplus is maximised.

10.   True **T** or False **F**.   Assume a competitive market.

a)   When all costs and benefits are accounted free market is efficient in allocation.   *T*

b)   When community surplus is maximised, the market is efficient in allocation. *T*

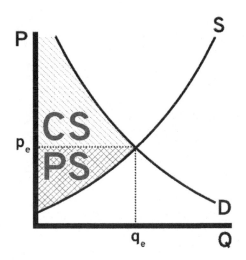

c)   Allocative efficiency means the price of the last unit of the good sold is equal to cost of making the last unit of the good.   *T*

d)   Efficiency in allocation occurs when there is no way for an economy to reallocate resources or goods such that some stakeholders are better off without others being worse off in production or consumption.   *T*

11. Explain using an example the meaning of deadweight or welfare loss.

If a tax is implemented, the deadweight loss is the loss of community surplus due to failing to produce units with benefits above cost.

12.   Using an appropriate diagram explain how a sales tax creates a deadweight

or welfare loss. Show also the resulting changes in consumer and producer surplus.

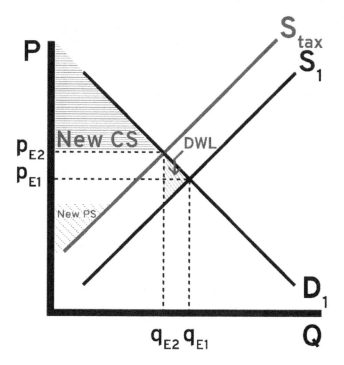

13.   Consider the case where a government introduces a price floor to support low income farmers and buys up the surplus. In the diagram below:

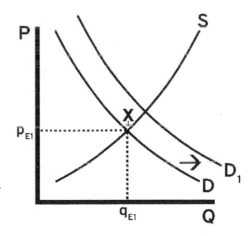

(a)   Label equilibrium price and quantity *Pe1, Qe1*.

(b)   Consumer surplus *Area 1,2,3* and producer surplus

    Area 4, 5?

(c)   If **Pf** represents the price floor, what is the excess supply?

    A to B

(d)   What is the new consumer surplus? **Area 1**

(e)   What is the new producer surplus? *Areas 2,3, 4 5 and 6*

(f)   The price floor has created a deadweight loss given by *Area 3, 5, 6, 7, 8, 9*

It is important to note that the deadweight or welfare loss represents the overall loss/allocative inefficiency to society resulting from using scarce resources for overproduction of the good. Society is producing too much of the good, much more than consumers want at the floor price.

14.   **Samsung Mobile Phone S4**

Which of the following is the **most** correct:

    A   An increase in the price of mobile phone calls will increase the demand for S4 and lower the producer surplus.

    B   The rise in the price of complementary goods to S4 will lower the demand for S4 and increase the producer surplus.

    C   The rise in price of inputs will increase the price for S4 and producer surplus will rise.

    D   The rise in demand for S4 will lead to an increase in both price and producer surplus.

Explain_D   *As demand rises, D shifts to the right which results in higher market price. Since supply curve stays the same, the producer surplus rises.*

15   One of the following will result in decreasing consumer surplus in the market for corn flakes:

   A   A successful advertising campaign for Kellogg's Corn Flakes.

   B   A successful advertising campaign promoting porridge as a healthier substitute option.

   C   A fall in the sales tax on all breakfast cereals.

   D   An increase in the level of subsidies given to corn farmers.

Explain_B *The demand for porridge rises and hence the demand for cornflakes falls. The cornflakes demand line shifts left and hence consumer surplus falls for cornflakes.*

16.   In 2014 Swiss voters had a referendum on introducing a ceiling wage rate (W_{max}) on CEO pay for all companies operating in Switzerland.

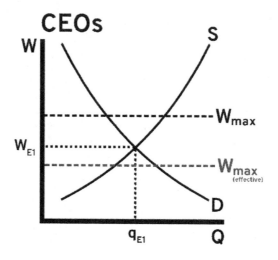

The introduction of W_{max}

   A   will mean wages of CEOs will be W_{max} soon after the vote.

   B   will attract new companies to relocate to Switzerland.

   C   will have no effect on the wages of CEOs.

   D   will lead to Swiss companies relocating abroad.

Explain_C   *If the ceiling is set above the equilibrium then the wage will gravitate to equilibrium level Pe1. For the ceiling to be effective, the ceiling must be set below equilibrium.*

17.   To support low income consumers the government introduces a price ceiling of $2, significantly lower than the $2.50 on each litre of milk current equilibrium price. What is the likely effect of this change?

    A   the supply of milk will rise.

    B   the taxpayer will have to buy the excess milk produced.

    C   the supply of yoghurt and cheese will rise.

    D   the demand line will shift to the right as consumers buy more milk.

Explain_C   *For producers, cheese and yogurt are relatively more profitable than milk because the price ceiling lowered the profit margin of milk.*

18   The government introduces a subsidy per tonne on corn as shown below.

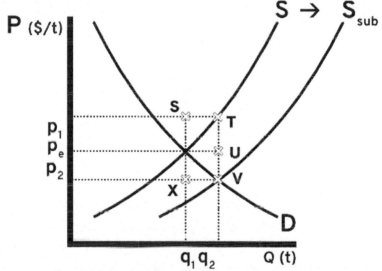

The total cost of the subsidy to the taxpayer is given by the area
    A   STVX

    B   P₁P₂TV

    C   P₁P₂SX

    D   P₁P₂UV

Explain_ B   *Size of the subsidy: price of subsidy per unit x quantity produced = Q2 x (P1-P2)*

19   The diagram below represents the demand and supply for a good.

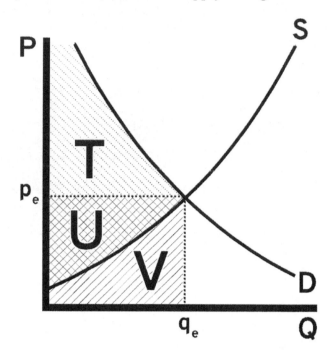

Which area represents the minimum amount producers are willing to accept to produce the equilibrium output.

A   Area T.

B   Area T + U.

C   Area U + V.

D   Area V

Explain D *Area U is producer surplus is difference between the minimum amount producers are willing to accept and market price.   Area V is referred to as transfer payments. It is the opportunity cost of using fops*

EVALUATION QUESTIONS   (Demand and Supply II: Applications)

20.   Evaluate the different ways of dealing with surpluses which occur when a price floor is introduced to both support incomes of farmers and ensure supplies.

- *Buy surplus and sell it abroad at below market price or free as part of aid*
- *Pay farmers to not produce, explained as green policy but may seem unethical*
- *Buy surplus and give it as part of food voucher to the very low income earners but ensure that it does not get released on general market.*
- *Buy surplus to store as part of a buffer scheme as long as some years would have p above floor level.*

21.   Evaluate the proposition that since all indirect taxes create deadweight/welfare loss, governments should not interfere in the free market.

- *Indirect taxes are there to raise revenue, needed for public goods and merit goods.*
- *Discourage anti-social behaviours (alcohol, cigarettes)*
- *May be part of regulating AD via fiscal policy to achieve Macro objectives*
- *Indirect taxes may be introduced to correct market failure and hence deadweight loss does not occur.*
- *If indirect taxes are say tariffs to deter imports then consumer choice suffers, global misallocation of resources and higher prices domestically. All indirect taxes cause some misallocation of resources, and loss of consumer and producer surplus.*
- *Discourages imports of some goods to favour domestic production*

22.   Evaluate the view that 'shortages created by rent ceilings in the housing market lead to inefficiencies and discourage landlords and developers from increasing supply.'

- *Allocative inefficiency: housing not sold at equilibrium*
- *Profit margins fall, landlords less likely to rent out apt and maintain the buildings.*
- *Developers use the resources in other more profitable ventures.*
- *Government may provide financial aid or subsidies to landlords and developers in order to encourage them to supply more housing. Opportunity cost arises as a consequence.*
- *Parallel market: some consumers with higher income may be willing to purchase housing above ceiling price because of the shortage. Since this increases profit margin for landlords and developers, they increase supply to those consumers via the parallel market. One example of market distortion.*

23.   For five years, straight after World War II, Britain continued its programme of food rationing. Comment on the rationale for such a programme. Would a free market system for food be more efficient and equitable or preferable?

Rationale: *-More equitable: ensures all households receive minimal amount of food. Valuable when food supply is limited, for instance after the war.*

         -Market distortion by government intervention: may not achieve allocative nor productive efficiency

For free market: *-Allocative efficient because food is transacted at equilibrium*

-Not necessarily equitable: does not ensure low-income household having food

   -If food supply is limited, the price of food will rise as demand rises, which leads to exacerbated inequality

Possible conclusion: Food rationing would be better for equity

24.   Comment on the view that a subsidy given to dairy farmers is preferable to introducing a price floor on dairy products such as milk, butter and yoghurt.

Subsidy:

   -Allocative efficient: daily products are supplied at new equilibrium price

   -Both consumers and producers benefit: consumers benefit from lower price of daily products and producers benefit from increase in sales and subsidy

   -Opportunity cost: subsidies are funded from taxpayers' money which could have be used for other projects

   -Suppliers may become dependent on subsidies e.g. US subsidising sugar industry for more than 200 years

Price floor:

   -Suppliers benefit from higher profit per unit/ incomes are ensured, but consumers are worse off with the high price

   -Market distortion: daily products are not supplied at market equilibrium

   -Excess supply: surplus may be stored as buffer scheme; cannot be stored for long periods and it cost to keep them. Buffer scheme may be effective in a crisis.

   -'Pay not to produce'- may be considered unethical.

Possible conclusion: Subsidy is better than price floor because there is less market distortion when subsidy is given.

25.   In most cities the traditional taxi system works through the issue of a limited quota of licenses which are set below the market equilibrium level of licenses. This causes a **'wedge'** (demand price > supply price).

(a)   Explain using a demand/supply diagram what is meant by a **'wedge'**?

-At the new price, the height of D tells the price, but the height of S tells what price was needed to get that much Qs. The difference is the wedge.

(b)   Evaluate the effect on the various stakeholders of the introduction of Uber taxis (sharing economy business model)?

Consumers benefit from:

    -Lower taxi service price

    -Taxi service is more easily available: less time loss

    -Increase in consumer surplus

Licensed taxi drivers lose from:

    -Lower price per service/ lower profit margin

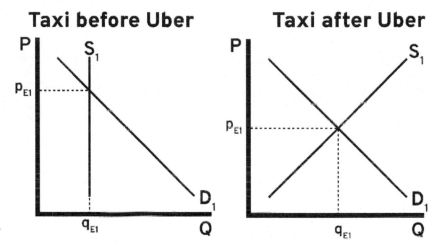

    -More competition within taxi industry: less service demanded/revenue earned per taxi

    -Loss in producer surplus

Society:

    -Benefit from freer and more efficient resource allocation

    -Less market distortion by government intervention

    -Job creation/ more demand for labour

Government:

    -Use fewer resources monitoring licenses and taxis in the long run if license is abolished

    -May use resources to monitor Uber company

    -Less unemployment benefits to be used

4 ELASTICITIES I

Economists use the concept of elasticity to study the change in behaviour of stakeholders such as consumers, producers and governments when the price of a good or related goods or disposable incomes changes.

PRICE ELASTICITY OF DEMAND (PED$_X$)

1.   Define price elasticity of demand for good X, (PED$_X$) in words.

PED measures the degree of responsiveness of Qdx as a result of a change in Px

2.   Write down the formula for PED$_X$

$$PED_X = \frac{\%\Delta Q_d}{\%\Delta P}$$

3.   If the quantity demanded for X rises by 27 % as a result of a fall in price of 30 %, the PED$_X$ is equal to:

$$PED_X = \frac{\%\Delta Q_d}{\%\Delta P} = \frac{+\,27\,\%}{-\,30\,\%} = -\frac{9}{10} = -0.9$$

4.   If PEDx = –3, then a 0.2 % rise in price will result in a fall in of **quantity demanded by 0.6 %.**

$$PED_X = \frac{\%\Delta Q_d}{\%\Delta P} = -3 = \frac{\%\Delta Q_d}{+\,0.2\,\%} \Longrightarrow \%\Delta Q_d = 0.2\,\% \times -3 = -0.6\,\%$$

5.   Let the demand equation be **Qd = 20 – 2P**. Fill in the demand schedule below.

P ($)	0	1	2	3	4	5	6	7	8	9	10
Qd	20	18	16	14	12	10	8	6	4	2	0

Calculate to 2 decimal places or use fractions, the pedx between the following prices:

   P=1 and P=2   PEDx = *–0.11*   Good X is elastic / ***inelastic*** / unit elastic

P=2 and P=3.   PEDx = −0.25   Good X is elastic / *inelastic* / unit elastic

P=3 and P=4   PEDx = −0.43   Good X is elastic / *inelastic* / unit elastic

P=4 and P=5   PEDx = −0.6   Good X is *elastic* / *inelastic* / unit elastic

P=5 and P=6   PEDx = −1   Good X is *elastic* / inelastic / **unit elastic**

P=6 and P=7   PEDx = −1.5   Good X is *elastic* / inelastic / unit elastic

P=7 and P=8   PEDx = −2.33   Good X is *elastic* / inelastic / unit elastic

P=8 and P=9 P   PEDx = −4   Good X is *elastic* / inelastic / unit elastic

P=9 and P−10   PEDx = −9   Good X is *elastic* / inelastic / unit elastic

Deduce the PEDx value for P=0 **PED$_X$ = 0**.   For P−10   **PED$_X$ = ∞**

What can you conclude about the pedx along a straight line:

The PED value varies along the line. Hence the slope of the demand line does not represent a particular PED value

6.   The total revenue (TR) is price of good X times quantity demand of X . (TR=P×Q). Calculate total revenue for the above demand equation.

P ($)	0	1	2	3	4	5	6	7	8	9	10
TR	0	18	32	42	48	50	48	42	32	18	0

7.   Draw the demand equation and total revenue function below:

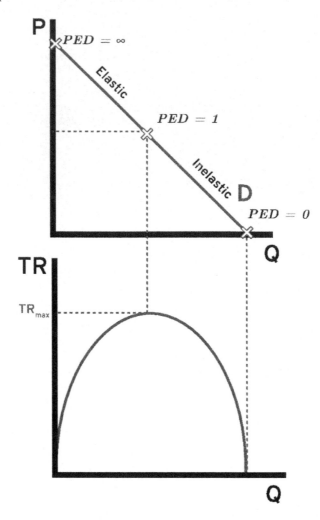

What conclusions can you draw from the above diagrams in terms of PED_X and TR?

In the elastic range of the demand line, if the price falls total revenue will increase

In the inelastic range, fall in price will results in fall in TR

TR is maximised when PED=1

8.   If price falls and total revenue increases then **Demand is price _Elastic_**

9.   If price rises and total revenue increases then **Demand is price _Inelastic_** 10. If price falls and total revenue decreases then **Demand is price _Inelastic_**

11.   If price rises and total revenue decreases then **Demand is price _Elastic_**

12.   If price rises or falls but total revenue is unchanged **Demand is _Unit elastic_**

13.   List 5 factors affecting the price elasticity of demand for a good.

-% of income taken by the product

-Habit forming/addictiveness

-Number and closeness of substitutes

-Time period allowed for response

-Broadness/narrowness of definition of product

14.   Using the list above explain why the ped is low or high for the following:

a)   Salt

Low PED, salt takes low percentage of income. It is a necessity hence there is low number of substitutes.

b)   Foreign holidays compared to domestic resorts

High PED, foreign holidays take up a higher percentage of income.

c)   Petrol short run compared to petrol in the long run

Low PED in the short run, not enough substitute to consider and compare because of lack of time compared to in the long run

d)   Kellogg's Corn Flakes compared to breakfast cereals.

High PED, Kellogg's Corn Flakes has narrow definition to breakfast cereals, hence Kellogg's Corn Flakes has greater number of substitutes compared to breakfast cereals.

PRICE ELASTICITY OF SUPPLY (PES$_X$)

15.   Define price elasticity of supply for good X, (PES$_X$) in words.

Measurement of degree of responsiveness of quantity supplied to the change in price

16.   Write down the formula for PESx.

$$PES_X = \frac{\%\Delta Q_S}{\%\Delta P}$$

17.   If the quantity supplied of X rises by 20 % as a result of a rise in price of 10 %, the PESx is equal

to:

$$PES_X = \frac{\%\Delta Q_S}{\%\Delta P} = \frac{20\%}{10\%} = 2$$

18.   If $PES_X = 1.5$, then a 20 % fall in price will result in a fall in supply of:

$$PES_X = \frac{\%\Delta Q_S}{\%\Delta P} \Rightarrow PES_X \times \%\Delta P = \%\Delta Q_S$$

$\Rightarrow 1.5 \times -20\% = -30\%$

19 *h.*   Let the supply equation be $Q_s = -10 + 2P$. Fill in the supply schedule below.

P ($)	6	7	8	9	10
Q_s	2	4	6	8	10

Calculate to 2 decimal places or use fractions, the pes_x between the following prices:

P= 6 and P=7 PESx = **6.00**   Good X is supply price *elastic* / inelastic / unit elastic

P=7 and P=8   PESx = **3.50**   Good X is supply price *elastic* / inelastic / unit elastic

P=8 and P=9   PESx = **2.67**   Good X is supply price *elastic* / inelastic / unit elastic

P=9 and P=10 PESx = **2.25**   Good X is supply price *elastic* / inelastic / unit elastic

20.   What does PESx =0 mean for the firm and for the consumer?

The value of PES=0 means that the firm has no ability or way to increasing supply as the price rises. This may be due to scarcity of product, such as the Mona Lisa, or the firm does not have immediate stock available to respond to change in price. For the consumers overall, this means that they are unable to consume more of that product even if they are willing to pay a higher price.

21. From the supply diagram below match the five values of PES$_X$

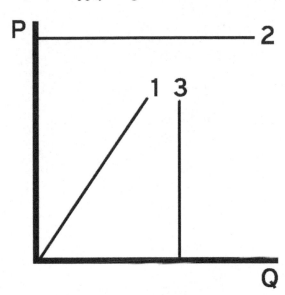
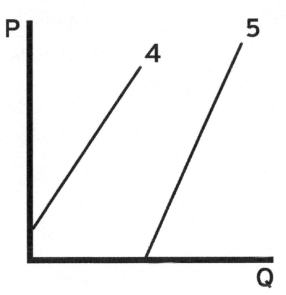

PES$_X$ = 0	Perfectly price inelastic	Line:	3
0 <PES$_X$ < 1	Price inelastic	Line:	5
PES$_X$ = 1	Unitary price elastic	Line:	1
1 <PES$_X$ < ∞	Price elastic	Line:	4
PES$_X$ = ∞	Perfectly price elastic	Line:	2

22. List 5 factors which make a product price elastic in supply?

   -Long time period available to adjust supply

   -Excess stocks/inventories

   -Lots of unused capacity

   -High mobility of factors of production/ lots of interchangeable FoPs

   -Lots of producers

-Short growth cycle: able to produce goods quickly

INCOME ELASTICITY OF DEMAND (YED$_X$)

23.   Define income elasticity of demand for good X, (YED$_X$) in words.

Measurement of responsiveness of quantity demand to a change in income

24.   Write down the formula for YEDx.

$$YED_X = \frac{\%\Delta Q_d}{\%\Delta Y}$$

25.   If disposable income rises by 8 % and as a result the demand rises by 4 % then YEDx = **0.5**. Product X is inferior / **necessity** / luxury.

26.   Define in terms of YEDx, a normal good.   **$0 < YED < 1$**

27.   Define in terms of YEDx, an inferior good.   **$YED < 0$**

28.   Define in terms of YEDx, a luxury good.   **$1 < YED$**

29.   If YEDx = –1.5, then a 20 % fall in income will result in **a rise in Q_d of 30 %.**

$$YED_X = \frac{\%\Delta Q_D}{\%\Delta Y} = -1.5 = \frac{\%\Delta Q_D}{-20\%} \Rightarrow \%\Delta Q_D - 1.5 \times -20\% = 30\%$$

CROSS ELASTICITY OF DEMAND (XEDA, B)

30.   Define cross elasticity of demand between two 2 goods A and B (XEDA, B) in words.

Measurement of degree of responsiveness of quantity demanded of good A on the change in price of good B.

31.   Write down the formula for XEDA, B

$$XED_{A, B} = \frac{\%\Delta Q_{D_A}}{\%\Delta P_B}$$

32.   Explain with examples the meaning of XED$_{A, B}$ = 0 *The value XED$_{A, B}$ means that good A and good B are not related.*

33.   Explain with examples the significance of XED$_{A, B}$ = –0.4

The XED value -0.4 means that good A and good B are weak complements. This is illustrated by printer and ink, if printer prices fall by say, 10 % then demand for ink will rise by 4 %.

34.   Explain using examples the meaning of XED$_{A, B}$ = 1.2

The XED value 1.2 means good A and good B are strong substitutes. This is illustrated by Coca-Cola and Pepsi

EVALUATION QUESTIONS   (Elasticity 1)

35.   Discuss how a mobile phone manufacturer can use the concepts of price, cross and income elasticities of demand in its business strategy.

Phone: price elastic, income elastic

PED: related to revenue

>   *-Decreasing the price of mobile phone increases the total revenue*

>   *-Advertisements & increase brand loyalty to lower PED value/consumers less price sensitive*

YED:

>   *-Place: -Manufacturers should sell their newest high-tech mobile phones in areas in which income is fast-growing (e.g. India)   (-Sell simple mobile phones in poor regions?)*

>   *-Features: provide signals of luxury such as design elegance when selling to high income earners and provide functional basics when selling to low-income consumers. Some features on mobile phone are more income elastic than others.*

>   *-As incomes rise some features decline in demand (inferior features) while others increase.*

XED:

>   *-Try to foresee which complements will fall in price, such as energy and increase the range.*

>   *-Produce many complementary goods, which help to create brand loyalty*

>   *-Reduce the substitutability of the phone.*

>   *-*

36.   Apply the concepts of price elasticity of demand and supply to explain why holiday resort prices are higher at Christmas than in the off-season.

>   *-PED measures the degree of sensitivity of demand for one good when there a change in its price*

>   *-Holiday resorts are price sensitive good because during the off-season the visitors tend to be low income groups such as pensioners. and it takes a high percentage of their income*

>   *-Christmas is one of the most popular days for holidays*

>   *-At Christmas, the consumer's sensitivity to price of holiday resort service decreases because:*

>   *-Increase in demand/necessity of Xmas celebrations.*

>   *-Hotel resorts may use advertisements as Christmas approaches*

> *-Limited PES over limited time span as space cannot expand and contract easily over the year.*

>   *e.g.) Hotel resort prices increases if the consumers are reserving the hotel resort near Christmas*

>   *-Lower PED value: quantity demanded falls less proportionally than the rise in price*

-The hotel resorts increase price to increase total revenue. Use PED and TR diagram.

37.   Explain why the demand for strawberries is likely to be more price elastic than for bread. How would your answer change if it were possible to store strawberries cheaply and easily?

-PED value increases with a narrower range of the definition of the good, greater number of substitutes, higher percentage of income, and greater necessity.

-Strawberry may have less necessity value than bread does/ for some, fruits are considered as desert, while bread provides calories and protein needed even at low incomes.

-Bread has a broader term than strawberry: strawberry is in the sub-category of fruits

-Bread hence has fewer substitutes than strawberry does

Cheaper and readily available storage of strawberries:

- Stored strawberries, e.g. frozen, become a substitute for fresh strawberries in season, so PED would increase

-Supply becomes more elastic: instead of a limited amount available when it is berry season, excess supply can be stored for off-season consumption. A similar substitute for bread exists in the form of (storable) pasta.

As a result, lower price due to high supply is less likely to be seen as temporary, and consumers may be less responsive (especially in the short run)

However, consumers may learn a wider range of recipes with strawberries when they become available year-round, thus expanding overall PED due to greater ability to substitute them in place of other fruit if price falls

38.   Explain the following situations using elasticities:

(a)   When an economy is in a boom period more new types of restaurants open than new supermarkets.

-YED measures the degree of demand sensitivity of one good to the change in income

-YED$_{RESTAURANTS}$>YED$_{SUPERMARKETS}$

Restaurants serve more expensive and higher quality food (and less labour of preparing meals) whereas supermarkets provides ingredient for cooking (cheaper but more work/labour)

-Boom period: households' incomes increase

-Consumers wishes to spend more of extra income on goods with higher quality goods/services and greater convenience.

(b)Overtime goods such as laptops change from being luxuries to being almost necessities making the demand curve for laptops steepen and supply curve flatten.

-Considered as 'necessity' due to: use for private home computing (instead of mainly office applications), combined with increasing complementary use of the internet, as well as familiarity by students who had them at school and grew used to their convenience. Necessity also comes from addiction to Facebook, games and sharing music, etc. with friends.

more price elastic as there more producers carrying more inventories

-Standard of living increases & higher income: more consumers available to purchase laptops, demand for laptops increases dramatically. As more others become connected the necessity of some connections increases.

-Technological advancement requires more highly skilled workers: more education on technology/computer: necessity of laptops increases as workers are becoming more mobile. Work and home separation lines are becoming blurred.

All of these mean that a higher price will be less likely to cause consumers to do without or substitute, so PED falls.

-Fall in cost of production & economies of scale with technological advance

> *-Fall in price of laptops*
>
> *-PES more price elastic, as resources are a smaller share of their total market, and thus more easily hired. Also, inputs with restricted supply have production substitutes invented.*

5 ELASTICITIES II (APPLICATIONS)

1.   The supply of maths textbooks is fairly price elastic while the demand is fairly price inelastic.

a)   Explain why this is probably true.

This is manufactured good, easy to increase supply. The demand is inelastic because it is more of necessity, forced to buy it due to recommendation by teachers. No close substitutes.

b)   The government is contemplating introducing a sales tax of 12 % on textbooks. Give one possible reason for this move and using an appropriate diagram show the incidence of the tax.

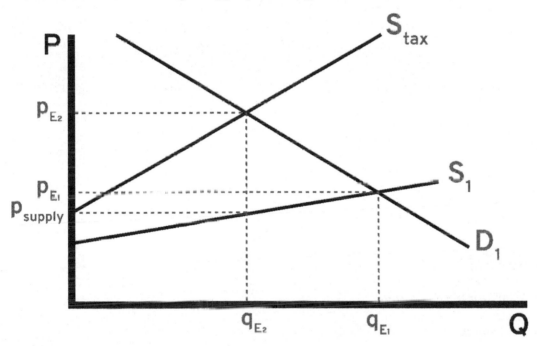

Raise tax revenue

Supply price = price the producer receives

c)   State the rule on the incidence of sales tax using price elasticities (PED and PES). *Since PE D< PES consumers pay bigger share of tax*

2 *b*.   The data below refers to demand and supply of tablet computers and laptops and income of the average household over time:

Year (a)	Price$_{tablets}$ ($)	QD$_{tablets}$	QS$_{tablets}$	Income ($)	QD$_{laptops}$
1	300	5 000	12 000	50 000	8 000
2	240	8 000	9 000	55 000	7 600

a)   Suggest a reason for the fall in price of tablet computers: *technological progress in production.* *(7000 oversupply in year and that leads to a fall in price)*

b)   Is the market for tablet computers in equilibrium. **Explain** *At both prices demand is lower than supply*

Calculate PED for tablet computers. (assume: income constant)

$$PED = \frac{\%\Delta Q_d}{\%\Delta P} = \frac{+60\,\%}{-20\,\%} = -3$$

d) Calculate the total revenue/sales for years 1 and 2 for tablets.

$$TR_1 = P_1 \times Q_1 = 300 \times 5000 = 1.5\ M\$$$

$$TR_2 = P_2 \times Q_2 = 240 \times 8000 = 1.9\ M\$$$

e) Did the fall in tablet prices increase or decrease total revenue for the manufacturers. How could this have been predicted from part (c)'s answer?

TR$_2$ > TR$_1$ predictable since demand is price elastic

f) Calculate the income elasticity of demand for tablet computers (YED$_{tablets}$) assuming constant prices.

$$YED = \frac{\%\Delta Q_s}{\%\Delta Y} = \frac{+60\,\%}{+10\,\%} = 6$$

g) What type of good is a tablet? Justify your response.

Very income sensitive. It is a luxury good.

h) Calculate PES$_{tablets}$ and suggest three reasons for the value

$$PES = \frac{\%\Delta Q_s}{\%\Delta P} = \frac{-25\,\%}{-20\,\%} = 1.25$$

It is price elastic because they are manufactured goods with many producers and a large inventory.

i) Calculate the cross price elasticity for laptops as a result of a change in the price of tablet and decide the type and strength of relation between laptops and tablets.

$$XED_{laptop,\ tablet} = \frac{\%\Delta Q_{d_{laptop}}}{\%\Delta P_{tablet}} = \frac{-5\,\%}{-20\,\%} = 0.25 \Rightarrow$$

The two are weak substitutes.

j)   Evaluate the reliability of the above data and your conclusions.

It depends on quality of market research. Sample size, time lags. All changes should be ceteris paribus, otherwise none of the calculations of elasticities are reliable.

k)   Suggest how a manufacturer could use the above data.

PED elastic YED was luxury XED weak substitutes between tablets and laptops. **Manufacturer can design high end tablets. Sell tablets cheap but higher price on accessories.**

l)   If the government imposes a specific tax on each type of computer what do you predict will be the incidence of the tax? **Since PED > PES, the producer will pay a bigger share of the tax**

3.   A football club increased the price of all its stadium tickets by 20%. The demand for standing room tickets fell by 30%, the demand for seat tickets fell by 50% and the demand for Box tickets went up 10%.

a)   Work out the ped for tickets for all 3 sections of the stadium.

PED standing room $= \frac{-30\%}{+20\%} = $ *-1.5 = price elastic*

PED seats $= \frac{-50\%}{\%20\%} = $ *-2.5*

PED box $= \frac{+10\%}{+20\%\%} = $ *+0.5 (possibly Veblen good, but substitutes are more expensive)*

b).   How are the 3 types of tickets related?   *They are all substitutes*

c)   Explain the behaviour of the consumers here and decide whether this behaviour is rational.

For Standing Room and seats the behaviour is rational because of the law of demand. However for Box tickets product may be a Veblen good, chosen for its snob value, so there is more demand when few can afford it.

4.   Which of the following pair of goods/services are likely to have a positive cross elasticity of demand?

        A   Cars and tyres.

        B   Cars and petrol

        C   **Cars and bus service.**

        D   Cars and parking spaces.

Explain C *They are substitutes*

5.   Income elasticity of demand for items bought in Morocco and France are:

Item	France	Morocco
Couscous	−0.20	0.30
Cigarettes	0.60	1.30
Lamb	0.30	0.45

        A   Cigarettes have low ped in France but a high ped in Morocco.

        B   An increase in the price of lamb will lead to a fall in demand for couscous in France.

C   Couscous is an inferior good in Morocco whereas lamb is a normal good in France.

D   Cigarettes are a normal good in France while being a luxury good only in Morocco.

Explain D   *because 0<YED<1='necessity'. And 1<YED*

6. From the demand line above it can be deduced that:

A   Apple iPad is a Veblen good.

B   the XED is negative and hence the 2 goods above are substitutes

C   the XED is positive and this means the 2 goods above are substitutes

D   iPad is a luxury good.

Explain C *As P_{iPad} rises, Qd for iPad falls, Qd for luptops rises.*

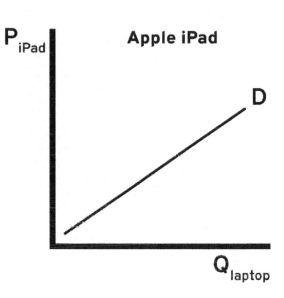

7 b   The demand curve for potato chips faced by a producer in the US is shown below.

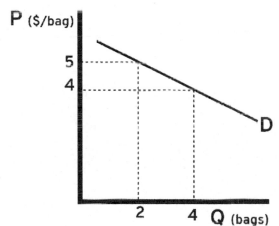

If the company cuts its price per packet from $5 to $4 then

A   total revenue will fall because the demand is price elastic.

B   total revenue will rise because the demand is price elastic.

C   total revenue will remain unchanged.

D   total revenue will rise because demand is price inelastic.

Explain__B _ *Q rises proportionately more than the proportionate fall in the price of rice.*

8.   The elasticities of demand for holiday resorts in the Bahamas are as follows

PED = –0.8   YED = +1.6

From the above data we can deduce that

A   an increase in income of 10% will lead to an increase in demand of 8%.

B   holidays to the Bahamas are price inelastic and hence a normal good.

C   an increase in the price of resorts will increase the total revenue for resort owners.

D a fall in income of 10% will result in a fall in demand of 1.6% for Bahamas resorts.

Explain C *Since product is price inelastic, increase in price will lead to increase in total revenue*

9 *b*.   You intend to borrow $600 000 at 4 % interest to buy an apartment. However if the interest instead is 6% and you decide to borrow $480 000. What is your interest elasticity of demand?

    A   +0.4

    B   –0.6

    C   +0.6

    D   –0.4

Explain:

$$IED = \frac{\%\Delta QM}{\%\Delta I} = \frac{-20\,\%}{50\,\%} = -0.4$$

10 *b*.   Assume Toyota has 2 special edition car models and the relevant sales and elasticities are as reported below.

Model	№ of cars (monthly)	XED with respect to petrol price
1800 cm^3	8 000	–2
1000 cm^3	16 000	+2

Ceteris paribus, if the price of petrol rises from $2 to $2.50 per litre then the total number of cars sold will

    A   rise by 4 000.

    B   remain unchanged.

    C   **rise by 12 000.**

    D   falls by 6 000.

Explain

$$\%\Delta P_{petrol} = \frac{new - old}{old} = \frac{2.50 - 2}{2} = 25\,\%$$

$$XED_{1800\,cm^3,\ petrol} = -2 = \frac{\%\Delta Q_{D_{1800\,cm^3}}}{\%\Delta P_{petrol}} \Rightarrow \%\Delta Q_{D_{1800\,cm^3}} = -2 \times \%\Delta P_{petrol} = -50\,\%$$

$$\Rightarrow \Delta Q_{D_{1800\,cm^3}} = Q_{D_{1800\,cm^3}} \times \%\Delta Q_{D_{1800\,cm^3}} = 8000 \times -50\,\% = -4000$$

$$XED_{1000\ cm^3,\ petrol} = +2 = \frac{\%\Delta Q_{D_{1000\ cm^3}}}{\%\Delta P_{petrol}} \Rightarrow \%\Delta Q_{D_{1000\ cm^3}} = +2 \times \%\Delta P_{petrol} = +50\ \%$$

$$\Rightarrow \Delta Q_{D_{1000\ cm^3}} = Q_{D_{1800\ cm^3}} \times \%\Delta Q_{D_{1000\ cm^3}} = 16000 \times +50\ \% = +8000$$

$$\Rightarrow \Delta Q_D = \Delta Q_{D_{1000\ cm^3}} + \Delta Q_{D_{1800\ cm^3}} = 8000 + -4000 = +4000$$

11. Which of the following groups will probably have the lowest PED for air travel?

    A   ***Business executives.***

    B   people who are afraid of flying

    C   students.

    D   retired couples.

Explain A   *Businesses have the least flexibility in travelling times.*

12. A sales tax will fall entirely on the consumer if the

    A   demand curve is perfectly elastic.

    B   supply curve is perfectly inelastic

    C   demand and supply curve are both unitary price elastic.

    D   ***none of the above.***

Explain D   *For the consumer to pay all the sales tax, the consumers must have demand as perfectly price inelastic or supply is perfectly elastic*

13. Consumer surplus will be zero if

    A   Supply is perfectly elastic.

    B   ***Demand is perfectly elastic.***

    C   Price elasticity of demand is 1

    D   None of the above.

Explain B   *In perfect competition, consumers are not willing to consume if price increases.*

14. The price elasticity of supply for a product is more inelastic

    A   the higher the number of firms in the industry.

B   the longer the product can be stored.

C   ***the longer the time required to make the product.***

D   the higher the interchangeability between the factors of production.

Explain   C   *Time lag: producers have less flexibility to supply as products cannot be made quickly.*

15   The diagram below shows the market for basketball shoes.

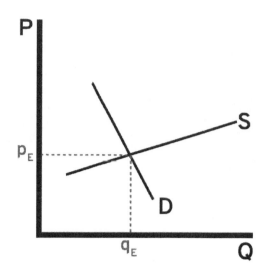

We can deduce from the above diagram that

A   the PED for basketball shoes is constant on a straight demand line.

B   the PES = 1 for basketball shoes in the above market.

C   the market is efficient and the community surplus is higher than the combined sum of consumer and producer surplus.

D   none of the above are correct.

Explain   D *because (**A**: PED is not constant on a demand line) (**B**: PES=1 when supply curve passes through the origin) and (**C**: Community surplus=consumer surplus+ producer surplus)*

16   If the government of Australia increases the tax on passengers using air travel, from $60 to $90 per passenger per trip in the economy class on internal flights the effect of the tax will be to:

A   increase producer surplus for airlines flying internally.

B   increase consumer surplus for passengers flying within Australia.

C   decrease consumer surplus of passengers flying within Australia.

D   increase tax revenue if the demand for internal flights is price elastic.

Explain   *The difference between what the consumer is willing to pay and he actually pays falls and thus the consumer surplus falls assuming PED is not zero.*

17 *b.*   A 10 % increase in sales volume ends up increasing a firm's total revenue by 10 % also. The PED for the firm's product is

   A   PED = 1. Unitary elastic.

   B   PED = 0. Perfectly inelastic

   C   PED = ∞. Perfectly price elastic.

   D   None of the above.

Explain   C   *rise in price will mean less consumer surplus.*

18 *b.*   Assume the pes for a good is 0.8. Initial price is $20 per unit and 500 units are supplied. The market price subsequently increases to $22. What is the total revenue for the firm after the increase in price assuming all production is sold?.

   A $11 880

   B $10 800

   C $ 1 540

   D   None of the above.

Explain A   *8 percent increase in units makes 540, and 540 times 22 is 11880*

EVALUATION QUESTIONS   (Elasticity II: Applications)

19.   Evaluate the view that since cigarettes are highly addictive high sales taxes will only drive smokers underground, making this policy counterproductive.

- *Explain the concept of ped and why it is low for cigarettes. Similarly explain high pes for cigarettes.*

- *Diagram to show low ped, high pes. This means that most of the tax will be passed on to the smoker.*

- *The lower the ped the higher the tax will need to be to elicit the required behaviour. However the higher final price relative to cost of actually producing the cigarettes the greater the danger of encouraging the development of smuggling/ illegal economy. Here quality control may be lost along with tax revenues but the health problems still remain at previous levels.   For this reason government use several complementary policies. Tax combined with education, ban in public places, like restaurants, airlines, trains and more recently in the car when there is the presence of a child. All the policies have drawbacks.*

- *Some governments have started promoting 'safer' substitutes such as e-cigarettes.*

20.   Copper, cocoa, and coffee are basic commodities which fluctuate more in price and output than manufactured goods such as cars and computer chips. Discuss the validity of this view.

- *Define ped and pes and explain why for commodities ped is low and pes is low in the short run. Similarly explain why both ped and pes is much higher for manufacturing goods.*

- *Put the above on two side by side diagrams, customised for commodities and manufactures. Show small shifts in demand and/or supply of cocoa leads to big rises in price. Much lower level of fluctuation for cars.*

- *Explain that this is more likely in the short run than in the long run as more options are available in the long run.*

21.   Using demand and supply diagrams along with elasticities, evaluate the view that 'drug education is preferable to drug prohibition.'

- *Hard drugs are particularly addictive and hence have a very low ped. The pes is usually elastic. Prohibition will simply reduce supply and raise prices. This encourages the black market even further leading to more producers who are attracted by the high profit margins. The higher profits increase the power of the drug barons.*

- *Drug education is a slow process but the results are particularly strong at early education levels. Programmes require funds which entail an opportunity cost. Poorly designed programme may have no effect.*

- *Use diagram which moves from normal d & s diagram to one where demand decreases due to successful education. D1 shifts left to D2.*

- *Most policies today are aimed at drug education, rehabilitation, promoting safer substitutes, prosecution of suppliers and drug takers in the case of hard drugs. Success rates vary from place to place.*

22.   A city government introduces a specific tax per square metre of land. Evaluate the view that land-owners and developers will be disproportionately affected and hence will not be willing to build apartments or rent out properties.

- *Since land is a fixed asset (fixed in supply unlike say bread) and it has no substitutes, the tax will be completely passed on to the land developer.*

- *For the land developer the cost of the land for any development will rise. This is a rise in the fixed cost. This is one of many component cost of development. The supply of any one particular type of land use say apartments will fall. Higher prices mean some demand for apartments may fall and profits may also fall. Some developers may be deterred from supplying apartments if they are unable to pass on the higher cost to the renter.*

- *Use 2 diagrams. One diagram for landowner whose supply is fixed. (all the tax passed on to land developer) and one standard diagram for land developer. At the developer stage the number of substitutes in terms of uses rise.*

23.   Examine the merits of the state giving rent subsidies to low income households wishing to rent apartments with low price elasticities of supply in the city.

- *In the free market the forces of demand and supply determine equilibrium price and quantity. At this equilibrium price/rent there may be many who cannot afford the rent due to their low incomes. These low income workers are needed to enable cities to function and remain competitive against other cities. They often work in a labour market which is in surplus and suffering from depressed wages. There is macroeconomic failure in the labour market. The government hence steps in and regulates or rations a certain section of the low income housing market.*

- *Here low income households are given money to pay towards their rent.   The demand line shifts to right. The pes is low and hence most of the subsidy ends up in raising apartment rents. New developers or landlords are more likely to enter the market and increase supply in the long run.*

- *This method brings some relief to the lowest income households. New apartments are encouraged to be developed. There is a fair degree of exploitation of the system. Tax payer picks up the tab. These funds may be limited and have an opportunity cost as other programmes are deprived of resources. There is a fair degree of deadweight loss (show on diagram) as resources are used up in setting up, implementing and policing this subsidy. Government in poor countries may not have funds. There is also a distortion in terms of land use away from non subsidy uses to subsidy uses.*

-

24.   A government decides to raise the minimum wage for unskilled workers. Evaluate the effects of this policy on stakeholders if:

(a)   both demand for and supply of workers is wage **inelastic**.

- *(a) Diagram with low ped and low pes for labour market. An increase in minimum wage will have very little effect unemployment. This is because supply of labour (move along the same supply curve) changes very little and so does the demand for workers. A really big wage increase may be needed to have a big change. The workers may enjoy a higher standard of living without losing their jobs. Employers may be able to pass on the rise to customers through higher prices especially if the products/services are price inelastic and target to the well-off in society.*

(b)   both demand for and supply of workers is wage **elastic**.

-    *(b) Diagram where both D & S are flatter (wage elastic). The supply of labour will respond positively and employers will cut back the numbers employed dramatically. The result is a big gap between demand for labour and supply of labour. High level of unemployment especially if consumers of products have very low incomes or if there are many lower price substitutes from abroad.*

6 MARKET FAILURE

1. Define market failure.
    When marginal social cost does not equal to marginal social benefit for the last unit produced.

2. Define marginal private cost (MPC).
    The cost of factors of production, the amount that must be charged to the fee paying individuals

3. What is the MPC of owning a car?
    Price of car, insurance, servicing, petrol, tolls

4. Define external cost (EC) using the example of owning a car.
    The cost of activity to the third party. For a car, third party cost could be the pedestrian (neither buyer nor seller)

5. Marginal Social Cost (MSC)
    MSC=Marginal private cost + External cost

6. Define marginal private benefit (MPB).
    The additional satisfaction or utility that a buyer receives from consuming an additional unit of a good or services

7. What is the MPB of getting an eye test?
    Benefit of seeing clearly, security, personal enjoyment

8. What is the external benefit (EB) from an eye test?
    Reduced probability of accidents affecting the rest of society

9. Marginal Social Benefit (MSB)
    MSB=Marginal private benefit + External benefit

10. A. Market Failure occurs when not all costs and benefits are taken into account. **_True_** / False.
    B. Last unit will not have MSC equal to MSB   **_True_** / False.

11. List 5 examples of market failure.
    -Positive externality in production: Bees for honey production leading to pollination for farmers, multinational corporation installing fibre optic cables which also helps new businesses to form.
    -Positive externality in consumption: Vaccination, eye test, safe sex
    -Negative externality in production: pollution from factories, oil spills, nuclear energy production
    -Negative externality in consumption: Cigarette, alcohol abuse, obesity

12. MSB > MPB is the definition of demerit / **_merit_** goods .

13. MSC > MPC is the definition of **_demerit_** / merit goods

14.   List 3 examples of **negative externalities of production**.

> *-Pollution from factories (smog, inhale toxics constantly, higher health service cost, less clean air to breath. Illustrated by China)*
> *-Oil spills (marine ecosystem destroyed/die)-Nuclear explosion (Chernobyl/Fukushima; contamination of radioactivity, cancer, weird species coming from Japan)*

15.   Illustrate and fully label **negative externalities of production** in the diagram below using free market price and quantity as P_{FM} , Q_{FM} and society's optimum price and quantity as P_{SO}, Q_{SO}. **Note: (so = society's optimum)**

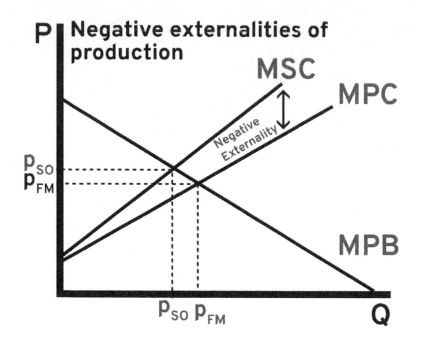

Here the free market partially fails since it **over-produces ($Q_{FM} > Q_{SO}$)** and **under-prices ($P_{FM} < P_{SO}$)** compared to society's optimum.

16.   List 3 examples of **negative externalities of consumption**.

> *-Cigarettes smoking (smoking deteriorates the smokers' health and harms third party via second-health smoke)*
> *-Obesity (obesity deteriorates the health of that individual, health problem, more cost for health service using tax payer's money, lower productivity. See US and many developed countries)*
> *-Alcohol/drug abuse (harms the mental, physical health, less productivity, violence and crime in that area, more money goes to health service)*

Illustrate and fully label **negative externalities of consumption** in the diagram below using free market price and quantity as P$_{FM}$, Q$_{FM}$ and society's optimum price and quantity as P$_{SO}$, Q$_{SO}$.

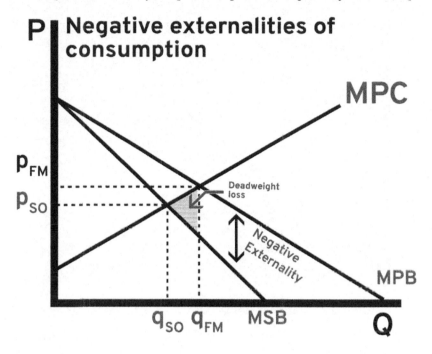

Here the free market (FM) fails since it **over-produces (Q$_{FM}$ > Q$_{SO}$)** and **under-prices (P$_{FM}$ < P$_{SO}$)** compared to society's optimum

17.   List 3 examples of **positive externalities of production**.

   -Bees and honey (bees helps pollination for fruits)

   -Training (If a worker is trained before the work, that worker is more efficient hence saves cost of training for the company)

   -Plantation of new trees (more oxygen and less carbon dioxide, feel more fresh)

Illustrate and fully label this in the diagram below using free market price and quantity as P_{FM}, Q_{FM} and society's optimum price and quantity as P_{SO}, Q_{SO}.

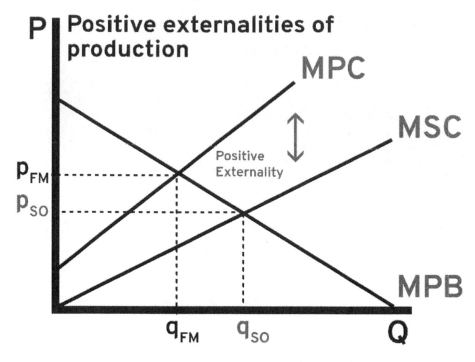

Here the free market fails since it **under-produces (Q_{FM} < Q_{SO})** and **over-prices (P_{FM} > P_{SO})** compared to society's optimum

18.   List 3 examples of **positive externalities of consumption.**

> *-Education (increase quality of human capital; higher skills/productivity in communication make other workers more productive, less money to health services)*
> *-Vaccination (less money on health services, less chance of contagion, increase productivity)*
> *-Hybrid car (reduces pollution/emission by purchasing hybrid car)*

Illustrate and fully label **positive externalities of consumption** in the diagram below using free market price and quantity as P_{FM}, Q_{FM} and society's optimum price and quantity as P_{SO}, Q_{SO}.

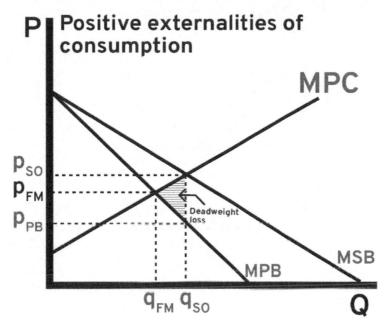

Here the free market fails since it **under-consumes ($Q_{FM} < Q_{SO}$)** and **over-prices ($P_{FM} > P_{PB}$)** compared to society's optimum. P_{PB} represents the price consumers will need to pay to ensure society's optimum level of consumption. P_{SO} represents society's price if *all* costs and benefits are internalised.

19.   Vaccinations are considered by economists as an example of merit goods.

(a)   Explain why vaccinations are considered as merits goods.

> *MSB vaccination > MPB vaccination*
> *The full benefits of vaccination is greater for society than for the fee paying individual*
> *Receiving vaccination gives beneficiary effects to the community by reducing chance of spreading disease, improved health, less money on health services, increase productivity*

b)   Draw and label appropriately, the diagram below showing the case for vaccination.

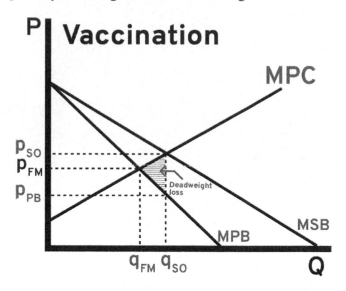

c)   When all costs and benefits are included we have socially optimum/efficient level of production. Show this in the diagram above as Q_{SO}.

d)   What does the shaded area depict and explain what does it means?

__Shaded area shows deadweight loss. It represents the resources that are misallocated under the free-market because of market failure. Area between MPC and MSB for omitted units.__

e)   Is the marginal social cost (MSC) less or greater than marginal social benefit (MSB) at the free market output Q_{FM}?

__Marginal social cost is less than marginal social benefit at the free market output because the market ignores the fact that vaccination benefits the third parties. There are no external costs.__

f)   Would an introduction of an indirect tax be appropriate to remove the deadweight loss.

__No, introduction of an indirect tax does not remove, but increases the deadweight loss. The supply curve shifts left, as the tax, discourages producers from producing vaccination. The government might be better off using a subsidy to remove deadweight loss.__

20.   Market failure in a free market economy can occur when

A   the costs of pollution are already taken into account by the free market.

B   a tax on cars which use diesel is introduced to reduce pollution.

C   no property rights have been allocated.

D   private firms are contracted out by the government to provide schools.

Explain C *is an example of tragedy of the commons because the there is no ownership of land, which leads to abuse of resources. The sustainability is threatened.*

21.   **Market for Ebola vaccine**

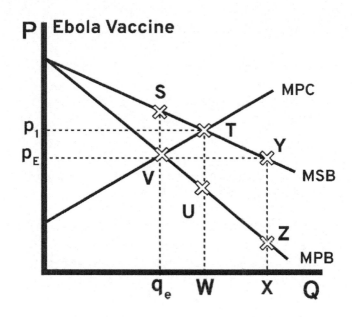

At the current equilibrium price level Pe and quantity Qe,

   A   there is no market failure.

   B   there is market failure since society's optimum price is P1.

   C   *free market under produces by the amount QeW when compared to society's optimum.*

   D   there is market failure and government could subsidise by yz per unit to correct this failure.

22. The US government has provided aid to Haiti to rebuild the destruction of its public goods. Select the statement which is **true** regarding public goods.

   A   Public goods such as schools can only be provided by the government.

   B   Public goods are rivalrous such as street lighting but not excludable.

   C   Private sector will not provide sufficient and charge too high a price for poor consumers.

   D   **Private sector will fail since pure public goods are non-rivalrous and non-excludable**.

Explain D   *Public goods are example of complete market failure because they are non-rivalrous and non-excludable, private sectors will not provide them under the free-market unless the government intervenes. (Only provided in free market if goods are rivalrous and excludable)*

23.   A waste disposal company was caught illegally dumping in the local lake and found guilty by the courts. The above incident shows one of the following;

    A   Free market does not work, and the government should nationalise the company.

    B   **Free market does work since property rights are clearly defined and exercised.**

    C   There is a strong need to increase taxes on waste disposal companies.

    D   None of the above.

Explain *B*   *The property rights are defined and fringed upon, hence the company was found guilty by the courts. This therefore shows that free market is working efficiently.*

24.   The diagram below depicts all the costs and benefits of producing a good.

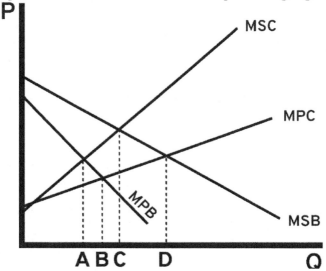

From society's point of view what level of output is considered efficient.

          A   B   **C**   D

Explain C   *All costs and benefits are fully considered, internalised. MSB=MSC at point C*

25.   A coal power station in Poland pollutes the atmosphere and suffocates trees in both Poland and the nearby country of Germany. Which one of the following is an example of the external costs in this case?

    A   Costs to the power station of installing new technology to reduce pollution.

    B   **The cost of planting new trees in Germany and Poland.**

    C   The cost of cleaning up the dead trees in Poland.

    D   The damage done to trees in both Poland and Germany

26.   Which of the is following is the best example of a public good?

    A.   postal services

    B.   airports

    C.   public/state schools

    D.   fireworks display on New Year's Eve.

Explain D   *is non-rivalrous and non-excludable*

27.   List 5 policies governments can use to correct market failure.

        -Subsidies
        -Indirect taxation
        -Cap-and-trade scheme
        -Quotas
        -Advertisement
        -Legislation
        -Property rights and buffer schemes.

28.   List 5 problems/side-effects government face in correcting market failure.

-   *Opportunity cost of implementing policies: taxpayers' money*
-   *Difficult to determine the size of externality*
-   *Deadweight loss to monitor/maintaining policies*
-   *Possible government failure: failure caused by inappropriate government intervention*
-   *Policies not always efficient: loopholes*
-   *May discourage private sectors from producing if the policies strongly disadvantages the private sector. Companies may translocate to country with looser legislation.*
-   *Lobbying.*

EVALUATION QUESTIONS   (Market Failure)

29.   Evaluate the proposition that government intervention in the market for sugary drinks and junk food is justified.

- *Government intervention usually takes place if the consumption of these result in significant negative externalities of consumption, external cost (EC > 0)*
- *Define market failure with MSB<MPB (EB <0).*
- *Diagram with examples of costs to third parties. Diagram must be customised.*
- *Free market partially fails as it under prices and over produces these products.*
- *Government intervention can take the form of taxation, subsidies, and regulations on where to consume, regulation on contents, awareness campaigns.*
- *Size of taxation depends on PED (low PED will need high level of tax), size of externality, required revenues to finance other campaigns and pay for clearing up healthcare problems.*
- *Food lobby are going to come kicking and screaming. Just like the cigarette companies, the airlines for smoking, car companies for seat belts.*

30.   Evaluate three methods of reducing the external costs of smoking.

- *Define market failure and external costs in terms of smoking. (what is the negative externality of consumption for cigarettes).*
- *Diagram customised. Low PED and high PES, explained.*
- *Method 1: Tax per packet of cigarettes. Tax will have to be high since PED is low. Most of tax paid by consumer. Debate on quantifying the size of externality. Too high a tax and danger is that the market goes underground. Tax revenues lost, legitimate factories shut down with jobs lost. Smokers are voters who may revolt. Cigarette companies leave the country, or they focus on lobbying or they come after kicking and screaming.*
- *Method 2: Education. Raising awareness on the dangers of smoking. Process slow and requires resources. Young more responsive than the older generation who are firmly addicted. Young may rebel as education represents the establishment and big brother.*
- *Countries have had reasonable success.*
- *Method 3: Regulations on content of cigarettes, advertising rules, places where smoking not allowed to protect the innocent bystanders e.g. in building, planes, railways, workplaces, bars and restaurants. Lobbying by cigarette firms may make rules introduction more difficult. Personal freedom used as an excuse. Loss of jobs, bars lose clients. Evidence shows new customers attract to smoke free environment more than compensates*
- *Usually governments end up using all three methods when they become serious.*

31.   Evaluate the view that free markets can never exist since producers/sellers **always** have more information than consumers/buyers on products.

- *Define free market as where forces of demand and supply came together to determine equilibrium price and quantity.*
- *Simple D & S to determine equilibrium p & q. Here consumer surplus + producer surplus = community/social surplus. There is no deadweight loss and there is allocative efficiency.*
- *Behind the D curve lays the assumption that the consumer aims to maximise utility from a given level of income. However, if the consumer cannot calculate the level of utility than she/he may be paying too much or too little. This is clearly seen when we buy a product that we come to regret as it did not bring us the assumed level of satisfaction. Companies often use advertising to influence the consumer's perception of utility.*

- *In other areas such as doctors, plumbers, tutors, realtors, car mechanics, there is a problem of asymmetrical information where the sellers usually have more information on the product than the buyers. It is in their interest to sell the buyer more than they need.*
- *For insurance companies the problem may be reversed as buyer of insurance does not always reveal all the information that the insurance company wishes. This is why many forms of insurances have very long and detailed forms which need to be filled and vetted before the insurance companies accept the customer.*
- *D & S are essentially distorted and there is mispricing than under full information.*

32.   Explain why overfishing is considered an example of market failure. Evaluate the policies available for governments to correct this type of market failure.

- *Define market failure as MSC not equal to MSB. Explain with example and diagram.*
- *Overfishing is when rate of fishing exceeds the rate of replenishment of stocks.*
- *Explain 'tragedy of the commons' for fishing. Problem of lack of property rights.*
- *Government needs to step in and assign property rights to a newly created body. Eg parks and public spaces or coastline.*
- *If the problem relates to more than one country eg ocean, space then international cooperation required in assigning property rights or limiting/rationing the use of the ocean by issuing fishing quotas.*
- *Evaluation involves the degree to which countries agree, implementation, policing. Not easy if there are many non- cooperative parties involved or the rules are weak.*

33.   Evaluate the view that creating a market for tradable permits to reduce air pollution is always preferable to setting strict environmental standards because it offers greater efficiency.

- *Air pollution is an example of market failure where MSB does not equal MSC. Here the problem is that the atmosphere lacks property rights and that the problem is global and hence requires joint country solution.*
- *To internalise this negative externality free market introduces a market for trading permits. Explain this using a diagram.*
- *Environmental regulations set minimum standards of behaviour. These standards can be set too high (seriously damaging economic activity) or set too low (no significant effect on pollution controls). Firms, countries, free riders look to exploit any loopholes. Governments use up scarce funds in policing the standards. Lobby groups manipulate and distort the process.*
- *With trading permits too many may be issued (supply>demand) and permit price end up too low and hence insufficient to bite into a firms costs and persuade them to change their behaviour. Firms buy permits in low price markets from countries with surplus permits. Some firms may relocate to more 'business friendly' regions and continue polluting and gain an advantage over firms who do reduce their pollution. Some jobs lost due to relocation. Bad behaviour rewarded over good behaviour.*
- *Global standards need to be set and rigorously policed.*

34.   Evaluate the arguments behind the decision by many Swiss cities to subsidize the purchase of electric bicycles.

- *Define market failure as MSB does not equal MSC.*
- *For bicycles MSB>MPB (merit goods) resulting in external benefit >0 since the use of pedal and electric bicycles lead to less traffic congestion since there is a lower level of car traffic and cleaner air at peak times. Journey times quicken and clean air benefits all. Diagram to illustrate.*
- *Government intervenes to promote greater consumption of merit goods using subsidies, advertising or education, and regulation.*
- *Subsidies bring down the cost of production and subsequently the price. The larger the external benefit the larger the subsidy. Quantifying this is not an exact science.*

- *Subsidy towards electric bicycles as oppose to pedal bicycles is aimed particularly to encourage the older generation to remain active. This brings very strong health benefits and cost savings.*
- *Other indirect benefits are less repair costs on roads since the lower level of car traffic.*
- *Note: there is an opportunity cost for government funds being used to finance the subsidy.*

35.   To what extent would you consider internet piracy a 'free rider' problem? Evaluate the policies available for a government to deal with this issue.

- *Market for internet downloads suffers from the free rider problem because the product can be consumed without paying for it. In addition since the marginal cost of one more download is almost zero, the product is non-rivalrous. Together the internet download market is behaving as if it is a private market when essentially it is closer to being a public good.*
- *Cost of excluding the non-payer can be very high in both monetary terms and non- monetary terms. Internet companies would like the taxpayer to use up all the policing resources to ensure their property rights are fully protected. (piracy vs privacy issue). Irony is that these companies are keen to avoid paying taxes.*
- *We now have a double free rider problem. (consumer and producer)*
- *In the MC=0 economy the free market and hence most efficient solution is to bring the prices of these products down through competition and less government intervention such that piracy is not economically viable. The internet companies gain less per unit but their audience/reach is global. Heavy duty government protection simply preserves the companies' monopoly profits.*
- *The gains from the applications of the internet are currently not shared equitably and the problem or free rider arises.*

36.   Checking a book out of the school library and not returning it on time creates a negative externality of consumption.

(a) Explain the negative externality here.

- *(a) Not returning a book on time means the rest of borrowers are denied access. (time element crucial since the borrower has had enough time to read the book). Diagram*

(b) Discuss the merits of charging a huge fine instead of a small fine.

- *(b) Theory of nudge. Too high a fine either scares some readers from borrowing in the first place as they worry about the stress of missing the deadline or not being able to afford the high penalty. Too low a fine and the user simply ignores the deadline and hence others denied access. There internet ebook technology, MC=0 can be employed to resolve this problem more efficiently without denying the writers from equitable rewards. This is the same problem as what level of parking charges to set.*

7 PRODUCTION, COSTS & REVENUE (HIGHER ONLY)

PRODUCTION

The relationship between the factors of production (inputs) that a firm uses and the resulting output is known as the production function. The production function in the short-run is governed by the law of diminishing returns whereas in the long run the returns to scale determine the nature of the relationship between inputs and output.

1. Define short-run: *the period of time during which at least one factor of production is fixed/constant*

2. Define long-run: *the period for which all factors of production are variable*

3. State the law of diminishing returns: *As more and more variable factors are added to a fixed factor there comes a point beyond which each additional variable factor will contribute less and less to the final output. (short run concept)*

4. Define total physical product (TPP) in words: *Final quantity of output produced using inputs*

5. Define average physical product (APP) in words and formula:

   Average physical output/product; amount that an average worker produces

   $$APP = \frac{TPP}{Input}$$

6. Define marginal physical product (MPP) in words and formula

   The additional amount that the next unit of input produces.

   $$MPP = \frac{\Delta TPP}{\Delta Input}$$

7. Assume a mango farmer has a fixed piece of land and equipment/physical capital. The farmer is able to increase or decrease the number of workers. The farm is faced with the following production function in the short run:

Labour	TPP (100 kg)	APP (100 kg)	MPP (100 kg)
0	0	0	—
1	43	43	43
2	160	80	117
3	351	117	191
4	600	150	249
5	875	175	275
6	1152	192	277
7	1372	196	220
8	1536	192	164
9	1656	184	120
10	1750	175	94
11	1815	165	65
12	1860	155	45
13	1885	145	25
14	1875	133.9	–10

a) Fill in the values for APP and MPP above.

b) At what number of workers does the law of diminishing **average** returns set in? *8th worker*

   Explain: *The average falls from when the 8ᵗʰ worker is added*

c) At what number of workers does the law of diminishing **marginal** returns set in? *7ᵗʰ worker*

   Explain: *The value of MPP begins to decrease from the 7th worker. Additional worker, 8th worker, contributes less than the previous worker.*

d)   Verify that the above data can be shown in the 2 diagrams below. Diagram 1 depicts the relationship between labour and TPP. Diagram 2 depicts the relationship between labour and APP and MPP.

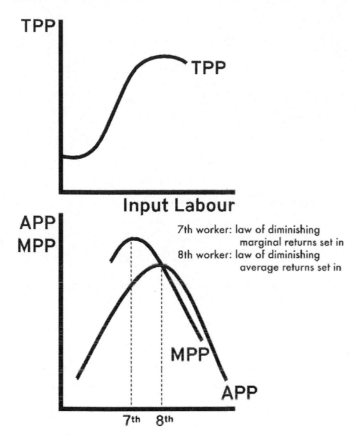

e)   From the above diagram, we can describe the relationship between average values and marginal values.

   If MPP > APP then APP will   <u>*rise*</u> */ fall / stay constant.*

   If MPP < APP then APP will   *rise /* <u>*fall*</u> */ stay constant.*

   If MPP = APP then APP will   *rise / fall /* <u>**stay constant.**</u>

COSTS

The full cost of producing a given level of output is known as total cost (TC). Total cost is made up of fixed cost (FC) and variable cost (VC). TC = FC + VC

8.   Define fixed costs (FC): *Fixed costs are costs which do not vary with the level of output*

9.   List 5 examples of FC for a pizzeria:

   -Rent

   -Interest payment

   -Building insurance

   -Loan for machinery

   -Cost of manager

   -Cost of land

10.   Define variable costs (VC): *Variable costs are costs that rise directly as output rises and fall when output falls.*

11.   List 5 examples of VC:

   -Wages for piece workers

   -Costs of raw materials

   -Costs of fuels

   -Cost of photocopying

   -Cost of shipping to customer

12.   Define and explain using an example marginal cost (MC): *Cost of producing an additional unit of goods: cost to the school for teaching one extra student*

13.   The MC of producing one more digital download is higher / *lower* than the MC of producing one more loaf of bread.

Explain: *The MC of producing digital download is negligible/almost zero compared to that of producing bread which still requires more flour, transport, oil etc.*

14.   Complete the following:

a) TC / Q = **AC**   b) (TC – VC) / Q = **AFC**   c) AC – AFC = **AVC**

d) Sum of MC = **VC**   e) Sum of MC + FC = **TC**

15.   The existence of FC for a firm implies that the firm is operating in the long run / ***short run.*** In the long run the firm has many more options in how it uses its inputs. It can expand or even shut down altogether. This means all costs are fixed / ***variable*** in the long run.

16.   Cost ($) data for a firm is given below.

Output	Total Costs ($)			Average Costs ($)			Marginal Costs ($)
q	FC	VC	TC	AFC	AVC	AC	MC
0	**116**	**0**	116	—	—	—	—
1	**116**	24	**140**	116	**24**	**140**	**24**
2	**116**	**44**	**160**	58	22	80	**20**
3	**116**	**60**	176	**38.7**	20	**58.7**	**16**
4	**116**	84	**200**	**29**	21	50	**24**
5	**116**	124	**240**	23.2	**24.8**	**48.0**	**40**
6	**116**	180	**296**	**19.3**	30	**49.3**	**56**
7	**116**	**252**	**368**	**16.6**	36	**52.6**	**72**
8	**116**	**340**	**456**	**14.5**	**42.5**	57	**88**
9	**116**	**514**	**630**	**12.9**	**57.1**	70	**174**

a)   Complete the above table of costs.

b)   Using the above data sketch two diagrams below. Diagram 1 depicts the relationship between output and FC, VC and TC. Diagram 2 depicts the relationship between output and AVC, AC and MC.

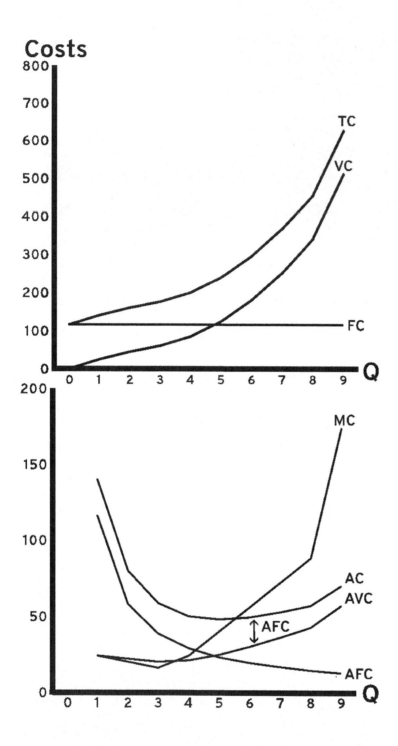

c)   At what level of output does diminishing marginal returns set in: **_3rd output_**

d)   At what level of output do diminishing average returns set in: **5.5th output**

e)   Does the relationship between marginal cost and average cost still hold as in the previous question Q16 ?   **_Yes_**

f) The MC curve must **always** cut the AC curve at minimum AC   *T.* / F

g) If the firm's fixed costs rise what happens to the following curves:

average cost curve: *Rise/ moves upward*

marginal cost curve: *Unaffected*

fixed cost line*: Shifts upward*

variable cost curve: *Unaffected*

total cost curve: *Shifts upward*

If the short run period is characterised by the law of diminishing returns then the long run equivalent is returns to scale.

17. Define economies of scale: *The output produced increases more proportionally to input added. Alternatively when all inputs (Fops) in the production process rise by X% and the resulting output rises by more than X%. Here the long run average costs are falling as the size of the factory expands.*

18. List 5 examples of economies of scale.

-*Bulk purchasing economies*

-*Transport economies*

-*Technical economies*

-*Managerial economies*

-*Financial economies*

19. Define constant returns of scale: *The output increases at same proportion to input added, when all inputs vary. Alternatively when all inputs (Fops)in the production process rise by X% and the resulting output rises by exactly X%. Here the long run average costs remain constant.*

20. Define diseconomies of scale: *The output increases less proportionally to input added. Alternatively when all inputs (Fops)in the production process rise by X% and the resulting output rises by less than X%. Here the long run average costs rise as the plant size expands.*

21. List 5 examples of diseconomies of scale

- *Communication problem*

-*Logistic problems/organisation*

-*Storage*

-*Demotivation*

-*Mistakes costs are bigger*

22.   Define the Minimum Efficient Plant Size (MEPS) and explain what this means for different sizes of firms: *The minimum a firm must produce to arrive at minimum long run average cost. This means that here smaller firms are able to compete with large firms in terms of average costs.*

23.   Draw an envelope curve which expresses the relationship between the short run and long run average and marginal costs.

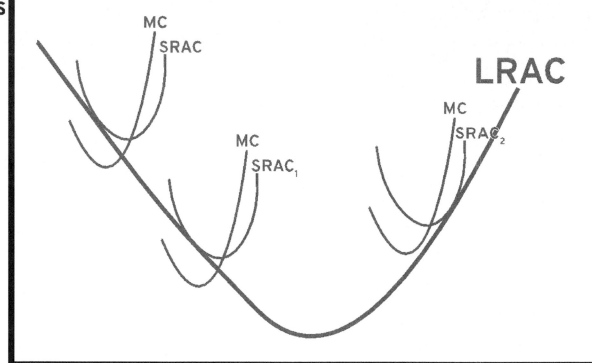

REVENUE

24.   Define total revenue (TR)/total income for a firm and state the formula.

   The total income the company receives from selling its output.   *TR = P x Q*

25.   Using the formula for average revenue (AR), show how the demand line is the same as the AR line

   AR= Total Revenue / output = P.   With Q on the horizontal axis gives the demand line.

26.   Define marginal revenue (MR) in words and formula

   The added income the firm receives on the next unit sold.

   MR = change in total revenue / change in Q

27.   State the relationship between MR and AR.

   If MR_ >AR, then AR is rising. If MR=AR, AR is constant. If MR< AR, then AR is falling.MR line is twice as steep as AR line.

28.   TR = sum of *MR.*   ***True***

29.   For the data below complete the revenue table:

Price ($)	Quantity Demanded (Q_d)	TR ($)	AR ($)	MR ($)
0	10	0	0	=
1	9	9	1	9
2	8	16	2	7
3	7	21	3	5
4	6	24	4	3
5	5	25	5	1
6	4	24	6	−1
7	3	21	7	−3
8	2	16	8	−5
9	1	9	9	−7
10	0	0	10	−9

30.   Draw and fully label the 2 diagrams below. The top diagram shows the relationship between output and AR and MR. The bottom diagram is a direct projection to show the relationship between output sold and the TR.

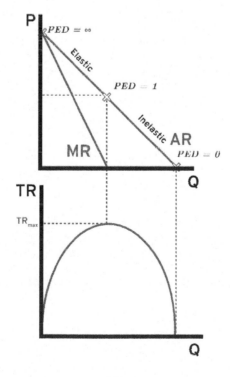

31.   List 5 advantages a large firm has over a small firm

Transport economies of scale, financial economies of scales, marketing economies of scale, more likely to be a price maker (company has market power), government favouritism, cost of research and development per unit is spread.

32.   List 5 advantages small firms have over large firms

Greater customisation, more flexible in changing, more local support, family keeps control of the company, less need to satisfy shareholders and the share market, niche marketing, no diseconomies from communication issues, etc.

33.   Diminishing returns to production come about because

A   more production can only be sold at a lower price.

B   extra production and consumption brings less and less satisfaction.

C   inputs are not always interchangeable.

D   none of the above.

Explain C   *At least one factor of production is fixed and others are not interchangeable*

34.   A firm notices that its short run average cost rises when its produces more or less. This means:

A   the firms is experiencing constant returns to scale.

B   the firm is currently producing at minimum average costs.

C   the firm is currently maximising its profits.

D   the allocation of resources is efficient at the moment.

Explain B *The firm is producing at minimum average cost.*

35   A firm has noticed that doubling all its factors of production has resulted in output more than doubling. This means:

A   the firm is experiencing decreasing returns to scale.

B   the firm's profit will rise.

C   the law of diminishing returns has not set in yet.

D   none of the above.

Explain D   *The company is experiencing increasing returns to of scale.*

36.   Which one of the following is good example a fixed costs:

    A   the tax paid on the profits it makes.

    B   the cost of energy used in making the product.

    C   **the interest costs the firm pays on the bank loan it has taken out.**

    D   the cost of raw materials used in the production.

Explain C   *Interest cost. It depends on size of loan, not the size of output.*

EVALUATION QUESTIONS   (Production, Costs & Revenue)

37.   Distinguish factors which shift the production function in the short run and average costs in the long run.   *Define short run and long run production function.*

- *In short run one of the FoPs has be constant. If labour, raw materials, machinery or entrepreneurship change in values then production function will shift. Use diagram to show this shift.*
- *In long run all FoPs have to change. The scale of production can change and thereby new technology changes the method of production. The internet, 3D printing has the capacity to shift the long term relationship between inputs and the corresponding output.*

38.   What effect do major inventions such as the internet have on the production function?
- *The internet changes the relationship between the FoPs. The production process becomes more capital intensive. The resources needed to produce one more unit fall with music download. The shape of production function will change. In the long run the production function will shift upwards as each unit of input results in higher level of output.*

39.   Using cost and revenue diagrams explain how price of laptops and tablet computers have fallen significantly over-time when demand has steadily increased.

- *Demand line (AR line shifts out due to get level infiltration of laptops and tablets in people's lives).*
- *LRAC curve shifts down as with greater scale of production there are various economies and dynamic efficiencies to be achieved.*
- *The profit margins (AR – AC) rise. This attracts new players to compete. Supply rises and prices fall to encourage a greater take up of these products. Use diagrams.*

40.   To what extent would you agree that large firms are more efficient than small firms?

- *Define efficiency particularly production efficiency. Large firms usually gain from economies of scale.*
- *List and explain with examples each of the economies of scale. Use diagram to illustrate.*
- *However, there are sectors where scope of economies of scale is very limited as the customer cherishes customisation, personal service, and specialisation. Areas such as doctors, tutors, piano teachers, personal shopper, lawyers, personal trainers, hair dressers focus on this. Here large firms are not more efficient.*
- *There is also the case where due to the technical nature of the production process a small bakery or brewery can produce as efficiently as a large producer due to the minimum efficient plant size (MEPS) being achieved at low output. Diagram to illustrate.*

41.   If globalisation offers huge benefits from economies of scale then why do so many small and medium size enterprises operate profitably in the world today? Discuss.

- *Define pure globalisation as the free movement of FoPs and finals goods and services across the world. Global companies can then fully use economies of scale in production and marketing to maximise their profits.*
- *List the many different types of economies of scale with a diagram of the LRAC.*
- *Small and medium size enterprises (sme) exist or several reasons. The meps (minimum efficient plant size) allows sme to have the cost advantage as the large firms. The sme offers products which are customised that large players find no gains. The sme serve a narrow audience and too small for economies to be achieved, such as Ferrari and Bang & Olufson. The sme has crucial technology which the large players lack, e.g. Bose sound systems. The sme may be protected by the government eg. Lots of small local breweries in Germany. The sme may not be interested in expanding and seeking new finance as it may mean loss of control. The sme may be family owned and it wants to stay that way.*

42.   The law of diminishing returns is no longer relevant since world output of agriculture is higher than ever before. Discuss this view.

- *State the Law of diminishing returns, (As more and more variable factors such as fertilizers or workers are added to a fixed factor, land, there comes a point beyond which each additional variable contributes less and less to the final output, agriculture produce)*
- *Agriculture output has been increasing per unit of land but at a decreasing rate in recent years. This implies that the law of diminishing returns in working.*
- *However whenever there is a technological breakthrough such as gene manipulation the equation changes and yields accelerate until this new technology becomes fully exploit.*
- *So the law holds provided the level of technology is constant.*

43.   To what extent is it realistic for a business to halve the price of its product and expect to double its total revenue?

- *Total revenue = P x Q*
- *Best to answer this question by introducing numbers:*
- *P1 = 200, P2 = 100   TR1 = 1000 ,   TR2 = 2000 therefore QD1 = 5 and QD2= 20*
- *For the above to work PED = 6   Demand has to rise by X4*
- *Product has to be very, demand price elastic.*
- *Discussion on what features this good must have.*
- *Overall unrealistic expectation in most cases.*

8 GOALS OF FIRMS & ISSUES FOR FIRMS (HIGHER ONLY)

1.   List 5 goals of a firm

- *Max profit*

- *Max market share / volume of sales*

- *Max Revenue*

- *Breakeven (Charities)*

- *Allocative efficiency (Nationalised company)*

- *Production efficiency*

- *Profit Satisficing*

- *Corporate Social Responsibility*

2.   List 5 barriers to entry for a firm wanting to enter a market.

- *Technical barriers*

- *Patent and copyright, trademarks*

- *Lack of finance / High start-up cost*

- *Government licenses*

- *Economies of scale and insufficient demand*

- *Collusion by incumbent firms*

- *Market structure.*

3.   Define X-inefficiency and illustrate with an example

This is when a firm spends resources on an activity/project which does not generate higher profits (ex: company provides a bigger office for manager but this does not translate into higher productivity). More recurring in a monopoly and oligopolies.

4.   Define efficiency in production .

This is where the firm combines FOPs to achieve lowest AC.

5.   Define dynamic efficiency and provide an example

This is the continuous/ incremental improvements in reducing AC. Memory sticks are the same size but are able to carry huge amount today compared to say 3, 5 or 10 years ago

6.   Explain with appropriate examples the difference between implicit costs and explicit costs.

Explicit costs are any costs to a firm that involve direct payment of money.

Implicit costs is when a firm which already owns FOPs and uses them in one department instead of another department. There is an opportunity cost of using FOPs within the firm.

Profit

In economics the total profit a firm's earns comprises of normal profit and abnormal/supernormal/economic profit.

7.   Define normal profit and explain why is considered as part of costs.

Normal profit is the minimum profit a firm must earn in order to stay in the same line of activity (opportunity cost of the FOPs that firm uses).

8.   Define abnormal profit and explain the role it plays.

Abnormal profit is any profit above normal profit. Businesses are attracted by the prospect of earning abnormal profit.

9.   Profit can be calculated in 3 ways.

   a)   Profit $=$ TR **TC**.

   b)   Profit $=$ (ΛR ΛC) $\times$ **Q**

   c)   Profit = Sum of MR - (Sum of **MC** + FC)

10.   If a firm wishes to maximise its profits or minimise its losses then it must keep producing the revenue it receives from the last units of production it sells (MR) is equal to the cost of producing that last unit (MC).

   a)   If MR > MC the firm should produce *more* / less / stop.

   b)   If MR < MC the firm should produce more /*less* / stop.

   c)   If MR = MC the firm should produce more / less / *stop.*

11.   In the cost and revenue diagram below indicate the profit maximising level of output (Q*) and price (P*) the firm must follow and shade in the area representing maximum profit.

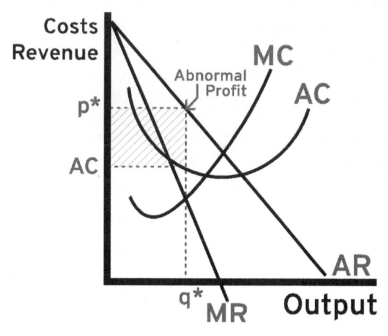

12.   Define external economies of scale and list 3 examples.

This is when the LRAC falls for all firms in the industry.

- Tech advancement available to all firms in one industry.

- Availability of specialized workers from the local university (chemists for drug companies)

- easy access to motorway/freeway to move material helps all firms in the area

13.   In the short run a pizzeria will continue to produce as long as :

    A   marginal cost is below average cost.

    B   marginal cost equals marginal revenue.

    C   average revenue is greater than average variable cost.

    D   marginal cost is higher than average fixed cost.

Explain C *In the short run a firm will carry on producing as long as the price covers the costs of the ingredients in the pizza (avc).*

14.   A kid's cake home delivery company is willing to deliver at a rate of $1 per piece of birthday cake for the first 50 pieces. For orders 51 pieces and more the price per piece falls to 90 cents for all pieces. What is the marginal revenue for the 51st piece?

    A   +$0.90

    B   +$1.00

    C   +$1.10

    D   −$4.10

Explain D *TR for 50 pieces = $50 TR for 51 pieces = $45.90 therefore   MR = $-4.10*

15.   A profit maximising firm operates in 2 different market with different price elasticities of demand. This is possible by :

    A   preventing resale from low price market to higher price market.

    B   MR = MC in each of the markets.

    C   price in market with lower ped is higher than price in higher ped market.

    D   All the above.

Explain D *Successful price discrimination requires all the above conditions.*

16.   For a company AVC = $2,   Output = 20 000,   FC = $80 000

If this company's goal is to earn normal profit only, what price should it charge?

            A $4   B $10   C $4   **D $6.**

Explain D *Normal profit requires TC = TR   This occurs at price = $6*

17.   Abnormal/supernormal/economic profit for a firm is when the profit level achieved is higher than the opportunity cost of using the current factors of production.   **_True_ / False**

EVALUATION QUESTIONS   (Goals & Issues for Firms)

18.   To what extent is an accountant's view of profit different from an economist's view of profit?

- *For an accountant profit is simply the surplus left after costs are taken away from sales revenue.*
- *For economists total costs are opportunity costs of using the factors of production. The entrepreneur here using his/her time in this activity for which there is an opportunity cost. This effort requires a reward and is referred to as normal profit. Normal profit is part of costs. The surplus left after costs are taken away from sales revenue is known as abnormal profits. It is the desire for abnormal profits that attract new businesses to enter this line of activity and produce and compete. A new successful and very profitable product I phone by Apple soon attracts other electronic companies into this market.*

19.   Comment the view that a firm can maximise profits by minimising costs.

- *Use a diagram to show max profit occurs when firms produce until MR=MC.*
- *Here average costs may or may not be at a minimum.*
- *Minimum average cost may for the Ferrari Car company may be at 1million cars a year. However to sell this huge number the price would have to be much lower than the current price in order to find 1 million buyers per year.*
- *Abnormal Profit = total revenue – total costs may end up being lower than before.*

20.   Examine the view that high barriers to entry serve no purpose but to protect profits of existing firms.

- *Define and list the different barriers to entry.*
- *Draw a diagram for a firm which is making abnormal profits. New firms are attracted by this level of profit to start up and produce. If the barriers to entry were weak as in perfect competition and monopolistic market structure then the consumer would gain from more supply, more choice and lower prices. Here it is clear that high barriers will prevent this from happening and it would serve the interests of the existing firms.*
- *However the high barriers enable the existing firms to continue making abnormal profits which in turn could be used to finance new ideas, finance R&D, finance innovation and quality and raise standards. This would also benefit the consumer.*
- *It is hence for the government regulatory body to decide on a case by case basis.*

21.   Discuss to what extent is the use of the profit motive to produce **everything,** realistic or even desirable.

-   *The profit motive serves to direct resources to areas where the returns are the highest for a given level of risk. This leads to allocative efficiency in the use of resources. Goods and services which are valued the most by the market are produced. Consumer sovereignty. This is a very convincing argument for deciding what gets made.*
-   *However, for public goods the free market and hence the profit motive completely fails and leaves society with no national defence as an example. For merit/demerit goods the free market only partially provides these goods. Here the profit motive does not serve society well. Processes which lead to positive or negative externalities are left unchecked under the profit motive. There are cases where there is asymmetrical information and hence valuations are distorted and hence the profit motive is misjudged.*
-   *There are many other drivers/reasons such as altruism as to why goods are produced. Guilt, ego, shame, fame, greed and fear are also other forms of motivators.*

22.   Is it possible for a firm to maximise both profits and revenue/sales at the same time?

-   *Define profit max (MC=MR), and revenue max (MR=0)*
-   *Draw diagram showing that most of the time the marginal cost of production is above zero and hence it is not possible to maximise both.*
-   *However the two are compatible when MC=0=MR. The closest real life example is the digital economy. Here the MC of one more download is almost zero. Explains why there are so many young technology billionaires. Their products serve a global audience and MC=0.*

23.   Using marginal analysis explain the differences between profit maximisation, production efficiency, allocative efficiency, revenue maximisation, break-even in terms of price and output for a firm. (use cost and revenue diagrams)

-   *Use a theory of the firm diagram and show points where MC=MR (profit max), Min AC (production efficiency), P=MC=AR (allocative efficiency), MR=0 (revenue maximisation) and AC=AR (break-even).*

9 PERFECT COMPETITION (HIGHER ONLY)

1.   List 5 assumptions/characteristics of perfect competition.

-Homogeneous products

-Perfect knowledge (same access to information, knows all info about prices)

-No economies of scale

-Each firm is small and insignificant

-Firms are price takers

-No barriers to entry

2.   List 5 stylised examples of perfect competition.

   -Production of cabbages (agriculture), foreign exchange, carrots, apples, milk.

   (*These are essentially homogeneous goods.*)

3.   In perfect competition what is the difference between the industry's demand curve and the demand curve for a single firm. Explain why.

   -Industry's demand curve: downward sloping (law of demand)

   -Demand for a single firm: horizontal (firms are price takers)

4.   The PED for the firm's demand line/average revenue (AR) is

   PED = Infinity and beyond

5.   In perfect competition P = AR = MR for the firm   *True* / False

6.   What does perfect knowledge mean to the consumer and to the producer?

Consumer: knows all the prices & features of all the products in the industry

Producers: each producer knows all the costs & price structures of all other producers

7.   What does freedom to enter and exit mean and what are its implications on profits earned in the short run and long run?

Freedom to enter and exit means there are no entry or exit fees required. This makes it very easy to set up a new firm and compete or to sell out and leave an industry.

Short run: 3 possibilities: Normal profit/abnormal profit/loss possible

Long run: only normal profits available

-If firms had been earning abnormal profit, new firms would enter the industry. Overall supply would rise. Price would be driven down until those abnormal profits are eroded away to restore long run equilibrium of normal profits.

8.   All firms in perfect competition have the same AC curve in the long run.   ***True*** / False

9.   Do individual firms in perfect competition advertise? Yes / ***No***   Why?

-Price takers: firms can produce and sell as much as they wish and no need to advertise if they are by definition unable to raise price without demand falling to zero.

- Advertisement = cost

-Perfect knowledge implies no fooling

10.   In the short run a perfectly competitive firm can make ***normal profit / abnormal profit / losses***. *All three outcomes possible.*

11.   In the long run firms in perfect competition profits earn ***normal*** / abnormal / loss. **Explain** *No barriers to entry*

    -If firm had been earning abnormal profit, new firms would be attracted to enter.

    -If firm had been making losses, other loss making firms leave the industry.

12.   Is perfect competition market structure conducive to innovation? Yes / ***No***

Explain *No barriers to entry*

    -Perfect knowledge: new technology spread to competitors and freely available.

    -Property rights not protected, discouraging investors from taking on risk on

    innovation and any rewards will be short lived.

13.   Use diagrams below to show a firm in perfect competition making **normal** profits.

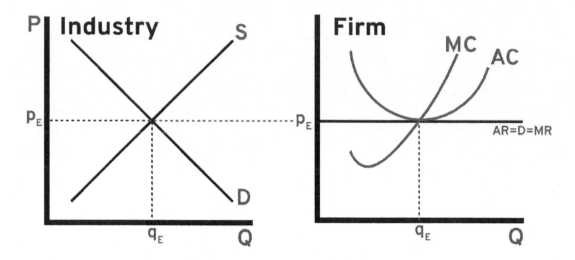

14.   Use diagrams below to show a firm in perfect competition making **abnormal** profits.

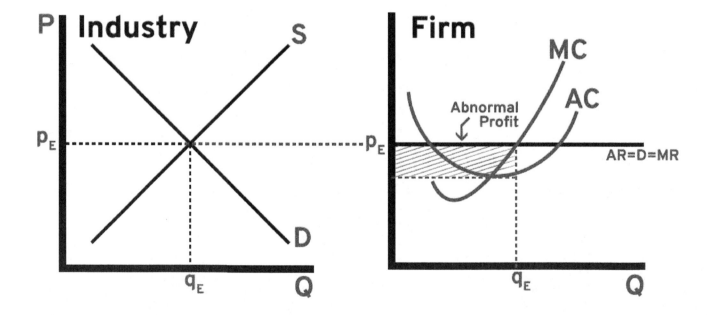

15.   Use diagrams below to show a firm in perfect competition making a **loss**.

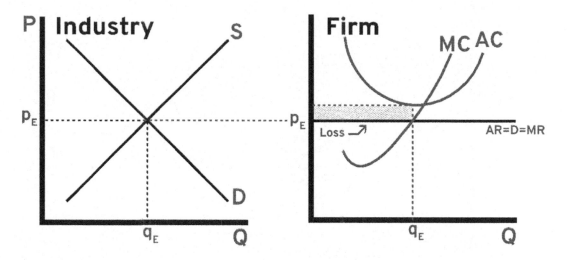

16.   Use diagrams below to show a firm in perfect competition facing **shutdown**.

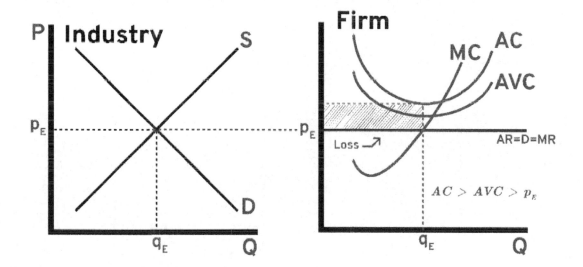

17. Draw the long run equilibrium situation for a firm in perfect competition. Show the condition $P = D = AR = MR = LRAC = LRMC = SRAC = SRMC$ holds.

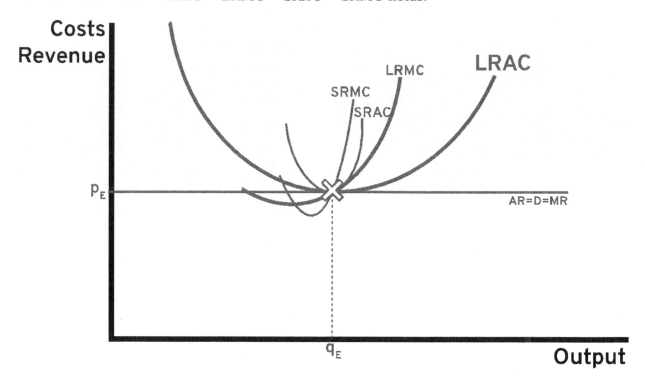

18. A firm in perfect competition is faced with the following situation

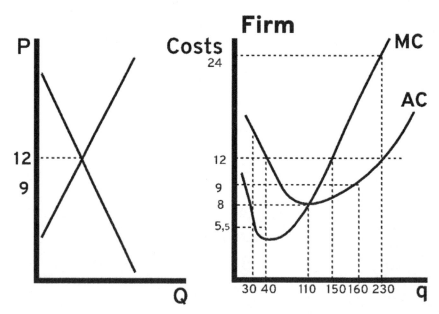

a) The current free market equilibrium price is $p = \$12$.

b) For the firm the profit maximising level output is $q = 150$ and price $p = \$12$.

c) Calculate the amount of profit the firm is making here. $TR - TC = (12 \times 150) - (8 \times 150) = \$600$.

d)   The profit made above is normal / ***abnormal***. **Explain**. *Since AR > AC at profit maximising level of output, the profit is abnormal (profit above the opportunity cost of using all the factors of production).*

e)   Do you expect new firms to enter the industry? *Yes* / No **Explain** *New firms are attracted to this industry as it offers abnormal profits assuming the same level of risk as before.*

f)   If the free market price falls to $9 per unit the firm will earn a ***profit*** / loss. **Explain:** *AR>AC still and it makes an abnormal profit.*

g)   The firm is justified in producing 230 units if the price is _*P = 12 dollars* .

h)   At what level of production is the firm efficient in production? *Q = 110 units.*

i)   If the firm produces 230 units at the market price of $12, it makes a profit / loss**. Explain** *Zero abnormal profits/break-even. Here only normal profits are made.*

19.   In the long run a firm in perfect competition:

    A   makes abnormal / economic / supernormal profits.

    B   is not efficient in production or in allocation since it too small.

    C   will erect strong barriers to entry.

    D   none of the above.

Explain._D   *Only normal profit in the long run because no barriers to entry & allocative and productive efficiency achieved.*

20.   Which one of the following is **not** a feature of perfect competition?

    A   perfectly elastic demand curve for each firm.

    B   product is homogenous.

    C   a large number of firms and consumers.

    D   barriers to entry and exit is not free.

Explain_D   *Under perfect competition, barriers to entry and exit is free.*

21.   At the current level of production, for a firm in perfect competition, the MR is greater than MC. To maximise profits this firm should:

A   increase advertising and output and reduce price.

B   increase output and with price unchanged.

C   decrease output and increase price.

D   decrease output with price unchanged.

Explain_B *Firms cannot influence price because of perfect knowledge and because firms are price takers. The only way to increase profit is by increasing output at given industry price while keeping average costs below the price.*

22.   For long run equilibrium in perfect competition which one of the following is **not** a necessary requirement:

A   MR = MC for each firm.

B   MC < AC for firm.

C   Long run AC is at its minimum.

D   MC = AC.

Explain_B   *MC=AC in long run/ Choice A, C, D are compulsory*

23.   In perfect competition, the short run supply curve for the whole industry is derived by adding up all firms':

A   average fixed costs.

B   marginal cost curve above minimum average variable costs.

C   marginal cost curve above minimum average cost curve.

D   average cost curve part which lies above marginal cost curve.

Explain_B   *In the short run, the firms must at least cover its average variable cost*

24.   If under perfect competition the industry is in long run equilibrium then which of the following applies?

	Level of firms' profit	Allocative Efficiency	Production Efficiency
A	**normal**	**yes**	**yes**
B	normal	no	yes
C	supernormal	yes	yes
D	supernormal	no	no

Explain_A   *Normal profit- no barriers to entry; allocative efficiency P=MC; Production efficiency, output produced at min AC.*

25.   A firm in perfect competition will stop production in the short run if:

A   MR < AC

B   it makes less than normal profits.

C   AR > MC.

D   AR < MC

Explain_D   *AR=P;   MC related to average variable cost*

EVALUATION QUESTIONS   (Perfect Competition)

26.   Evaluate to what extent the model of perfect competition is realistic.

-    *Define perfect competition market structure in terms of its features.*
-    *Describe the role of a model.*
-    *The closest example of a market where there huge number of buyers and sellers is the foreign exchange market. Even here with manipulation from the various central banks the market is not perfect. The model is static and assumes an self-adjusting mechanism where the norm is equilibrium. In reality this is hardly true.*
-    *Diagram.*
-    *The model of perfect competition is intended not so as to create a realistic view of the world but rather to explain behaviour, its consequences and the effects on stakeholders.*
-    *Overall perfect competition model only explains a few aspects of reality.*

27.   Discuss to what extent internet commerce move markets back towards perfect competition.

-    *Define perfect competition in terms of its features.*
-    *Internet allows new sellers and new buyers to enter the market. The global market place expands.*
-    *In terms of physical products there are transaction costs of shipping and foreign currencies transfer. In terms of download market there is only the currency exchange. In addition here MC=0 in the digital economy. MR earned becomes profit. We should hence expect many new producers and lower prices and software innovations. Here the market structure moves towards perfect competition.*
-    *However in the high street, physical retailers will find themselves less cost competitive when compared to internet retailers. The growth of Amazon.com shows this. These retailers either start their own online space, or partner themselves with well-known online retailers. The market over the longer run may be dominated globally by fewer players and hence the internet commerce moves away from perfect competition and more towards oligopolistic market structure.*

28.   Explain the process by which allocative and productive efficiency is achieved in the long run equilibrium in perfect competition.

-    *Define perfect competition market structure in terms of its features.*
-    *Define and explain meaning of allocative and production efficiency.*
-    *Diagrams to show 4 possibilities in the short run (define), (abnormal profits, normal profits, losses and shut-down). In the short run P=MC and hence always efficient in allocation. However minimum AC is not guaranteed.*
-    *In the long run (define) with no barriers to entry or exit the firm can only earn normal profits. Draw long run equilibrium case. Here firm achieves both efficiencies.*

29.   Leisure boats are made of plastic/fibre-glass resin based on oil. If there are no barriers to entry in this sector, explain using diagrams the effects of a large fall in the price of oil on profits in the short run and long run of boat manufacturing firms operating under perfect competition.

- *Define perfect competition market structure in terms of its features.*
- *Fall in the price of oil means, under competition, fall in the price of resin. Costs of making leisure boats fall.*
- *In the short run the fall in variable cost (define and apply for resin) shift the AVC, AC and MC down for the firm. Profit levels rise (diagram)*
- *In the long run new firms attracted by any abnormal profits with enter and produce.*
- *For the industry, the supply curve shifts right leading to a fall in the market price of boats. Diagram .*
- *Lower price means AR, MR falls for each firm (firm is a price taker). This carries on until all abnormal profits eroded away and normal profits restored (long run equilibrium diagram)*

30.   Evaluate the view that a perfect competition market structure is preferable to an imperfect competition since it leads to greater level of efficiency, more consumer choice and automatically prevents consumer exploitation in the long run.

- *Define perfect competition (pc) market structure in terms of its features.*
- *Define allocative efficiency, production efficiency, X-efficiency and dynamic efficiency.*
- *Define long run.*
- *Imperfect competition entails a downward sloping AR and MR lines.*
- *Diagrams (long run equilibrium for perfect competition and imperfect competition)*
- *Point out that perfect competition achieves allocative, production and X-efficiency whereas imperfect does not and hence pc preferred. Consumer choice may be higher but the good is homogenous. (choice between producers but not between products).*
- *Imperfect competition preferred when choice matters, when economies of scale may be so huge that prices are lower and output greater (monopoly diagram), when R&D results in innovation and falls in LRAC due to dynamic efficiency gains.*

10 MONOPOLY (HIGHER ONLY)

1.   List 5 assumptions/characteristics of monopoly

      -Strong barriers to entry/exit

      -Imperfect knowledge

      -Single dominant firm producing in an industry

      -Price setter

      -No close substitute

      -Huge economies of scale likely.

2.   List 5 stylised examples of monopoly. *(Utility industry)*

      -Electricity

      -Tram (Geneva)

      -Water

      -Sewage

      -Garbage collection

3.   List 5 sources of monopoly power

      -Government owned (or natural monopoly which can be government owned or privately owned.)

      -Buying other rival companies

      -Copyright/patent

      -Ownership of crucial resources (e.g. rare metals)

      -Economies of scale

      -Exclusive license from the government

4.   A monopolist's demand and costs of production data is shown below. Complete the table below.

Demand		Revenues ($)		Production Costs ($)			Profit($)
Q	P	TR	MR	TC	MC	AC	Profit
0	30	0	—	10	0	**0.00**	−10
1	28	**28**	28	**16**	**6**	16.00	**12**
2	26	52	**24**	26	10	**13.00**	**26**
3	24	**72**	**20**	**40**	**14**	13.33	**32**
4	22	**88**	**16**	**58**	18	**14.50**	**30**
5	20	**100**	**12**	**80**	**22**	16.00	**20**

a)   Calculate the output where profits are maximised. *Q=3*

b)   What is the level of maximum profit? *Profit=$32*

c)   It this monopolist chooses to maximise revenue, what output and price will achieve this? *Q=8 P=14*
Why? *MR=0 at Q=8 and P=14, assuming demand continues to follow pattern, linear function.*

5.   Below is the long run situation for a profit maximising monopolist.

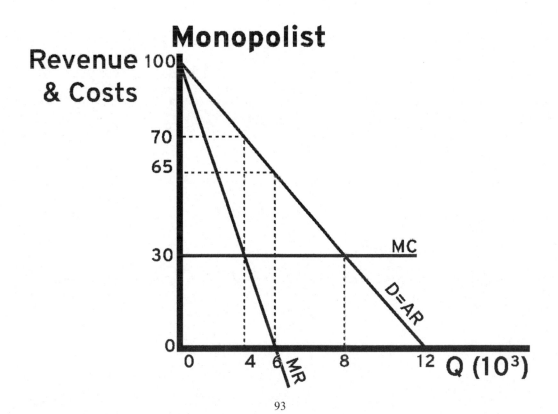

a)   Write down price and output for this monopoly. *P* = 70 Q* = 4000*

b)   At the profit maximising output the monopolist is experiencing economies of scale. **True** / _**False**_.
Explain *MC = AC is constant returns to scale*

c)   Calculate the maximum profit the monopolist can make.

Profit per unit at P* = 70 – 30 = 40   *Output Q*= 4000*

Total profit = 40 × 4000 = \$160 000

d)   Calculate the consumer surplus at profit maximising level of output

   Consumer surplus = B×H / 2 = 4000 × (100 – 70) / 2 = 2000×30 = \$60 000

e)   Calculate the size of the deadweight loss at profit maximising level of output

   Deadweight loss = Base × Height / 2 = 40 × 4000 / 2= \$80 000

f)   To achieve efficiency in allocation the price and output needs to be at

   P = 30 Q = 8 000   **Explain** *P=MC=AR*

g)   At what price and output does the monopolist maximise total revenue/sales

   P = 65 Q = 6 000   **Explain** *MR=0*

h)   What is the value of the PED at revenue maximising output? **PED** *= 1*

6.   A monopolist reduces the price of its product to increase its market share up to the output at which it just earns normal profit. What is the probable objective of the firm?

        A   Profit maximisation in the short run

        B   Minimise loss.

        C   Maximise revenue

        D   Maximise sales volume.

Explain D *To increase market share, to enter the market and to lock out the competition*

7.   The presence of X-inefficiency is most likely when:

    A   the market is in perfect competition.

    B   the dominant firm has high market share and many patents in place.

    C   new firms are entering the market.

    D   all of the other forms of efficiency have not been achieved.

Explain _B_ *All consumer surplus captured by the monopolist. Costs subtracted.*

8.   A monopoly supplier of water is fined as a result of abusing its position and exploiting the consumer. The water regulator and the legal system are forcing the monopolist to reduce its prices. The most likely effect of this is

    A   the monopolist will ignore the court's decision.

    B   an increase in consumer surplus.

    C   increase new investment.

    D   increase producer surplus.

Explain B *as price falls the difference between what the consumers are willing to pay and the new lower price, rise.*

9.   A monopolist is currently benefiting from economies of scale. The government is replacing this monopoly with perfect competition. The effect of this move on price and output is:

    A   price will rise, and output will increase.

    B   price will fall, and output will rise.

    C   price will fall but output indeterminate.

    D   indeterminate for both price and output.

Explain D   *The size of the resulting economies lost is unknown.*

10.   **'A monopolist can either set the price for its product or the output but not both.'** This is

    A   not possible because consumers' incomes are limited.

    B   possible only if it is a pure monopoly.

    C   not possible since the government will not allow it.

    D   none of the above.

Explain__A *Imagine if a firm could set both price and quantity. Then it would simply produce one unit and price it at infinite. Ultimately it is the consumer's income which is a limiting factor.*

11.   A profit maximizing firm sells in two markets Y and Z, monopoly and perfect competition respectively. In market Y as a monopolist it sells 500 units at $50 a unit. In market Z, perfect competition, it sells 700 units at the given price. Total output is 1200 units and average cost is $25. This firm's economic profit will be:

A   **$12 500 in total.**

B   indeterminate.

C $4000 in total.

D $1000 in market Y and a loss in market Z.

Explain A   *Profit in market Y = TR-TC, profit in market Z= 0, normal profit only*

12.   A drug company's patent expires on one of its drugs. What is the effect on this monopolist's demand curve?

A   The demand curve will shift right with a lower PED.

B   **The demand curve will shift left with a higher PED.**

C   The demand curve will shift left with lower PED.

D   The demand will shift right with a higher PED.

Explain B   *Some customers will buy from new entrants, and many will be willing to switch.*

13.   If an industry operating under perfect competition becomes a monopoly. Assuming the monopolist has the same supply curve and is profit maximising, the effect on output and price will be:

A   lower output and lower price.

B   higher output and higher price.

C   unchanged output and higher price.

D   **none of the above.**

Explain D   *Lower output and higher price*

14.   The diagram below refers to a **natural monopoly**.

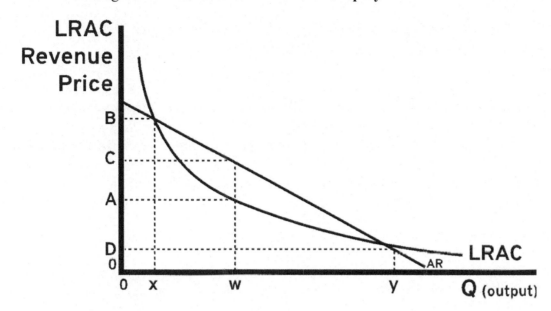

The profit maximising price and output will be

A   price A,   output ow.

B   price B,   output ox.

C   price C,   output ow.

D   price D,   output oy

Explain_C_ *At ow output the difference between AR and LRAC is the greatest, and the corresponding price C enables this.*

EVALUATION QUESTIONS   (Monopoly)

15.   Comment on the view that a monopoly is a result of technological superiority and higher economies of scale and hence should be encouraged and promoted.

- *Define monopoly in terms of its features.*
- *Microsoft can be used as an example supporting the view.*
- *List the other ways monopoly power can arise. The barriers to entry need to be introduced and maintained.*
- *Natural monopoly case result from economies of scale large fixed costs when product delivered through a grid system.*
- *Some monopolies may be exploitative and based around on keeping barriers high.*

16.   What may be the reasons for breaking up a monopoly?

- *Define monopoly in terms of its features.*
- *Prevent consumer exploitation on price, quality and service.*
- *Technological breakthrough (telecoms and airlines)*
- *Prevent monopsony which exploits workers.*
- *Reduce X-inefficiency*
- *MEPS position has changed allowing more than one company to compete and be profitable.*
- *Promote allocative efficiency.*
- *Promote competition and R&D.*
- *Government prefers free market than to use up resources in extensive regulation.*

17.   How do monopolies protect their profits?

-Use resources to create and maintain high barriers for entry, such as high set up costs.

-Protect intellectual property.

-Practice predatory pricing to keep new comers out.

-Buy up potential threats.

- Monopolisation of a natural resource needed to produce the product.

-Protection from the government, including partnership and lobbying.

18.   Evaluate the proposition that monopolies should be outlawed since they are a cause of market failure where price is higher than marginal cost leading to deadweight loss.

- Welfare loss is the loss of community benefit, in terms of consumer and producer surplus, that occurs when a market is supplied by a monopolist rather than a large number of competitive firms.

-Market failure: Prices and quantity of supply is set by the monopoly

-Less choice for consumers

-Productively inefficient

-However, natural monopolies are in favour of the society because of their high fixed costs

- Exploit economies of scale allows low cost of production which can be passed onto the consumers

19.   Evaluate the view that a monopoly market structure is preferable to an oligopoly market structure because while they both achieve economies of scale, a monopoly does not waste resources in duplication of infrastructure and advertising.

-    *Define monopoly in terms of its features.*
-    *Define oligopoly in terms of its features.*
-    *Case of natural monopoly supports the above view. (diagram)*
-    *Arguments against the view is based on the merits of oligopoly. Additional merits for oligopoly are dynamic efficiency (diagram of falling LRAC), more choice, competition and abnormal profits leading more R&D spending. Greater non price competition. More job creation.*

20.   Assess the merits of monopoly market structure compared to monopolistic market structure.

-    *Define monopolistic competition in terms of its features and examples.*
-    *Define monopoly competition in terms of its features and examples.*
-    *Monopoly preferred:*
-    *when high profits are needed to make necessary investments in research and development,*
-    *when there are huge economies of scale to be gained from avoiding duplication costs. Tap water, electricity, gas, are all delivered via a grid system requiring huge initial set up costs (Natural monopoly case),*
-    *when there is huge potential for achieving dynamic efficiency. Diagram. (falling LRAC,)*
    -Large scale is required to be able to compete on a global scale. (steel production)t level

    -Monopoly not preferred when the abuse their power and set higher prices and offer less

    Choice than under a monopolistic market structure..

    -Monopolistic market structure preferred:

    when choice/variety are very important (restaurants, hairdressers, tutors, doctors)

    when there are no economies of scale to be achieved and no further innovations needed.

11 MONOPOLISTIC COMPETITION (HIGHER ONLY)

1.   List 5 assumptions/characteristics of monopolistic competition

-lots of small firms

-product differentiation

-many substitutes

-imperfect knowledge

-downward sloping demand line implying some brand loyalty

-no barriers to entry

2.   List 5 stylised examples of monopolistic competition

Butcher, baker, hairdresser, restaurant , personal trainer and doctor.

3.   Assume the bakery industry in a city operates in a monopolistically competitive market structure. Currently the typical bakery is earning abnormal profits in the short run. Show this in the diagram below.

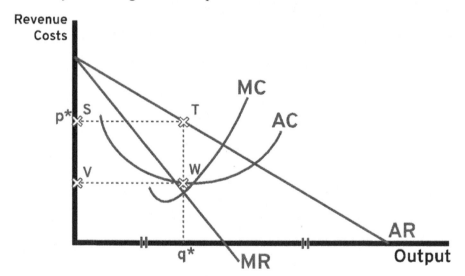

a)   Indicate the profit max level of output and price   ***P*, Q*.***

b)   Mark the max abnormal profit area with the letters   ***STWV.***

c)   Is profit max price P* in the elastic or inelastic range of the demand line.

Elastic range / inelastic range. **Explain**   *operating where MR>0*

d)   Is this typical firm achieving efficiency in allocation or production?   **Yes/_No_**

Explain *Not efficient in allocation since P>MC. Not efficient in production since not producing at lowest AC*

e)   Explain what will happen in transition from the short-run above situation to the long run

In LR only normal profit as new firms enter, increase market supply, reduce market price and thus firm's demand, and so erode abnormal profits into normal.

f)   Draw a new diagram to illustrate the long run situation for a typical bakery.

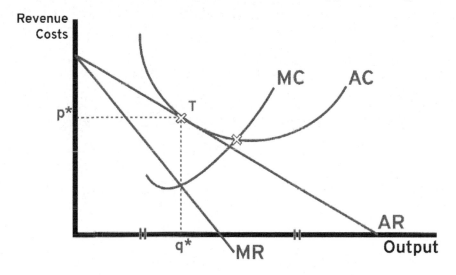

g)   In the long run is allocative and production efficiency achieved? Yes / *No*

4.   Which of these are normally supplied by a firm in monopolistic competition?

a)   Glass for windows.   Yes / **_No_** **Explain**: *Glass is homogeneous industry requires economies of scale which is favoured by large firms (economies of scale cannot be provided by small monopolistic competition)*

b)   Food court in a shopping mall. **_Yes_** / No **Explain**: *Each food stand is differentiated*

c)   Hairdressing salons. **_Yes_** / No **Explain**: *Individual store is small, and it provides personalised services*

d)   Bags of cement.   Yes /**_No_** **Explain**: *Cement is homogeneous and requires economies of scale which is favoured by large firms (economies of scale cannot be provided by small monopolistic competition)*

e)   Supermarkets.   Yes / **_No_** **Explain**: *Products are standardised and requires economies of scale.*

f)   Lawyers, doctors, tutors.   **_Yes_** / No **Explain**: *Not much in economies of scale, provides specialised service.(but relatively strong barriers of entry)*

g)   Electricity in the home.   Yes / **_No_** **Explain**: *Electricity is homogeneous and requires economies of scale which is favoured by large firms (economies of scale cannot be provided by small monopolistic competition). Strong barriers of entry.*

h)   Smartphones.   Yes / **_No_** **Explain**: *Strong barriers of entry, goods are not homogeneous, economies of scale required*

5.   An industry in monopolistic competition is currently in long run equilibrium. Explain how this industry adjusts in the short run and the long run as a result of the following changes:

a)   An increase in tax which raises the fixed cost for every firm. **Explain:**

Short run: -Fall in profit: MC/VC does not change=point of intersection between MC=MR does not change (increase in FC)

Long run: -No fixed cost/all costs are variable,

        -Increase in AC,

        -Optimal price and quantity affected

        -Firms start to make losses (only normal profit earned in long run) so some will shut-down unless the tax is entirely passed to the consumers

b)   A significant fall in raw material cost that reduces the marginal cost.

Explain: *Short run   -P* decreases whereas Q* increases,   -Profit may increase*

Long run: -New competitors enter the industry all attracted to abnormal profit due to absence of barriers to entry.   -Normal profit restored

6.   Decide which of the following are true and which false when comparing monopolistic competition with perfect competition in the long run.

a)   Monopolistic competition will have a higher price.   **_True_** / False

Explain: *P>MC in monopolistic competition whereas P=MC in perfect competition. P is greater than min AC in monopolistic competition while P=MC in perfect competition*

b)   Monopolistic competition will have lower average cost.   True / **_False_**

Explain: *Monopolistic competition does not produce at minimum AC whereas perfect competition produce at minimum AC.*

c)   Monopolistic competition will bring more customised products. **_True_** / False

Explain: *Products are differentiated whereas products are homogeneous under perfect competition*

d)   Monopolistic firms' profits will be higher.   True / **_False_**

Explain: *Firms under both market structures earn normal profit in the long run*

e)   Monopolistic competition will have more barriers to entry.   True / *False*

Explain: *No barriers of entry exit in both market structures in the long run*

7.   Monopolistic competition model is characterised by:

   A   economies of scale.

   B   homogenous products.

   C   few large sellers:

   D   customized/specialized/tailored or personalised services.

Explain: **D**   *Products are often heavily differentiated under monopolistic competition*

8. to 10.   Examine the diagram for a monopolistically competitive firm below;

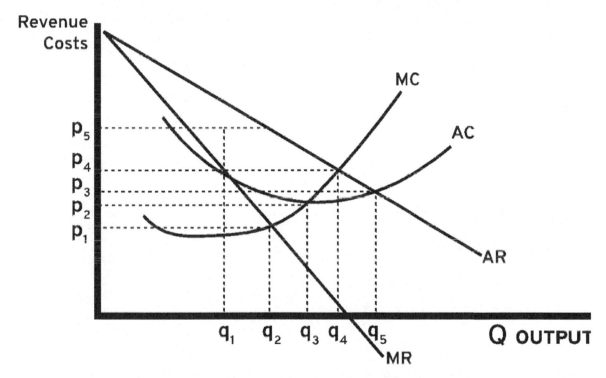

8.   The monopolistic firm can earn normal profit at price:

   A   P1

   B   P2

   C   **P3**

   D   P4

Explain: C   *Normal profit at AC=AR*

9. For profit maximisation the price and output will be:

A P_1Q_2

B P_2Q_3

C P_4Q_4

D P_5Q_2

Explain: D *Profit maximisation at MC=MR*

10 The above firm is currently producing in the ***short run*** / long run.

Explain: *In the long run, the firm under monopolistic competition earns only normal profit. However, the firm is currently earning abnormal profit*

11. Which one of the following is **least** likely to be present:

A price taking.

B price setting.

C product differentiation.

D price discrimination.

Explain: A *Because individual firms in monopolistic competition produces differentiated goods, the firms are price setters*

12. A monopolist and a firm in monopolistic competition share which of the following features?

A Efficiency in allocation and production.

B No barriers to entry.

C Always make normal profits in long run.

D An ability to set the price.

Explain: D *Price setting is a common characteristic in monopoly and monopolistic competition*

13.   Which one of the following is a defining characteristic of an industry operating under monopolistic competition?

        A   there are significant patents and barriers to entry.

        B   all firms only make normal profits.

        C   there are only a few major buyers and sellers.

        D   **there are differences in the product features of the firms.**

Explain: **D**   *Products are differentiated under monopolistic competition*

EVALUATION QUESTIONS   (Monopolistic Competition)

14.   Evaluate the costs and benefits of monopolistic competition for consumers and producers.

-   *Define monopolistic competition in terms of its features and examples.*
-   *Diagram to illustrate a firm under monopolistic competition.*
-   *Evaluation in terms of efficiency (allocative, production, X-efficiency and dynamic efficiency define), customer choice, price, profits, economies of scale,*
-   *Consumers gain from choice, personalised services, specialised and customised products. Use examples to illustrate (personal trainers, restaurants, hair dressers, doctors etc)*
-   *Consumers lose from not having benefits from standardisation, economies of scale, higher prices that perfect competition, lack of major innovative products, and loss from unrealised efficiencies.*
-   *Producers gain from brand loyalty (price premium), offering consumer choice.*
-   *Producers lose from lack of economies of scale, normal profits only in the long run, lack of funds to finance R & D.*

15.   Assuming advertising is a fixed cost then analyse how a very successful advertising campaign affects short run and long run profits of a firm competing in a monopolistic competition.

-   *Define monopolistic competition in terms of its features and examples.*
-   *Successful advertising means revenues rise more than cost of advertising.*
-   *Diagram to show shift in AR and MR to the right.*
-   *The new MC =MR line is such that price is higher and quantity sold higher resulting in higher profits in the short run. Show abnormal profits case.*
-   *In the long run with no barriers to entry and abnormal profits potential, new similar firms enter the industry. Industry supply rises, prices fall until normal profits restored.*
-   *Diagram to show long run equilibrium.*

16.   Discuss why the fast food sector operates under monopolistic competition whereas the telecom sector functions in an oligopolistic market structure.

-   *Define monopolistic competition in terms of its features and examples.*
-   *Define oligopolistic competition in terms of its features and examples.*
-   *The main reason is the size of the fixed cost required to start a telecom company compared to a fast food place.*
-   *Another reason is that telecom sector's product is essentially homogenous whereas in the fast food sector customers crave for choice and personalisation.*
-   *Finally needing a grid system to deliver the product entails disruption, duplication of infrastructure and long term government licensing where the firm can only make a reasonable return if the total number of users are shared among only a few producers.*

17.   Using examples distinguish between monopolistic and monopoly and decide which is preferable.

- *Define monopolistic competition in terms of its features and examples.*
- *Define monopoly competition in terms of its features and examples.*
- *Monopoly preferred:*
- *when high profits are needed to make necessary investments in research and development,*
- *when there are huge economies of scale to be gained from avoiding duplication costs. Tap water, electricity, gas, are all delivered via a grid system requiring huge initial set up costs (Natural monopoly case),*
- *when there is huge potential for achieving dynamic efficiency. Diagram. (falling LRAC,)*
- *Large scale is required to be able to compete on a global scale. (steel production)t level*
- *Monopoly not preferred when the abuse their power and set higher prices and offer less choice than under a monopolistic market structure..*
- *Monopolistic market structure preferred:*
     o   *when choice/variety are very important (restaurants, hairdressers, tutors, doctors)*
     o   *when there are no economies of scale to be achieved and no further innovations needed.*

12 OLIGOPOLY (HIGHER ONLY)

1.   List 5 assumptions/characteristics of oligopolistic competition

   -Few large firms dominate the industry

   -Strong barriers to entry

   -Economies of Scale

   -Interdependence of behaviour between dominant firms

   -Price setters

2.   List 5 stylised examples of oligopoly

   -Smartphones, Airlines, Cars, Coffee capsules, Manufactured chocolates

3.   Oligopolistic firms often have a degree of pricing power. *__True__* / **False**

4.   What does a 3,5,7 firm concentration ratio measure? *Percentage of market supplied by that number of largest firms*

5.   What does the formula **(P – MC) / P** aim to measure ?

Pricing power of a firm/ the percentage the firm can raise the price of its products

6   Use the formula **(P – MC) / P = – 1/PED** to compare a simple price taking farmer in perfect competition with an firm in oligopolistic competition such as Apple.

Perfect Competition: $PED= \infty$, $-1/PED = \infty^{-1} \approx 0$ *(No pricing power)*

Oligopolistic Competition: *0<PED <1, much higher pricing power*

7.   Oligopolists are characterised by independence / *__interdependence__* of behaviour on the strategy for production and marketing. Marketing strategy comprises of the

   Marketing Mix (4Ps: *price, product features, promotion, place/mode of distribution*).

8.   Explain the difference between independence and interdependence of behaviour in terms of the demand curve.

Independence: one single downward sloping demand line

Interdependence: no set demand line

9.   The Kinked Demand model of oligopoly is one of hundreds of possible scenarios of independence / *interdependence* behaviour.

10.   What is the aim of the Kinked Demand model?

To explain price stability/ why sometimes prices and output remains constant despite the change in cost

11.   The validity of the Kinked Demand model depends upon the validity of its 2 assumptions. What are these 2 assumptions?

-Rival firms do not change their prices/do not follow when one firm raises the price of its product

-Rival firms also lowers the price when one firm decides to drop its price

12.   Are these 2 assumptions always true? Yes / *No.*

   Explain: *Not necessarily/ interdependence/example of possible demand line*

13.   Below is a diagram of the Kinked Demand model. It combines 2 demand lines to produces a 'kink.' Explain why this happens

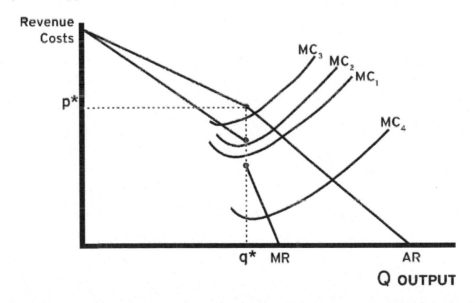

Firm increases the price: the demand falls significantly as the rival firms do not follow that firm and some customers switch away. Here PED>1 and hence TR falls. Firm lowers its price: demand does not grow as much because rival firms follow by also lowering their price. So no customers switch away from one firm to another as expected in the standard model which uses ceteris paribus assumption. Here PED<1 and once again TR falls. New demand occurs only because of lower prices in the whole industry. So increasing or decreasing the price from P* results in fall in TR. There is less incentive to move away from P*.

a)   What happens to price and output when marginal costs rise from MC_1 to MC_2 ?

Explain: *P* and Q* is stable.   No change in MR/vertical: firms absorb increase in marginal cost*

b)   What happens to price and output when marginal costs rise from MC_1 to MC_3 ?

Explain *Q* falls whereas P* increases. At MC_3, the firms no longer absorb the higher costs and hence have to pass on to consumers*

c)   What happens to price and output when marginal costs fall from MC_1 to MC_4 ?

Explain: *Q* increases whereas P* falls. Producers drop their price to become more competitive/attract more consumers*

14.   What does collusion in oligopoly mean?

Collusion: When few large firms set some agreements between themselves and act as a single firm (example of market failure: monopoly)

15   List 5 ways in which oligopolistic firms can collude.

-Set price

-Set output

-Divide up the market

-Collude to reduce power of workers

-Collude to put pressure on suppliers (behave as monopsony)

16.   List 5 benefits to firms of colluding.

-Higher prices and profit

-Strengthened barriers to entry

-Reduce output saving costs

-Monopsony behaviour leads to lower price paid for raw materials

-Lower wages paid to workers as firms collude

17.   List 5 reasons why collusion is usually **not** in the public interest.

   -Less choice

   -Higher price

   -Less innovation

   -Less competition

   -Lower wages (greater inequality)

   -Lower quality /"shrinkflation")

18.   List 5 examples where oligopolists have been caught colluding.

   -Airlines

   -Drug companies selling vitamins for cattle

   -Oil companies

   -Diamond

   -Auction Houses (Christie's, Sotheby's)

   -Banks

   -Insurance companies

19.   List 5 conditions which are likely to lead to collusion.

   -Market dominated by very few large players, including <u>one</u> especially large

   -Market saturation

   -Strong barriers to entry

   -Similar cost structures

   -Very similar product

   -Monitoring and policing is easy

20.   Formal, open, non-tacit collusion is illegal. However, firms can still indulge in **tacit** collusion. Tacit collusion is difficult to detect as there often is no paper trail. Which of the following are examples of tacit collusion?

a)   prices set according to some well-known reference price point. *Yes* / No

b)   firms follow the dominant firm in pricing. *Yes* / No

c)   firms charging different prices to different consumers. Yes /*No*

d)   one firm makes a public announcement about its pricing intention and very shortly afterwards all the other oligopolists follow. *Yes* / No

e)   oligopolists secretly get together and make deals. Yes / *No*

f)   oligopolistic manufacturers give preferential discounts to their distributors. Yes / *No*

The behaviour of firms in oligopolistic competition is better understood through the application of game theory. In game theory 2 rational firms make strategic decisions to maximise their self-interest by trying to estimate/predict the rival's behaviour. Here firms adopt one of two strategies, **maximax** and **maximin**.

21.   Define maximax and maximin.

   Maximin: Choosing the best of the worst situation for lowest risk

   Maximax: highest risk with highest reward

22.   Define Nash equilibrium/Dominant strategy.

Nash equilibrium: there is no incentive for any player to change strategy, given the strategies of the other players. Note sometimes this means there is a conflict between following individual self interest and collective interest. (contradicts Adam Smith's invisible hand)

23.   Two European discount supermarket chains, Aldi and Lidl have recently started expanding in Switzerland. Each company must now choose between 2 locations, Zurich North and Zurich South. The estimated daily profit payoff matrix is shown below in Swiss Francs for the firms.

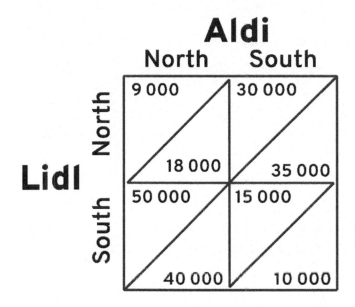

a)   If Aldi chooses the Zurich South location then which location should Lidl choose? *Zurich North* **Explain**: *Gains 35 000 because there is no competition*

b)   Does Lidl have a dominant strategy? *yes* / no **Explain**: *Dominant strategy: Lidl goes to South*

c)   If both firms are able to collude then where should each locate?

Aldi should go to Zurich North and Lidl should go to Zurich South **Explain** *Both firms earn the highest profit at that point*

24.   Which of the following behavioural tendencies of oligopolies are considered to be in the interest of society?

a)   Not efficient in allocation.   *No*

b)   Usually enough profits for research and development.   *Yes*

c)   Economies of scale usually.   *Yes*

d)   Strong barriers placed to maintain market power.   *No*

e)   Strong barriers needed to reward innovation.   *Yes*

f)   X-inefficiency often present.   *No*

g)   Oligopolies influence governments for self interest.   *No*

h)   Oligopolies enjoy external economies of scale.   *Yes*

i)   Oligopolies overtime achieve dynamic economies.   *Yes*

j)   Oligopolies often come up with new products.   *Yes*

k)   Matured oligopolies are more likely to collude.   *No*

l)   Firms practice tie in sales to handcuff consumers.   *No*

m)   Advertising here is often persuasive and wasteful.   *No*

25.   In which market structure would you expect to find a firm consider other firms' possible reactions when it decides to change its price?

    A   oligopoly.

    B   perfect competition.

    C   monopolistic competition.

    D   monopoly.

26.   In a city the four main supermarkets are operating in an oligopolistic market structure. The most popular product is the fresh 20 cm Margherita pizza and the supermarkets are holding their price stable. Which of the following could be a reason for this?

    A   The supermarkets must be colluding.

    B   The supermarkets prefer to compete on non-price factors to avoid a price war.

    C   The price is set based on costs only.

    D   If one supermarket reduces its price all the others will keep their prices unchanged.

Explain: **B** *Oligopolistic firms often focus on price stability and compete on non-price factors*

27.   In the kinked demand curve model one of the assumptions is that:

    A   all the oligopolistic firms have falling average costs as their output rises.

    B   an oligopolistic firm expects that its consumers have lower PED when the price rises and

            higher PED when the price it charges falls.

    C   an oligopolist expects its competitors to match any price decreases.

    D   an oligopolist will raise its price when one of its rival firm raises its price.

Explain: **C** *One of definition*

28.   A firm in equilibrium is faced with the following;

market price = $2   **average cost = $2**   **marginal cost = $2**

This firm must be in which of the following market structures?

A   oligopoly.

B   perfect competition.

C   monopoly.

D   monopolistic competition.

Explain: **B** *Flat demand line, P=MC=AC=MR=AR*

EVALUATION QUESTIONS   **(Oligopolistic Competition)**

29.   Price rigidity in oligopolistic competition is a result of price fixing. Discuss.

Define price rigidity.
Features of oligopoly
Price fixing may cause price rigidity where firms collude. This is likely to happen in a saturated market with few large sellers, producers, similar cost structures, similar cost structures, lack of growth, similar cultures, strong barriers to entry and easy for firms to police each other. Here firms collude to avoid a price war and maximise profits.
Alternatively price rigidity may be explained by the Kinked demand model. Here the assumptions result in prices remaining stable/fixed even if costs change. This is not price fixing even though the end result is the same.
Some firms use a 'follow the leader' pricing to avoid a price war and focus on non-price factors to compete.

30.   Evaluate the factors which favour the formation of cartels.

-    *Define cartel and give examples such as OPEC, De Beers Diamond, and Maple Syrup in Canada.*
-    *Draw diagram to show how market moves from free market to vertical supply line (cartel supply is set below free market supply).*
-    *Cartels most likely to occur when there are a few large players, similar cultures and cost structures and technologies used, market has matured and not much more room for growth. Member quotas have to be agreed on and policed.*
-    *Law of the land has to be cartel friendly.*

31.   Evaluate the view that it is the producers who gain more than consumers in oligopolistic market structure.

-    *Define oligopolistic market structure in terms of its features.*
-    *Producers gain from having strong barriers to entry which enables them to keep their abnormal profits.*
-    *With on a few competitors, firms can gain from strong pricing power as Apple, Microsoft, Coca Cola have. Pricing power measured by (P – MC)/P*
-    *Strong product differentiation and non generic complements/accessories allow firms to reduce the PED for their products.*
-    *Firms here gain from not having to compete on price but rather on non-price factors.*
-    *Producers gain from having sufficient profits to use further R&D and price discrimination and differentiation to gain/squeeze further valued-added.*
-    *Producers gain from higher profits due to economies of scale. Examples include consumer durables, food, airlines, and car producers.*
-    *Consumers gain from more choice of products, new products arising from greater degree of innovation eg: Nestlé's Gluten free corn flakes., downloads , shopping online due to fast internet.*
-    *Consumers lose since there are fewer firms than under perfect competition. P>MC.*
-    *Greater real choice is debatable in terms of quality/illusion of quality. Putting another stripe on toothpaste or having a coloured aspirin with vitamin C probably does not result in greater utility as much as it benefits the producer.*
-    *Consumer can lose from greater degree of collusion and lobbying power of oligopolists.*
-    *Consumer may also lose from choice fatigue (too much choice)*

32.   Explain the difference between independence and interdependence of behaviour in the context of market structures.

- *Oligopolistic market structure is faced with Interdependence of behaviour where marketing strategy(4ps) of one firm is based on possible reactions from rival firms. 4ps are price, product features, promotions, place/mode of distribution. Interdependence means there is no ceteris paribus assumption as in other market structures. There are many scenarios of behaviour and the Kinked demand curve is just one of many possibilities. This is the rise of game theory.*
- *Independence of behaviour means firms make decisions on the 4ps assuming ceteris paribus, no reactions from rivals. The ceteris paribus assumption results in a single demand line.*

33.   Comment on the view that oligopolistic market structure is preferable to all other types of market structures since it offers benefits of size and sufficient consumer choice.

- *Definition of oligopolistic market structure in terms of features using examples to illustrate.*
- *Significant economies of scale and strong barriers to entry allow firms to retain abnormal profits and use them to compete further in terms of price and non-price factors. This results in greater choice and standardisation for consumer. New markets can result from innovation eg. Drug treatments and internet services. Perfect competition does not offer variety and MC higher due to lack of economies of scale. Product variation limited.*
- *Oligopolies especially in saturated markets may be tempted to collude and lobby for favours to maintain the status quo (the car industry unwilling to give up polluting diesel). The quality of choice is debateable. P>MC and firms not producing at allocative, production or X efficiency levels of output.*

13 ODDS AND SODS (HIGHER ONLY)

Price Discrimination

1.   Define price discrimination (PD).

This is when the firm sells the same product at different prices to different groups of consumers. Alternatively charging different prices to the same consumers for different quantities.

2.   List 5 examples of PD.

Restaurants, utility companies, airlines, cinemas, internet downloads, hotels, bars and hairdressers.

3.   For successful price discrimination a firm must be a ***price setter*** / price taker it must be able to combine / ***separate*** the different markets in terms different PES / ***PED***. Goods must not be able to be resold from a ***low price to high price*** / high price to low price market. In the high price market, the PED will be ***less elastic*** / more elastic.

4.   Define and illustrate with a diagram and example third degree PD.

This occurs when a firm separates its consumers into different groups and a different price to different groups but the price is the same within the group.

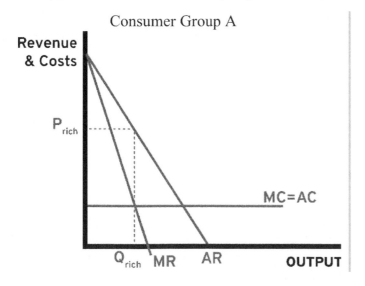

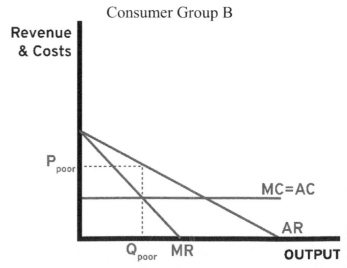

5. A firm successfully practicing PD can enjoy which of the following benefits?

    a) increase in total sales and its help increase its market share   *Yes*

    b) higher total revenue   *Yes*

    c) economies of scale   *Yes*

    d) greater power to keep new competitors out   *Yes*

    e) PD extremely profitable in the digital ($MC = 0$) economy.   *Yes*

6. The rest of society benefit from PD in which of the following?

a) deadweight loss resulting from the implementation of PD.   *No*

b) higher sales leading to higher tax revenue for government.   *Yes*

c) higher tax revenue from higher profits.   *Yes*

d) more markets, more sales, more jobs created.   *Yes*

e) low income consumers benefit from lower prices   *Yes*

f) higher income consumers pay higher price.   *Yes*

g) PD firms gain less than rest of society loses overall   *No*

7.   Examine the diagram for a firm below.

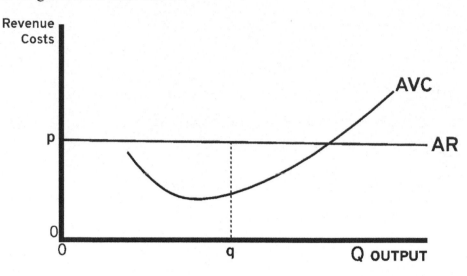

Which one of the following pieces of information is necessary to decide whether the firm is in short run equilibrium at production level 0Q?

    A   **MC curve.**

    B   MR curve.

    C   AC curve

    D   AFC curve.

Explain _A *MC is necessary to work out profit maximisation.*

8.   Examine the diagram showing TR and TC below for a firm.

The situation above describes which one on the following?

    A   monopoly in long run

    B   oligopoly in short run

    C   **perfect competition in short run**

    D   monopolistic firm in long run

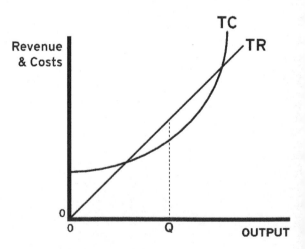

Explain C *A linear TR implies a flat AR and a flat MR and this is one of the features of a firm in perfect competition.*

9.   The city of Glasgow has 2 bus companies operating from the city centre to the airport. Both the Red Bus Company and the Blue Bus Company have to submit the annual timetables which are legally binding. The choice is between am and pm departures and the corresponding payoff matrix in British Pounds is given below.

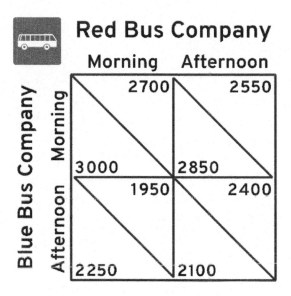

a)   The above market structure is perfect competition /*oligopoly* / monopolistic competition / monopoly.

    Explain *The 2 companies' behaviour is interdependent.*

b)   If the Red Bus Company chooses the pm departure time then what departure time should Blue Company choose?

    AM departure as it means the Blue company can earn either 3000 or 2850 and this is better than any PM departure pay-off.

c)   What is the dominant strategy for the Blue Bus Company? *This is when the 2 strategies, maximin (worst outcome is least bad) and maximax (best possible result) lead to the same strategy*.

    Explain___*AM for both players leads to dominant strategy.*

d)   There is no dominant strategy for Red Bus Company. **Yes / *No***

    Explain *Red Bus Company gains from choosing AM in all cases as its dominant strategy.*

10.   Assume a firm in the short run has the following cost structure diagram.

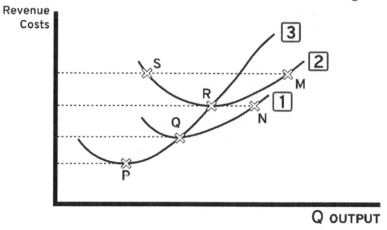

a)   Curve I is   AC / _AVC_ / MC / TC

b)   Curve II is   _AC_ / AVC / MC / TC

c)   Curve III is   AC / AVC / _MC_ / TC

d)   What determines the shape of the above cost curves? *The law of diminishing returns.*

e)   Describe how the average fixed cost (AFC) can be determined from the above cost curves.

AFC is the vertical difference between the AC and AVC (AC – AVC). AFC decreases as output rises as fixed costs are spread across an increasing level of output.

f)   Below what price will the above firm shut down. *Q*

Explain *Below price Q the AVC is not being covered. If the price of pizza does not even cover the cost of the ingredients it will not be possible for the restaurant to cover its fixed costs or overheads.*

EVALUATION QUESTIONS   (Odds & Sods)

13.   Examine the view that in the real world since firms set their own prices not knowing the demand curve for their products, there is no free market.

- *In real world full demand curve is not known. Theory uses static analysis. Firms look at similar products and price accordingly. They often fine tune their pricing and conduct marginal analysis. Ceteris paribus assumption is a weakness. With this narrow window of data free market functions and is sufficient. Firms often price according to 'what the market can bear'. The existence of 'surge pricing' pricing is an indicator that there is a free market at work in real time.*

14.   Price discrimination merely redistributes consumer surplus to the producer and creates no net value to society. Discuss the view.

- *Most price discrimination (PD) merely redistributes income from one group to another and hence the <u>net</u> value to society in fact falls as scarce resources are used up in designing and implementing pd.*
- *However if the firm's <u>survival</u> depends on PD then society gains due to the continuation of choice. Example of a doctor working in a remote village which has a few rich residents and many very poor residents. Unless the doctor practices PD, he will not be able to make a living and will be forced to leave. Without PD the village will not have a doctor.*

15.   To what extent is it true that the more competition there is within each industry the better?

- *More competition leads to lower prices, greater choice and efficiency in allocation and production (define the types of efficiencies), especially if the product is homogenous, there are no economies of scale, there is no further room left for innovation (foreign exchange market, market for cabbage and commodities). Here more competition is preferred. In contrast, discuss the natural monopoly case.*

16.   Discuss why a monopolist or an oligopolist is able to increase profits by separating its market. What are the effects of this on stakeholders?

- *The practice of separating market is known as price discrimination (PD). PD also means charging a different price to different groups according to their price elasticity of demand (PED). The firm must be a 'price maker'. Low PED groups are charged a higher price than higher PED groups. Resale has to be prevented and the cost of separation viable.*
- *Diagram of 3rd degree PD with examples such as market for music download, eBooks.*
- *Stakeholders are consumers, producers, workers, government.*
- *Low income consumers gain from price being lower than single price model.*
- *High income consumer loses out from a higher price and loss of consumer surplus.*
- *Producers gain from greater revenues, profits, market share, pricing power, economies of scale and additional barrier to entry.*
- *Workers in these firms gain from more employment opportunities, higher wages from higher productivity perhaps.*
- *Government gains from more indirect and direct tax revenue.*
- *Keep in mind pd is usually only a distribution of income from one group to another. Overall in most cases there is no net welfare gain to society.*

17.   To what extent do the goals of firms' conflict?

- *Goals can be profit maximisation (MC = MR), revenue/sales maximisation (MR = 0), breakeven (AR = AC), welfare maximisation (P = MC = AR), profit satisficing.*
- *Diagram to show the first four above.*
- *Conclusion is that firm can achieve only one at any point in time, not more.*
- *However, in the real world firms do not know all these curves and hence do not know the relevant price and quantity. They compromise and work on increasing 2 goals at a time, profit and revenue for example. Some CEOs also aim for profit satisficing to keep shareholders happy.*
- *Please note in the digital economy (market for downloads) where MC=0 (very close to 0), the goals of profit maximisation and sales maximisation is possible. (draw a diagram)*

18.   Evaluate the view that since monopolistic competition results in more consumer choice than oligopolistic competition, government regulation should ensure small firms are not taken-over or merged into larger firms.

- *Define monopolistic and oligopolistic market structures through there features and examples..*
- *Most cases monopolistic firms exist when consumer wants lots of variety economies of scale are limited. However in the restaurant business some economies of scale may be possible and hence the rise of McDonalds, Starbucks etc. This shows customer wants variety and standardisation at the same time.*
- *Government's role is limited to setting and policing the food safety standards and consumer rights. Evidence based policy is better here as economic theory is found lacking.*

19.   All heath care and education should be provided under free market as it leads to efficiency and consumer sovereignty. Evaluate this view.

- *Define free market (forces of D & S determine equilibrium price and quantity), no deadweight loss and allocative efficiency achieved.*
- *Some healthcare is considered as merit goods (MSB > MPB). Define and illustrate using examples of vaccination and eye tests.*
- *Here free market partially fails since free market does not recognise positive externality of consumption. Free market over prices and under produces merit healthcare and primary education goods. This means government has to correct this market failure.*
- *In types of healthcare and education where there are no externalities free market can function fully. Government's role is simply to set and police standards, rules of engagement.*

20.   The provision of clean drinking water requires resources and investment. This can only be achieved efficiently under free market. Discuss this view.

- *Similar answer as above Q20. Government could charge P=MC to ensure basic rights and maximise welfare of society.*

21.   Evaluate the economic arguments from firms' point of view in the decision to remove all restrictions on opening hours for retail shops.

-    *Each firm weighs up costs and benefits of increasing opening hours.*
-    *Some firms may extend the hours as revenues may rise even after incurring higher costs.*
-    *Currently in Switzerland very small retailers depend upon having exclusive rights on opening on Sunday as they would not survive against the large players during the rest of the week. This law allows more diverse players to exist and increase consumer overall choice. (the Swiss law says the owners and family have to be working in their shops on Sundays)*

14 MACROECONOMICS: INTRODUCTORY CONCEPTS

This workbook, so far, has focused on behaviour at the individual, micro level. When behaviour is studied at the aggregate level, macro level the outcomes and policy implications are quite different. It is important to note the whole is greater than the sum of the parts.

1.   Decide which of the following are micro issues and which are macro ?

a)   John will buy a second-hand car if the price of a new one rises.   *micro* / macro

b)   There is a nationwide strike by truckers.   *micro* / macro

c)   Sales taxes are rising from 10% to 12% from Friday.   micro / *macro*

d)   Comfy furniture is installing 3D printing machine to raise productivity and profits for the company.   *micro* / macro

e)   The overall spending in the economy is predicted to fall.   micro / *macro*

g)   The gas industry is going to be privatised starting next year.   *micro* / macro

h)   Interest rates falls are raising demand for loans on housing.   micro / *macro*

i)   The number of job vacancies are falling.   micro / *macro*

j)   The computer industry is doubling the size of its workforce.   *micro* / macro

2.　　We use the **circular flow of income** to make a model of the economy.　Draw the circular flow income below and label the real flows of goods and services in one colour and the monetary flows in another colour.　Make sure the following are included: Consumer spending on domestically produced goods and services (Cd), Investment spending (I), Government spending (G), Value of Exports (X), Value of imports (M), Savings (S), Tax revenue (T), and payments to factors of production (Y) as monetary flows.

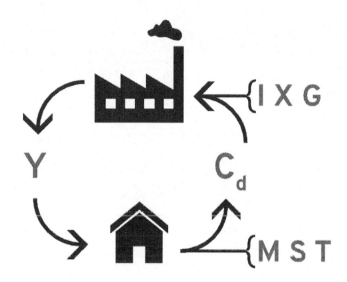

a)　　Define injections (J) and give a real-world example for type of J.

This is a monetary injection J, in the circular flow of income in the form of I, G, X.　The new metro system (CEVA) in Geneva will mean fops are being used to create value.

b)　　Define leakages/withdrawals (W) and give a real-world example of each type of W.

Here spending power is being removed from the circular flow of income in the form of S, T, and M.　A rise in sales tax from 19% to 23% in Greece will mean that the circular flow of income will shrink as more purchasing power is removed from the economy.

c)　　Define aggregate demand (AD) in the economy.

This is the sum of all expenditure on goods and services being produced in the economy.　It comprises of Cd + I + G + X or C + I + G + X - M

d)　　The value of total production of final goods and services in an economy for a given period of time is known as *GDP.*

e)　　Use the above diagram to define equilibrium in the economy.　*AD = AS　or　Total J = Total W*

f)　　Describe the process using the above diagram on what happens when exports (X) rise.　*When X rise firms receive payments for the sales of their output.　They pay for the fops. Households use these rewards to purchase goods and services, finance government services which in turn makes use of more fops.　Total economic activity rises.　The expanding circular flow of income results in economic growth and employment.*

g)   Describe what happens in the circular flow diagram when savings (S) are stuffed under the bed instead of being deposited in the bank. *Banks have less money (FOPs) to lend out to borrowers, to entrepreneurs to make new investments. Less money is received by the firms which in turn produce less and pay less for fops. Households receiving less income, spend less and pay less taxes. All the sectors shrink as economic activity slows and the circular flow contracts.*

h)   Describe what happens when firms decide to increase investment (I). *New spending means more fops are used and paid for. Households receiving this income increase their spending on goods and services. More activity is generated resulting in the expansion of the circular flow of income.*

3.   Decide which of the following are withdrawals, W, and which are injections J. Also decide whether there is a rise or a fall in the values.

a)   The government wins the bid to host the Olympics.   W / *J* / *rise* / fall

b)   The exchange rate strengthens, and more foreign holidays are taken.   *W* / J / *rise* / fall

c)   Firm bring forward their investment decisions in preparation of the coming Olympics

                                                                                  W / J / *rise* / fall

d)   Government increases taxes on high income earners and redistributes this via lower taxes on low income earners.   W / J / *rise* / fall

e)   People invest more money in their savings account at the bank.   *W* / J / *rise* / **fall**

f)   Government reduces state pensions.   W / *J* / rise / *fall*

To measure the size of the economy and the changes overtime governments collect data on incomes, production and its value and the expenditure on goods and services. This figure is known as the GDP.

4.   Gross domestic product (GDP) measures

        The value of all final goods and services being produced in the economy in a given period of time.

The 3 methods of measuring GDP are the expenditure method, the product method and the income method. AD = Y = AS

5.   Briefly explain the expenditure method (AD).

        Add up all the spending made on consumption of domestically produced goods and services Cd, spending on investment goods and services I, government spending G and the value of exports sold X.

6.   Briefly explain the product/output method (AE/AS).

Sum up the value of all final goods and services produced by each firm in each sector.

7.   Briefly explain the income method (Y).

Add up all the rewards given to the fops for their use. Wages + interest + rent + profits.

8.   List 7 difficulties in calculating/computing accurate GDP figures.

Inaccurate data, undeclared income, valuation of government services, valuation of owner occupied housing, valuing depreciation, valuing unfinished stock, double counting, household production, barter services, valuing 'do-it-yourself production.

9*.   What is the difference between GDP at market prices and GDP at factor cost?

GDP at factor cost   = GDP at market prices – indirect taxes and + subsidies.

10.   What is the difference between Nominal GDP and Real GDP?

GDP real = GDP nominal – inflation.

11.   Explain and give 2 examples of what is Net Property Income from Abroad.

This is returns to fops owned abroad by the citizens of this country take away rewards given to fops owned by foreigners in this country. Example 1: Foreigners own factories in this country which give profits which are then repatriated abroad. Example 2: Citizens of this country working abroad repatriate some of their salaries back to this country.

12.   Explain and give 2 examples of depreciation.

This is the total spending on wear & tear/maintenance of a country's capital stock. Example 1: Repairing roofs on buildings. Example 2: Fixing potholes and bridges.

13.   Net Domestic Product NDP = GDP – *depreciation spending*

14.   Why do we normally remove the value of depreciation from GDP?

Explain *Depreciation spending does not add to the total capital stock but rather it maintains the capacity and efficiency of the current stock.*

15.   Define Gross National Product (GNP/GNI).

This is value of all final goods and services produced by a country's citizens both at home and abroad. Here we measure the contribution of a country's citizens.

16.   What is the difference in meaning between GDP and GNP?

GDP = GNP – *net property income from abroad.*

GDP measures the value of production in this country irrespective of nationality. GNP measures the contribution of the citizens of a country whether at home or abroad.

17.   For a less developed country GDP > GNP   ***True*** / False

Explain *Foreign companies are more likely to own assets in the poor country than vice versa. This makes net income from abroad negative.*

18.   For a more developed country GDP > GNP True / ***False***

Explain *For rich countries net property from income tends to be positive especially when compared to poor countries due to the influence of the multinationals.*

19   Using only the terms GDP, GNP, factor cost, market price, indirect taxes, subsidies, net property income from abroad, depreciation, work out the Net National Product (NNP at factor cost).

NNP at factor cost = **GDP at market price** *– indirect taxes + subsidies – depreciation + net property from income abroad.*

20 *h*.   Consider the data below in billions $ for **year 1**: C_d = 700, I = 100, G = 500, X = 70, M = 80, income from assets coming from abroad = 30, income from assets going abroad = 5, depreciation = 20

a)   Calculate for *year* 1 the value of GDP.   *C_d + I + G + X = 700 + 100 + 500 + 70 = $1370*

b)   Calculate for year 1 the value for GNP/GNI.

GNP = GDP + net property income abroad = 1370 + 30 – 5 = $ 1395

21 *b*.   Consider the data for **year 2**: $C_d = 750$, $I = 150$, $G = 600$, $X = 40$, $M = 120$, income from assets coming from abroad $= 50$, income from assets going abroad $= 5$ depreciation 25.

a)   Calculate for **year 2** the value of GDP. $= Cd+I+G+X = 750+150+600+40 = 1540$

b)   Calculate for **year 2** the value of GNP.

GNP = GDP + Net property income from abroad = 1540 + (50 – 5) = $1585

c)   From year 1 to year 2 the inflation rate is 1.5% what does this mean?

The same output has risen 1.5% in price. Real GDP has fallen.

d)   Work out the Real GDP for **year 2**. in comparison to year 1.

Real GDP for year 2 = Nominal GDP year 2 – 1.5%= 1540- 1.5%*1540 = $1516.9

e)   Has the economy grown in real terms or shrank and what does this mean for jobs, for investment, for government tax revenue?

Explain__ *In real terms the economy has grown. This means more goods and services have been produced, requiring more workers (unless it's a jobless growth). More investment will be needed and government will collect more tax revenue from profits, incomes and from sales taxes.*

22.   Define green GDP.

GDP that accounts for the value of resource depletion and environmental degradation

GDP green = GDP *– value of environmental degradation*   *e.g. pollution, externalities*

23.   Define GDPppp (purchasing power parity). *This is the value of output produced in an economy over a period of time, measured in terms of what the currency can actually buy.*

GDPppp for LDC > GDP market exchange rate for LDC

24.   List 5 uses of national income statistics.

-Helps policy makers to plan economic policies

-Helps compare performance between: similar countries, over time, between sectors

-Helps to figure out the level of inequality using the Gini coefficient and Lorenz curve

-Helps to measure size of black market

-Helps in formulating the HDI

25.   List 7 problems in using national income statistics as a measure of economic progress or standard of living **within the country**.

-Does not indicate the distribution of income: GDP per capita averages the income earned per person

-Environmental degradation not accounted

-Increase in GDP may be due to longer hours

-National Income statistics may include spending on regrettables e.g. military spending

-Increase in value of GDP & GNP due to debt spending

- due to more spending on correcting market failure & depreciation etc.

- due to greater stress and insecurity

26.   List 7 problems in using national income statistics as a way of comparing economics progress or standard of living **between countries**.

-Subsistence farming

-Household production

-Informal sector

-Fluctuation of exchange rate

-Inflation rate vary

-Cold countries spend more on heating than on Mediterranean countries

-GDP rises if one country spends more on regrettables than another country

27.   The difference between Net National Product (NNP) and GNP is:

A   net income from abroad.

B   indirect taxes and subsidies.

C   purchasing power parity (PPP).

D   **none of the above.**

Explain : **D**   *NNP = GNP- depreciation*

28 *b.*   If over a period of time nominal GDP went up by 8%, inflation of 2% and population rose 2%, then the change in real GDP per capita/head is:

A   a rise of 2%.

B   a fall of 2%.

C   a rise of 4%.

D   a rise of 3%.

Explain : **D** *Real GDP = Nominal GDP-inflation = +6%. GDP per capita: GDP/population = 6/2 = +3%*

29.   The problem double counting can be avoided when computing GDP by:

A   excluding values for exports and imports.

B   only including the final price after removing indirect taxes and subsidies.

C   only including private sector production and not government services.

D   none of the above.

Explain: **B** *GDP only accounts for value of final goods and services since this includes all the previous steps of production*

30.   Which one of the following should be included in the measure of GDP but is not included?

A   state pensions.

B   private pensions.

C   the purchase of a house in the neighbourhood.

D   household production.

Explain: **D** *Household production is output produced in an economy, but not included in the accounts because household production is not exchanged in the market.*

31.   Which one of the following is **not** an example of a transfer payment?

    A   State and private pensions.

    B   Child benefits paid to parents by the state.

    C   **Salaries of government ministers.**

    D   Profits divided by firms to their shareholders.

Explain C *Government ministers are paid in return for their services given in that year.*

32.   GNP - NNP =

    A   **depreciation/capital consumption.**

    B   net property income from abroad.

    C   Value of exports - Value of imports.

    D   inflation

Explain   A   *Reason stated in above question.*

EVALUATION QUESTIONS   (Introductory Concepts)

33.   Comment on the value and limitations of completely relying on GDP as a way of making international comparisons of living standards.

See answers to question 26

Useful only for comparison between similar countries

34.   To what extent is the use of green GDP compatible with economic growth?

Green GDP is compatible if economic growth is sustainable i.e. using renewable resources

Green GDP is not compatible if the rise of GDP comes from environmental degradation

35.   To what extent does an expanding circular flow of income imply a higher standard of living for a country?

    -Definition of circular flow of income

    -Draw circular flow of income and label the diagram

    -Circular flow of income measures value of output 3 methods: income, output, expenditure

    -Higher real GDP values imply more goods and services produced in an economy and hence higher standards of living

    -However, circular flow of income does not account for inflation, population   growth and distribution of income, environmental degradation and transfer payments

36.   Saving is considered a virtue. However if the savings rate is too high current spending will fall resulting in lower incomes and savings. Use the circular flow of income to explain this paradox of thrift.

    -Definition of circular flow of income

    -Draw and label circular flow of income

    -Illustrate what happens when savings (leakage) rise without corresponding investment: if savings recycles as investment then circular flow of income increases

The Classical and Neo-Classical economists believe that the economy tends towards a situation of equilibrium and deviations from this equilibrium is only temporary or obstacles are blocking the smooth move.

15 AGGREGATE DEMAND & AGGREGATE SUPPLY

Aggregate Demand

1.   Define aggregate demand AD. *This is total monetary value of all expenditures in the economy.*

2   List the 5 components of AD. $AD = C + I + G + X - M$ or $AD = Cd + I + G + X.$

3.   List 5 major determinants of Consumption, C.   *C depends upon the level of disposable income (Yd), level of interest rates (i%), level of inflation (P), level of taxation (T), level of wealth, level of debt, cultural tendencies, religious beliefs. Etc.*

4.   Consider the Consumption function C = f(Y) below. It represents the relationship between the level of consumption and the level of disposable income.

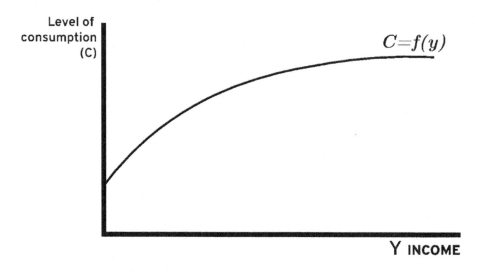

a)   Explain why the shape of the consumption function is a curve and not a straight line.

At low levels of income the desire/need to spend each additional $ of income received is much higher than at high levels of income. This is because at high levels of income the consumer is much closer to the point of satiation. MPC (poor) > MPC (rich).

b)   Define and explain the meaning of marginal propensity to consume (MPC).

This is the % of each extra $ received in income that is spent. MPC = change in C / change in Y

c)   Define and explain the meaning of average propensity to consume (apc).

APC = C / Y   This is the portion of total income that is spent overall.

5.   The Savings function S = f(Y) describes the relationship between the level of saving and the level of disposable income as shown below.

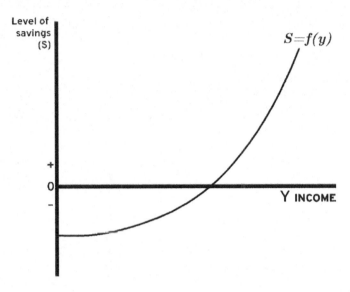

a)   Explain why the savings function starts below the origin, in the negative region.

At zero income there can be dis-saving occurring to finance consumption spending.

b)   Define and explain the meaning of marginal propensity to save (MPS).

This is the % of each extra $ received in income that is saved. MPS = change in S / change in Y

c)   Define and explain average propensity to save (APS).

APS = S / Y This is the portion of total income that is saved overall.

6 *b*.   In a simple and closed economy MPC + MPS = *1*

   Explain *This is because in the absence of the government sector and the foreign sector incomes can only be spent on consumption or saved. So mpc = 0.7 then mps = 0.3*

7 *b*.   In an open economy with the presence of all the sectors, withdrawals (W) come in the form of M, T, and S then   MPC + MPW = *1.*

   Explain *This is because MPW = MPS + MPT + MPM. In an open economy income can be spent, saved, can go to pay taxes, pay for imports and saved.*

8 *b*.   In the same vein   APC + APS = *1.*

9.   Is the MPC (poor) > MPC (rich).   *True* / False.

   Explain using the law of diminishing marginal utility of money. *As income rises each additional $ of income brings less and less satisfaction.*

10.   List 5 major determinants of Investment spending I.

I depends on the rate of change in income, level of i%, level of business confidence, level of government subsidies and taxes, level of inflation and price stability, stability of currency, stability of government.

11.   Consider the investment functions I = f(i) below.   It shows the inverse relationship between the level of investment and the rate of interest.

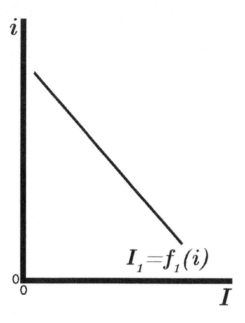 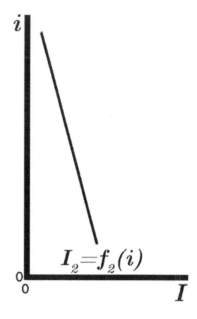

a)   Why is investment and interest rates inversely related?

As i% rise the cost of borrowing rises. The return on the investment falls as costs of production rise. Fewer investment projects will be considered viable.

b)   Investment function I_1 is more interest elastic than I_2 *True* / False.

Explain *When i% falls I1 firms are much more responsive and willing to take on new projects than in I2.*

12.   List 5 major determinants of Government spending G:

level of tax receipts, phase of the trade cycle, level of pensioners and students and unemployment, level of foreign obligations, level of government services, level of i% rates will determine the cost of borrowing through the issue of bonds. In a recession, automatic stabilisers kick in through the progressive tax and credit system. Discretionary spending may rise when a stimulus package is implemented.

13.   List 5 major determinants of Export Demand, X.

X depends on the level of economic growth in the global economy, the strength of the currency in terms of other competing currencies, the overall value PED for exports, level of government support for the export sector, the relative inflation rate, relative real i% rate.

14.   List 5 major determinants of Import demand, M.

M depends on the level of disposable income (Yd), the strength/weakness of the currency, the availability of domestic substitutes, the level of import taxes and restrictions, the price competitiveness of imports, the level of easy credit available for borrowing.

15.   Consider the AD "curves" below.

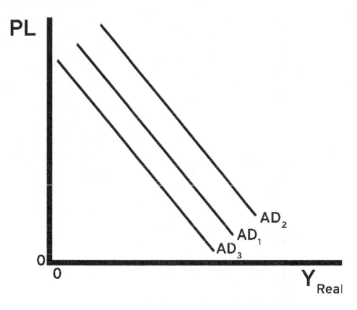

a)   Give 2 reasons for the downward sloping AD curve.

Real income effect: When the price level falls, ceteris paribus, the buying power of income rises, and more is spent. Real output rises. Interest effect: As the price level rises, lenders will demand higher compensation. This means higher i% rates which in turn will discourage Cd, I and G borrowing. However, the currency will strengthen and in turn imports will rise. Real output will fall.

b)   List 5 government policies which would increase AD1 to AD2.

Increases in G, reduction in income tax rates, decreases in sales taxes, more subsidies and tax breaks for I spending, imposition of import tariffs and quotas, greater trade promotion for the export sector.

c)   List 5 non-government policies which lower AD1 to AD3.

The central bank can increase the base i% rates, the central can increase the reserve requirement of the commercial banks to limit their ability to create loans, the central bank can raise i% rate tool to control inflation. This will strengthen the currency and discourage exports and encourage imports. AD will fall to AD3.

Aggregate Supply.

16.   Aggregate Supply (AS) is the total amount of supply of final goods and services produced in a given period of time at any given price level. The nature or shape of the aggregate supply curve competes between two schools of thought, Keynesian and Neo-Classical.

a)   Draw the Keynesian AS curve and explain the 3 phases of the curve.

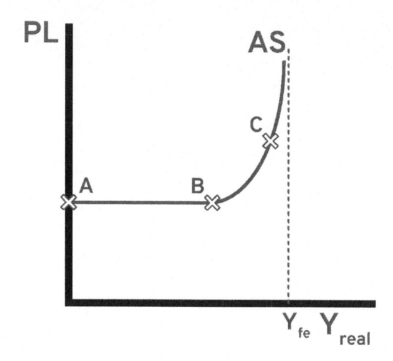

The section 'A' to 'B' implies that the economy is operating well below full employment output. There is lots of unused capacity and hence there is no pressure for prices to rise. 'B' to 'C' section implies that as the economic activity rises further there are some shortages of FOPs. Here price of FOPs rise as some sectors arrive at full employment faster than other sectors. Expansion or economic growth is accompanied by some inflation. In section 'c' onwards it is difficult to expand production in the short run without fuelling demand pull inflation (AD growth > AS growth).

b)   Draw Neo-Classical short run aggregate supply (SRAS) and the long run aggregate supply (LRAS) side by side.

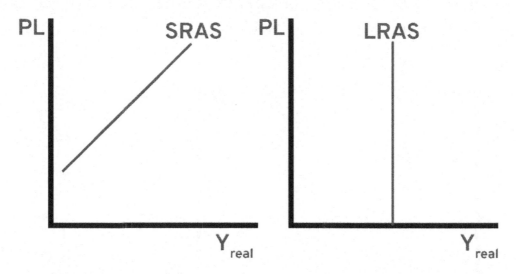

Explain the rationale for having 2 aggregate supply lines. *SRAS. In the short run rises in prices of fops and final goods can affect the level of supply put on to the markets. In the long run (LRAS) the supply available/potential depends upon the total level of fops and technology (quantity and productivity of fops) that can be made available.*

c)   List 5 factors which cause a shift in the SRAS line above.

  Costs of production (prices of FOPs). Taxes on goods, taxes on workers, subsidies, i% rates, numbers of firms, level of unused capacity.

d)   List 5 factors which cause a shift in the LRAS.

  Level of resources available in the country, quality / productivity of these fops, level of new investment, the discovery of new technologies, size of population, quality of the infrastructure.

Macroeconomic equilibrium occurs when AD = AS

17.   Draw and label AD/AS diagram (Keynesian or Neo-Classical AS) and explain the effect on the price level PL and real output Y_{REAL} in the short run and long run in each case.

a) Increase in export demand

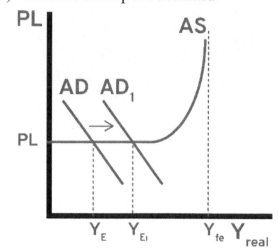

$$\Delta AD \times k = \Delta Y$$
$$\Rightarrow Y_E \rightarrow Y_{E1}$$
$$Y_{E1} < Y_{FE}$$
$$\Rightarrow PL \text{ constant}$$

b) A fall in the price of oil

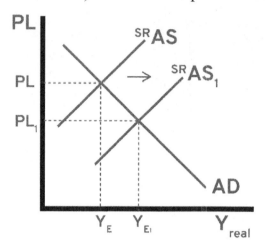

Costs of production fall
⇒ more supply, lower prices
and higher output.

c) A permanent rise in productivity.

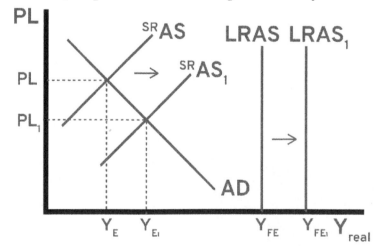

Higher productivity ⇒ Lower production costs
$$\Rightarrow PL \rightarrow PL_1, Y_E \rightarrow Y_{E1}$$
and capacity to produce rises
$$\Rightarrow LRAS \rightarrow LRAS_1$$

d) A fall in income tax rates.

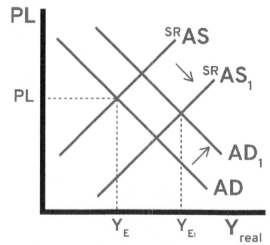

Ceteris paribus.
Greater incentive to supply labour
$$\Rightarrow SRAS \rightarrow SRAS_1$$
Working more ⇒ More Income
$$\Rightarrow AD \rightarrow AD_1$$

e) The discovery of new resources.

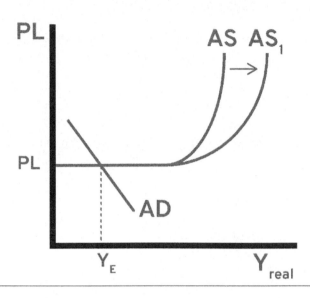

No short run effect. In the long-run the capacity to produce is increased.

f) A rise in overall wage costs

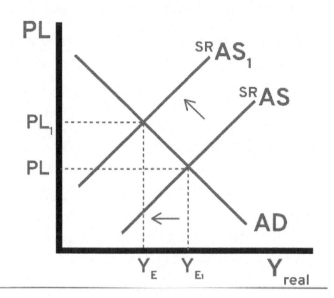

Rise in costs of production passed on to consumers via higher prices.

g) A massive infrastructure program.

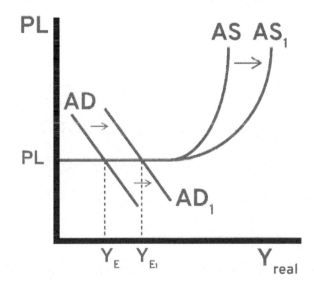

SR: During construction FOPs are paid for and $Y_{disposable}$ rises.
LR: Capacity rises

h) A fall in currency value.

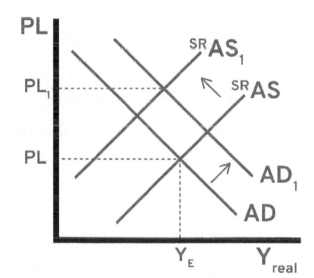

Demand Side: Exports rise and imports fall.
Supply side: Costs of production rise.

Multiplier

18 *b.*   Define the multiplier k, in words and state the 2 formulae.

This is the factor, k, by which an initial injection in the circular flow of income results in an increase in the level of national income after many rounds of spending. k = change in income / change in injection or k = 1/ (1 – mpc)

19 *b.*   If MPC poor = 0.8 > MPC rich = 0.5, show that the multiplier effect is greater for the poor that for the rich,   *k_{poor} > k_{rich}. k_{poor} = 1 / (1 – 0.8) = 5*

k_{rich} = 1 / (1- 0.5) = 2   therefore k_{poor} > k_{rich}

20 *b.*   State one implication of the above result for the government which is keen to make an injection into the economy to raise real income.

> *The government can target its limited funds towards the lower income groups if it wants to have a much bigger effect on income and economic activity. (bigger bang for the buck).*

21 *b.*   What will be the multiplier effect of each of the following?

a)   An increase state pensions for the less well off. **_Rise_ / Fall / Can't Say.**

Explain *poor pensioners have very high mpc and hence high multiplier value k.*

b)   A fall in the safety net provided by the state in provision of healthcare, pensions and education. Rise / **_Fall_ / Can't Say.**

Explain *these low income groups have the highest mpc. So value of k will be high and negative.*

c)   Fall in job security as a result of easier hiring and firing laws. Rise / **_Fall_ / Can't Say.**

Explain. *Workers to compensate increase their savings rate. The multiplier effect will weaken.*

d)   A rise in the rate of income tax. Rise / Fall / **Can't Say.**

Explain *If the government intends to spend all of the increased tax revenue then the net effect will be positive. Balanced budget multiplier value = 1 Otherwise it is unclear.*

e)   A greater willingness to outsource production and import. Rise / **Fall** / Can't Say.

Explain *Total leakages rise and this has a negative multiplier effect.*

f)   The young generation becoming thrifty. Rise / **_Fall_ / Can't Say.**

Explain *The MPS will rise leading to the lowering of the multiplier effect.*

22 *b*.   Given the following model of the economy:

government expenditure = 2000,   imports = 6000,   investment spending = 1000,

consumer spending = 18 000,   exports = 6000,   taxes = 1000,

marginal propensity to withdraw (MPW) = 0.25   Economy currently in equilibrium.

a)   Government budget surplus/deficit: *deficit of 2000 – 1000 = 1000*

b)   Balance of Trade: *Exports – Imports = 6000 – 6000 = 0 we have balance of trade balance*

c)   Meaning of mpw: *This is proportion of any additional increase in national income that leak out of the circular flow of income.*

d)   Meaning of equilibrium: *AD = Y or the total value of injections (I+G+X)= total value of withdrawals (S+T+M)*

e)   Equilibrium level of income Ye: *AD=Ye=C+I+G+X-M=1800+1000+2000+6000-6000=21000=Ye*

f)   The value of the multiplier: *Multiplier, k=1/mpw)= 1/0.25 = 4. Multiplier value = 4.*

g)   If the full employment equilibrium (Y_{FE}) is 29 000, then is the economy suffering from an Inflationary / *Deflationary* gap. **Explain $Y_E < Y_{FE}$ since 21 000 < 29 000.**

h)   Explain using the data how the government can achieve full employment.

An output gap of 8000 needs to be filled in order to reach full employment. The government needs to inject spending of 2000 since the value of the multiplier is 4.

23.   Define a deflationary/recessionary gap.

This is the difference between the current level of equilibrium real income and the full employment level of real income. ($Y_E < Y_{FE}$)

24.   Show a deflationary gap in the AD/AS diagram below.

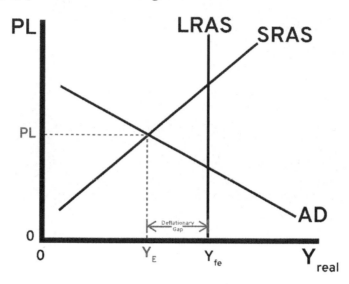

a)   List 3 reasons why a deflationary gap may be undesirable.

   1.Unused/under-employed FoPs means loss of production and hence lower standard of living.

   2. Unemployed workers means greater burden on rest of society socially and economically.

   3. Less need/desire for investment in R&D and innovations.

b)   To close a deflationary gap withdrawals / ***injections*** need to rise. This will have a ***positive*** / negative multiplier effect and Y_E will ***rise*** / fall to Y_{FE}. The gap will subsequently close.

25.   Define an inflationary gap.

   This is when the distance by which the current level of real GDP exceeds the long run full employment level of income. ($Y_E > Y_{FE}$)

26.   Show an inflationary gap in the AD/AS diagram below.

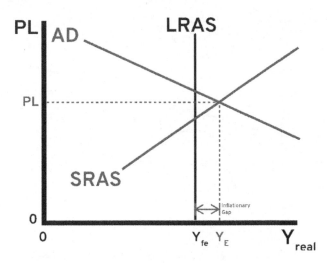

a)   List 3 reasons why an inflationary gap may be undesirable.

1. Massive shortages of FoPs results in accelerating inflation.

2. The rate of depreciation of the capital stock accelerates leading to more frequent break-down and shoddy quality of goods and services.

3. The rise in prices will make exports less competitive without a compensatory weakness in the currency.
4. Severe rises in fixed asset prices will show up in the housing market and the low-income groups will be particularly adversely affected.

b)   To close an inflationary gap **_withdrawals_** / injections need to rise. This will have a positive / **_negative_** multiplier effect and Ye will rise / **_fall_** to Y_{FE}. The gap will be closed.

27.   Define the trade/business cycle.   *This is the fluctuation in the level of economic activity over time. The cycle is inherent in free market capitalism.*

28. Look at the diagram of the trade cycle below.

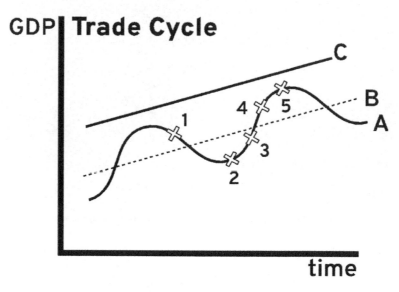

a) Name the 5 phases of the trade cycle above.

   1 *recession*,

   2. *trough/slump*

   3 *recovery*,

   4 *expansion*

   5 *peak*.

b) In the diagram above label the lines A, B, C. The vertical difference between line A and line C is called the *output gap.*

c) Explain the significance line B.

   this is the long term average rise in economic activity. China's trend line would be much higher than Switzerland, indicating that China is a faster growing economy starting from a lower base.

29.   An injection of government spending will be amplified by the positive multiplier effect subsequently affecting national income. However the multiplier effect will be diluted by which one of the following.

A   improvement in consumer optimism.

B   a rise in the marginal propensity to save (MPS).

C   a rise in interest rates.

D   a greater demand for exports.

Explain B. *If MPS rises, ceteris paribus, the value of the multiplier will fall and hence the multiplier effect will be diluted/weakened.*

30.   For an economy to be in equilibrium which one of the following is a necessary condition.

A   The level of injections must equal the level of withdrawals.

B   Savings must equal investment.

C   There has to be full employment.

D   Government budget has to be balanced. G = T.

Explain A *equilibrium means that the circular flow of income neither growing nor shrinking This occurs when AD = AS =Y or when J = W.*

31.   AD in the economy will rise as a result of changing tax policy to redistribute income from the top 10 % to the bottom 50 % only if

A   there is a government budget surplus.

B   the level of spending is higher for the top 10%.

C   the MPC for the poor is less than the MPC for the rich.

D   none of the above.

Explain D. *if MPC for the less well off is greater than the MPC well off, the multiplier effect will be greater.*

32.   In an open economy the national income will be in equilibrium when

A $S = T$

B $X = M$

C $S + G + X = I + T + M$

D   none of the above

Explain D *In an open economy with all the sectors, in equilibrium* $(S + T + M) = (I + G + X)$.

33.   An inflationary gap occurs when

A.   withdrawals exceed injections at full employment. $W > J$

B   government spending exceeds tax revenue $G > T$

C   aggregate demand is greater than full employment level of real income. $AD > Y_{fe}$

D   wages are rising fast.

Explain C. *This is possible in the short run only.*

EVALUATION QUESTIONS   **(Aggregate Demand & Aggregate Supply)**

34.   Use AD/AS diagram to explain the likely impact of an increase in infrastructure investment spending in the short run and the long run.

- *In the short run AD shifts right leading to an increase in GDP (actual growth) as FoPs are hired and paid and the multiplier effect takes place.*
- *In the long run LRAS shifts right as the economy's capacity to produce rises (rise in potential growth). Pick an major infrastructure project (China) as an example to use. Alternatively use the ppf approach.*

35.   Explain demand side and supply side consequences of an increase in personal income tax rate.

- *On the demand side, Y falls and less spending C takes place and hence AD falls. (ceteris paribus assuming no change in government spending). Firms output may contract.*
- *On the supply side there are two possibilities (a) Greater disincentive to effort results in fall in the supply of labour. (b) Workers respond by working longer hours to cover the shortfall in disposable Y. Evidence needs to separate income and substitution effects as well as labour market flexibility to respond to these changes.*

36.   "Keynes's solution to unemployment was higher public spending, which would add to income and through the multiplier process lead to more jobs." Evaluate this statement.

- *Define multiplier, use AD/AS to show increases in G will have a multiplier effect k, and AD1 rises to AD2 and Ye1 rises to Ye2. There is more actual economic growth and creation of jobs. This is however half the story.*
- *Keynes's solution also requires that governments reduce debts during boom times to enable this solution. Keynes's solution is particularly effective during deep recessions when household and private sector are both contracting and there is no crowding out. The role of monetary policy is to support fiscal policy.*

37.   Describe the likely economic effects of rising public sector debt levels.

- *Rising debt levels means government debt servicing may become harder. (debt servicing entails paying back a part of the principal and interest payments).*
- *Greater burden on the taxpayer, opportunity cost.*
- *Circular flow of income contracts especially if debt is in foreign currency and held abroad. Unemployment will rise and economic growth falls as withdrawals rise.*
- *Rising debt levels may be positive if debt used for productive purposes which result in long term higher than market returns. (R&D, infrastructure spending can lead to higher productivity of labour and capital.) Use internet technology as a good example.*

38.　　Every now and then the global economy experiences sudden economic shocks from terrorist attacks or the halving of oil prices in the course of a month or a major financial institution declaring bankruptcy. Explain using AS/AD the economic effects and evaluate some economic policies governments can use to dampen the adverse effects.

- *Short term consequences of shocks usually mean government and central bank step in and introduce discretionary expansionary fiscal policy and loose monetary policy to prevent permanent falls in AD. (As George Bush says, 'when the going gets tough, the tough go shopping')*
- *Long term consequences are policy changes to fight the last problem and try and prevent the next. Debts often escalate. Supply side policies come into effect. Results not known for many years.*

16 MACROECONOMIC OBJECTIVE I (INFLATION)

1.   Define inflation.

This is the sustained rise in the general price level in an economy over time .

2.   Price rises at the consumer/household level is measured by

consumer price index (CPI).

3.   Price rises at the production level are registered in the

producer price index (**PPI**).

4.   Describe how inflation is measured.

Measured using CPI and PPI. At the household level, the government records the weighted value of a basket of goods (which include household necessities, rent, food, personal care products, transport, heath care, education etc for the CPI) every year, and compares it to an arbitrarily assigned base year. From these figures the rate of inflation can be determined over several periods of time. For the producer the approach is the same except the contents of the basket will reflect production.

5.   A base year acts as a reference year and is given an index number.

100

6.   If the value of the CPI is higher than the base year there is *__inflation__* / deflation. Similarly, if the CPI number is below base year there inflation / *__deflation__*

7   Distinguish between inflation and the rate of inflation.

Inflation occurs when there is a rise in price levels. However, the rate of inflation looks at how quickly price levels are rising from year to year. Therefore, there can be increasing inflation (as PL increases), but decreasing rate of inflation (as the PL is not increasing as rapidly as before)

8.   Distinguish between inflation, accelerating rate of inflation, deflation, and disinflation.

Inflation is the rise in price levels, whilst accelerating rate of inflation is an increase in the rate of inflation. In other words, price levels are rising at a faster rate than previously. Disinflation is a decrease in the rate of inflation (PL are still increasing, just at a slower rate) whilst deflation is a decrease in price levels. Deflation is thus the opposite of inflation, whilst accelerating rate of inflation is the opposite to disinflation.

9.   The table shows year on year % change in CPI between 2009 and 2015.

Year	Change (%)
2009	18.0
2010	11.7
2011	8.6
2012	4.6
2013	4.9
2014	6.1
2015	4.5

Decide whether the following statements are true or false.

a)   The price level was at its lowest at the end of the period. True / *__False__*

       Explain *The CPI has increased every year, indicating an increase in price level*

b)   The price was at its lowest at the start of the period. *__True__* / False

c)   The price level fluctuated over the period. *__True__* / False

       Explain *The price level increased each year, but by varying percentages.*

d)   The price level was at its highest at the end of the period. *__True__* / False

e)   Has there been any deflation? Yes / *__No__*

       Explain *No, the price level has been increasing every year, indicating inflation.*

f)   Has there been any period of disinflation? *__Yes__* / No

       Explain *The rate of inflation has not increased steadily, but has decreased between certain years.*

10.   List 5 reasons why the basket to measure inflation is modified over time.

       1) Items become obsolete and are no longer bought or sold (e.g. typewriters)

       2) Changing consumer tastes or global awareness

       3) Bans of certain products (e.g. asbestos filled toys)

       4) Structure of the household changes and hence items bought and weights change.

       5) Changes in quality and changes in what the products can actually do. E.g. The smartphone has multiple uses.

11.   List 5 social and economic consequences of inflation.

1) Lack of faith in Governmental abilities (with hyperinflation).

2) Social unrest as savings can soon become worthless.

3) Rising inequality as only the very well off can afford certain goods and more likely be able to raise asset prices.

4) Development of black market trading in other currencies or goods.

5) Lack of international trade as returns become uncertain. Investment decisions difficult to make.

6) Loss of international competitiveness.

7) Groups whose incomes do not rise with inflation lose purchasing power.

12.   List and explain 5 types of inflation.

1) Cost push inflation: Increase in cost of production for firms, AS shifts to the left resulting in higher prices.

2) Demand pull inflation: AD grows faster than AS, AD shifts right leading to higher prices.

3) Imported inflation: depreciation in exchange rates makes imported goods and services more expensive to firms and consumers.

4) Wage push inflation: Higher wages result in higher costs for firms who may raise prices in return. Strong labour unions may then demand further increases in wages, which can lead to a wage price spiral.

5) Currency inflation: caused by increasing money supply in an economy by printing money and subsequent debasing of the currency.

6) Shrinkflation: here prices of products do not rise but the contents of the box falls.

13.   List 5 effects (positive and negative) of deflation.

1) Consumers benefit from lower prices for goods and services.

2) Producers benefit from lower prices of raw materials.

3) Low interest rates offered by Banks to try and encourage spending.

4) Lower profits for companies might lead to them laying off more workers, increasing unemployment.

5) Consumers may hold back on spending as they expect prices to fall even further in the future.

6) Workers find that the buying power of their wages rise.

For each statement below:

14.   Circle whether the price rises or falls and explain below.

15.   Show the consequences using an AD/AS diagram. Annotate with arrow and label the direction of change in the price level.

a) Ceteris paribus, a fall in consumption

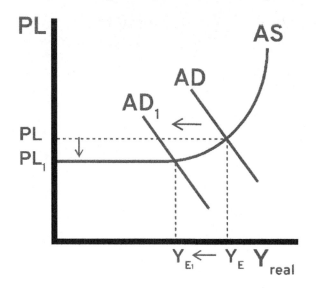

Rise / **Fall**

b) A rise in productivity of machines and/or workers

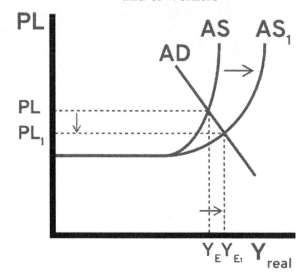

Rise / **Fall**

c) Rise in wages/ wage costs.

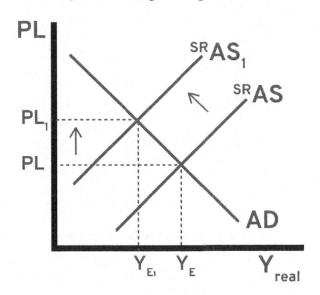

Rise / Fall

d) Government reduces spending but tax revenues unchanged.

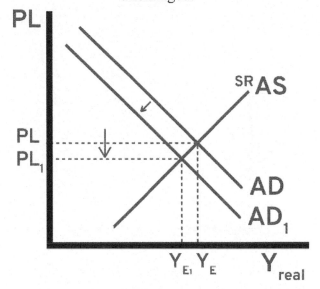

Rise / **Fall**

e) Ceteris paribus income tax rates rise.

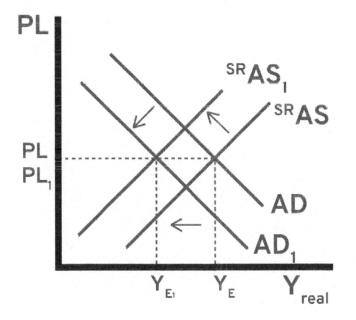

Rise / **Fall**

f) A major drought adversely affecting agriculture output.

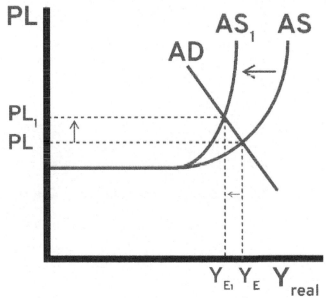

Rise / Fall

g) Money/credit supply rising faster than output

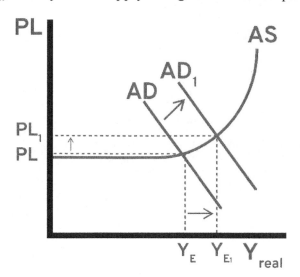

Rise / Fall

h) Firms increase investment spending (but factories not yet started production)

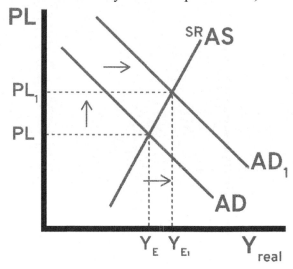

Rise / Fall

i) Major technical progress such as the internet.

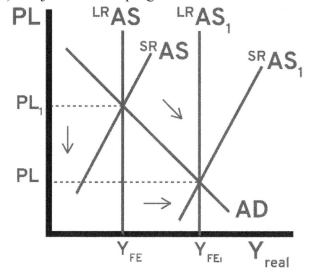

Rise / **Fall**

16 *b*.   CPI in year1 = 90. CPI in year 2 = 135. The rate of inflation from year 1 to year 2 is:

    A   45%

    B   35%

    C   *50%*

    D   −10%

Explain C   *Rate of inflation: (new-old)/old x 100 = (135-90)/90 x 100 = 50%*

17.   Disinflation is:

    A   a fall in the CPI.

    B   a rise in the price level.

    C   a rise in the CPI.

    D   *none of the above.*

Explain D   *Answer technically B and C, as disinflation is a decrease in the rate of inflation. Therefore, answer is none of the above, as none are specific enough.*

18 *b*.   The table below shows price changes for goods/services along with their weights.

	Year 1	Year 2	Weight
Good A	100	140	20 %
Service B	100	110	80 %

a)   In year 1 index number of 100 implies *This is the base year*

b)   What does a weight of 20 for Good A mean? *The good A takes up 20% of the basket value.*

c)   What does a weight of 80 for Service B mean? *Service B takes up 80% of the basket; it is therefore more influential to the overall price changes.*

d)   The rate of inflation from year 1 to year 2 is 116% / 25% / 6% */ 16%.*

Explain   *(new-old)/old x 100, ((0.2(140)+(0.8(110)-(0.2(100)+0.8(100)/(0.2(100)+ 0.8(100))= 16%*

$$\%\Delta \ = \ \frac{New}{Old} - 1 = \frac{(20\,\% \ \times \ 140 + 80\,\% \ \times \ 110)}{(20\,\% \ \times \ 100 + 80\,\% \ \times \ 100)} - 100\,\% = 16\,\%$$

19.   Which of the following is probably a consequence of inflation?

    A   a fall in the price of houses.

    B   a rise in demand for exports.

    C   a rise in the buying power of pensions.

    D   *higher wage claims from workers.*

Explain D   *Inflation causes real wages to decrease, prompting workers to demand higher wages to afford higher prices. Can lead to a wage-price spiral if this cycle feeds on itself.*

20.   The CPI depicts a weighted average of prices of goods and services. The weights are introduced

    A   *to reflect the relative importance of different goods in terms of income spent.*

    B   to reflect the changes in the quality of goods over time.

    C   to reflect the fact that some goods are more essential than others

    D   none of the above.

Explain   **A**   *5% increase in rents will have a much bigger effect on the value of the basket than an 100% increase in the price of salt.*

21.   If the CPI falls from 160 to 140 over a period of a year, ceteris paribus,

    A   the prices of all goods and services will fall.

    B   the cost of living will rise.

    C   the buying power of money will fall.

    D   *workers' incomes will buy more.*

Explain D   *fall in CPI means fall in price level of certain goods and services. This means that the real income of workers has risen, allowing them to be able to buy more.*

EVALUATION QUESTIONS   **(Macroeconomic Objective : Inflation)**

22.   Evaluate the view that price stability should be the most important objective of government economy policy.

- *Define price stability in terms of predictable and small increases in the CPI.*
- *Benefits of price stability for investment decisions, staying internationally competitive, preserving the standards of living of pensioners, workers in weak bargaining positions, students, savers and the unemployed.*
- *With price stability competitiveness is strength and hence fewer jobs lost. It helps government design policies to promote productivity.*
- *Opposite argument is based on price stability may at the expense of the other macro-objectives worsening. Trade-off with unemployment and worsening inequalities may not be acceptable because this can cause major social problems and slow down long term economic growth and job creation.*

23.   Discuss the problems that can result from a long period of high inflation in an economy.

- *Define inflation and measurement.*
- *Long periods of high inflation can cause falls in I due to uncertainty, loss of confidence in the currency, loss of international competitiveness (Britain compared to Switzerland).*
- *Investors and savers both demand higher i% to compensate. Continuous depreciation of the currency may lead to higher rates of imported inflation and further erosion of standards of living.*
- *Governments may find it more difficult to service debts if i% keep rising.*
- *The real value of debt may fall and this makes foreigners less willing to lend.*
- *Government/central bank may end up employing contractionary fiscal policy and tight monetary policy to control this inflation. Trade-off with higher unemployment and slow economic growth may be the outcome.*
- *Some groups continuously lose out as their incomes do not keep up with inflation.*

24.   Comment on the statement "if deflation of prices is undesirable then inflation must be desirable."

- *Define deflation and inflation and its measurement.*
- *Distinguish between price deflation and demand deflation. At the moment the developed countries are close to both. (secular stagnation)*
- *Price deflation maybe good and bad. Good: if deflation caused by technological progress leads to lower prices and greater spending power and jobs. (internet). Bad: if deflation is due to falling AD and the spare capacity in the economy increases. Here firms respond by reducing output and putting off new investment. Jobs are lost and long term economic growth suffers. Inequality worsens.*
- *Price inflation maybe be good if it is low, predictable and stable. There is an incentive to keep costs down and compete. Bad inflation is one which is the opposite. Here loss of competitiveness and confidence lead to many adverse effects.*

25.   Using appropriate diagrams explain how demand pull and cost push inflation can occur and describe two ways each type inflation can be controlled.

- *Define inflation and measurement.*
- *Define using diagrams and explain using previous example demand pull and cost push inflation.*
- *Government concerned about inflation because of its adverse effects.*
- *For demand pull inflation: Government can tame demand pull inflation using a combination of tight monetary and contractionary fiscal policy. Explain the mechanism.*
- *For cost push inflation: Government can use supply-side policies to increase LRAS by increasing the market efficiency of FoPs as well as final goods and services. Policies of privatisation, liberalisation, deregulation, labour market reforms and zoning regulations.*

17 MACROECONOMIC OBJECTIVE II   (UNEMPLOYMENT)

1.   Define unemployment.

People of working age who are actively looking for a job but who are not employed.

2.   Write down the formula for Unemployment Rate.

$$Unemployment\ rate = \frac{Number\ of\ Unemployed}{Labour\ Force}$$

3 *b*.   If 48 million people are employed and 6 million are unemployed then the unemployment rate is

$$Unemployment\ rate = \frac{Number\ of\ unemployed}{Number\ of\ employed\ +\ unemployed} = \frac{6}{6 + 48} = 11.1\ \%$$

4.   Decide if the following will increase or decrease the unemployment rate.

a)   More people retiring early. ***increase*** / decrease

Explain: *Retired people are not considered part of labour force (employed or unemployed). However denominator value falls but the numerator value stays same and hence unemployment rate falls.*

b)   The fertility rate rising. *increase* / decrease

Explain *large increases in birth rates are strongly correlated with high unemployment rates in the US. However no clear theory.*

c)   More people going to university. *increase* / decrease

Explain   *University students not part of employed or unemployed by definition. However labour force falls and denominator value falls, hence the unemployment value increases.*

d)   More of the long term unemployed are feeling rejected. increase / ***decrease***

Explain *Long term unemployment cause people to stop seeking for employment. The number of hidden unemployment increases. However, the unemployment rate decreases because these people are not defined as unemployment.*

e)   The school leaving age rising. increase / ***decrease***

Explain   *same as part (c).*

f)   The retirement age for women rising to the same level as men. increase / *__decrease__*

Explain: *Increase in retirement age for women increases the number of people employed and hence decreases the number of unemployed.*

5.   The number of working age population as a % of the labour force is the definition of unemployment rate / *__labour force participation rate__* / underemployment rate.

It measures the extent to the working age population that is economically active.

6.   If net immigration of working age population rises by 10 million will the labour force participation rate will   rise / *__fall__*.

7.   List 5 undesirable **social** consequences of rising unemployment.

- *Increased crime*

- *Increased homelessness*

- *Increased drug use*

- *Alcohol abuse and domestic violence*

- *Abandonment of children.*

8.   List 5 undesirable **economic** consequences of rising unemployment.

- *Fall in real GDP*

- *Loss of income for unemployed workers*

- *Fall in tax revenue for the government*

- *More unequal distribution of income*

- *Cost to the government of unemployment benefits*

9.   Define equilibrium unemployment.

Equilibrium unemployment is the rate of unemployment at which the demand for workers equals the supply of workers at the current wage rate. There can still be parts of the labour force unemployed.

10.   List 5 types of equilibrium unemployment.

- *Structural unemployment*

- *Regional unemployment*

- *Frictional unemployment*

- *Seasonal unemployment*

- *Technological unemployment.*

11.   Define disequilibrium/ real wage/ classical unemployment.

Disequilibrium unemployment: the rate of unemployment when the labour market is not in equilibrium

12.   List 2 types of disequilibrium unemployment.

- *Cyclical or demand deficient unemployment*

- *Real-wage unemployment*

13.   Define natural rate of unemployment (NRU) and state the types of unemployment here.

Natural rate of unemployment: rate of unemployment at working full capacity and where demand for labour equals to the supply of labour. There is only equilibrium unemployment.

14.   Label the labour market diagram below.

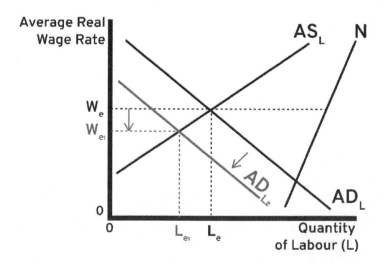

Labour Market

a)   Show in the diagram above the effect of a fall in economic activity. **Explain**

As the level of economic activity falls, less labour is demanded to reduce cost of production. ADl₁ shifts left. Unemployment rises.

b)   Show also the effect of an increase in the minimum wage rate. Does this have the same effect as an increase in the power of labour unions to negotiate higher wage increase? *yes* / **no**.

15.   Consider the PPF diagram below.

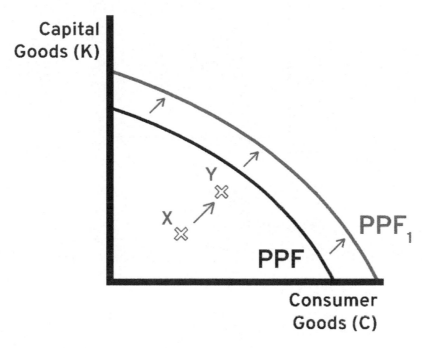

a)   Show in the diagram the effect of a fall in the unemployment rate.
        Explain: *Unemployment is an example of unused resources. Hence, the fall in unemployment rate indicates more employment of resources, and the point X moves to Y, closer to the PPF.*
b)   Show the effect of an increase in the net immigration of people of working age.
        Explain *Increase in net immigration of people of working age increases the size of labour force, increasing the total number of labour available. PPF shifts out PPF1.*
16.   A discouraged worker is not considered unemployed. *True* / False

        Explain *A discouraged worker no longer actively seeks a job*

17.   In the diagram below the LRAS has shifted from LRAS1 to LRAS2. This may have been the result of

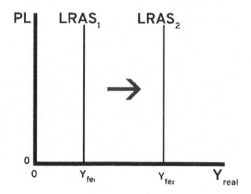

A   more automation or robots in manufacturing.

B   an increase in the school leaving age.

C   a rise a demand for workers as the economy recovers from a recession.

D   more job sharing.

Explain: A.   *Increase in automation or robots in manufacturing increases overall productivity, shifting LRAS1 to LRAS2.*

18.   Circle which type unemployment is likely to rise/fall if there are more robots in the service sector?

real wage or classical / frictional / ***technological*** / structural / seasonal / demand deficient or cyclical.

> **Explain:** *Robots, an example of technological development, replace labour, increasing technological unemployment.*

19.   Circle which type unemployment is likely to rise/fall if the interest rate rises?

real wage or classical / frictional / technological / structural / seasonal / ***demand deficient or cyclical.***

> **Explain**: *A rise in interest rate increases the cost of borrowing money; hence consumers and firms are likely to consume and invest less respectively. The level of AD falls, increasing the level of cyclical unemployment.*

20.   Circle which type unemployment is likely to rise/fall if there is more outsourcing of jobs to lower costs parts of the globe.

real wage or classical / frictional / technological / ***structural*** / seasonal / demand deficient or cyclical.

> **Explain**: *When jobs are outsourced to parts of the globe with lower costs, the demand for labour in such areas increases. However, the demand for labour in areas with high labour cost falls.*

21.   Circle which type unemployment is likely to rise/fall if there is a greater trend towards online application forms.

real wage or classical / ***frictional*** / technological / structural / seasonal / demand deficient or cyclical.

> **Explain**: *Increased use of online application form results in the fall in time looking for work due to speedier information connecting the employer with the potential employee.*

22.   Circle which type unemployment is likely to rise/fall if workers are able learn new skills more quickly.

real wage or classical / frictional / technological / ***structural*** / seasonal / demand deficient or cyclical.

> **Explain**: *Structural unemployment is when the demand for a particular labour skill changes over time. If workers are able to learn new skills more quickly, then they are able to find other jobs which require other labour skills of the demand of labour changes.*

23.   Circle which type unemployment is likely to rise if the minimum wage rate rises to 70 % of the national average.

***real wage or* classical** / frictional / technological / structural / seasonal / demand deficient or cyclical.

> **Explain**: *Employers are more likely to resist taking on new workers, some may lay-off current workers and some may focus on greater automation.*

24.   Circle which type unemployment is likely to fall if workers are more easily able to sell their homes and find rental accommodation in different cities.

real wage/classical / ***frictional*** / technological / structural / seasonal / demand deficient or cyclical.

> **Explain**: *Job mobility rises as it is easier for workers to relocate.*

EVALUATION QUESTIONS   (Macroeconomic Objective: Unemployment)

25.   Evaluate the proposition that full employment should be given priority over all other macroeconomic objectives.

- *Define full employment and state the macroeconomic objectives.*
- *Full employment given priority because high unemployment entails heavy costs to individual, to family and friends, to government, to the economy and attrition of skills.*
- *Circular flow of income full potential not realised.*
- *Point the difficulty of achieving full employment without accelerating inflation and the resulting problems.*
- *High opportunity cost of using government resources in trying to arrive at full employment.*
- *Governments often change the definition of full employment.*
- *Some pool of unemployed workers may be desirable from firms' point of view.*

26.   Discuss the reasons why some types of unemployment are easier to deal with than other types of unemployment.

- *Define unemployment and state measurement.*
- *Use diagram to distinguish between equilibrium and disequilibrium unemployment and list the types of unemployment associated with each.*
- *General demand deficient unemployment caused when economy goes in a recession is considered to be short term and hence resolved by loose monetary and expansionary fiscal policies.*
- *Spending and investment picks up and new jobs are created via the multiplier effect.*
- *Long term structural unemployment is much more difficult to solve especially as older workers find it difficult to retrain and find jobs which pay about the same as before.*
- *Many employers reluctant to invest in older workers, as they tend to be less malleable and comfortable with new technology (analogue to digital world) and those close to retirement.*
- *Time-lags are considerable before government policies show result.*

27.   Comment on the effectiveness of supply-side policies to reduce unemployment.

- *Define unemployment, measurement, supply side free market and interventionist policies focused towards reducing unemployment. Give examples.*
- *Effective supply side policies result in long term improvements in productivity.*
- *Use diagram to show right shift in LRAS.*
- *Here the rise in capacity and efficiency results in low inflation. Productivity rises associated with technological progress. Wages rise to sustain rises in spending causing greater employment opportunities.*
- *Ineffective supply side policies when time lags are long. Productivity gains not equitably shared between capital and labour. Government policy ill designed and risk reward ratio poor. Governments funds ill used.*

28.   Discuss to what extent are demand-side policies are more effective than supply-side policies lowering cyclical and structural unemployment.

- *Define cyclical and structural unemployment.*
- *Introduce diagram of labour market to show the above.*
- *Show how demand-side policies comprising of loose monetary and expansionary fiscal measures create jobs (cyclical unemployment falls) (AD/AS diagram).*
- *Structural unemployment may require fundamental re-balancing of the economy towards improving productivity and high value jobs. Here supply-side (increase LRAS) policies aim to increase quantity and quality of FoPs and final goods and services.*
- *Problems of time-lags and misdirection of resources can occur.*
- *Overall need a combination of the two to be effective.*

29.   Evaluate the view that since it is too difficult to achieve full employment, governments are better off focusing on reducing inflation.

- *Define unemployment and measurement.*
- *As economy gets closer to full employment the workers still looking for work tend to be the older ones, the ones with poor skills or obsolete skills. The risk reward ratio for government policy in helping these workers is poor and the opportunity cost too high.*
- *Government resources may produce a better return in tackling inflation (low hanging fruit). Focusing on achieving stable prices may bring more rewards in terms of job creation via price competitiveness and higher purchasing power of consumers.*

18 MACRO OBJECTIVE III (ECONOMIC GROWTH)

1.   Define economic growth. .

Economic growth is a rise in the real value of goods and services produced in a country in a given time period.

2.   Distinguish between **actual** economic growth and **potential** economic growth.

Actual economic growth is caused by an increase in aggregate demand. Potential economic growth is caused by an increase in aggregate supply. The difference between the two can also be shown on a ppf curve.

3.   How is **actual** economic growth measured?

A rise in the country's real GDP.

4.   How is **potential** economic growth measured?

A rise in the size of the labour market in terms of both quantity and quality of workers, rise in new investment, new resources found, technological improvements…

5.   Economic growth (actual and potential) can be expressed in 3 separate diagrams. (PPF, AD/AS, Business Cycle). Use the diagrams below to show actual and potential economic growth.

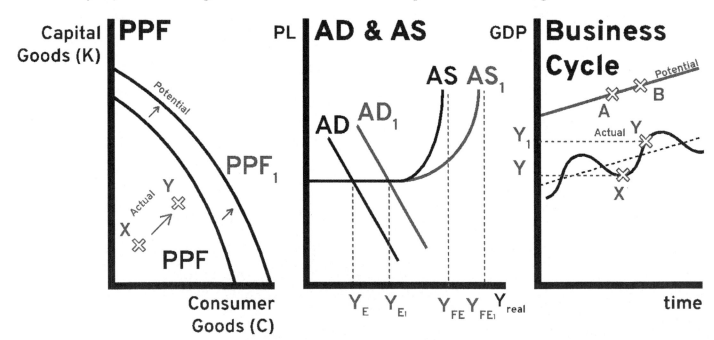

6.   List 5 factors which influence **actual** economic growth.

Since AD = C + G + I +X – M, (Consumption, Government expenditure, Investment, Exports, Imports) These are affected by interest rates, asset prices, consumer confidence, real wages, exchange rates, political stability, weather.

7.   List 5 factors which influence **potential** economic growth.

The factors that affect long run aggregate supply (LRAS):

1) *Size of labour force and its skills.(human capital)*
2) *Amount and quality materials available*
3) *Size and quality of infrastructure.*
4) *Amount and quality of capital stock.*
5) *The size and speed of technological progress.*

8.   Actual economic growth can be higher than potential growth rate. *True* / **False.**

True, in the short run if the economy has plenty of unused capacity. However, in the long run actual economic growth can only be within the limits of potential growth (inside the PPF curve)

9.   Decide whether the following affect growth **potential / actual / both / no effect**.

a)   Increase in the size of the labour force due to immigration. *potential* / actual / both / no effect. **Explain.** *Capacity rises but actual growth rises only when the immigrants work and produce.*

b)   Geologists find new gas reserves in the country with easy access. *potential* / actual / both / no effect. **Explain.** *Same as above. Easy access can lead to greater output now.*

c)   More government programs which provide new skills to long term unemployed workers. *potential* / actual / both / no effect.

     Explain. *These workers have more skills to make them employable.*

d)   Greater investment in fibre optics to increase the bandwidth and speed of the internet. potential / actual / *both* / no effect.

     Explain. *Actual growth during the construction stage and potential growth after the system is built.*

e)   As a result of the coming of both the Olympics and World Cup, firms expand and hire more workers over the next 2 years. potential / actual / *both* / no effect. **Explain.** *Same argument as above.*

f)   A 3 year war with destruction of capital stock and labour. potential / actual / *both* / no effect. **Explain. Wars destroy machinery, labour, skills, and infrastructure so both suffer.**

10.   List 5 desirable effects of economic growth.

1) ***Increases real disposable income***
2) ***Improves quality of life***
3) ***Lowers unemployment***
4) ***Higher tax revenues for the government***
5) ***Increases investment, FDI***

11.   List 5 undesirable effects of economic growth.

1) ***Growth may not be evenly distributed, or "trickle down"***
2) ***Growth may pollute the environment, and loss of bio-diversity***
3) ***Growth may use excess resources → may not be sustainable***
4) ***Inflation if AD>AS rate of growth.***
5) ***Worsening of balance of payments as imports sucked in.***
6) ***Over population***

12.   Define Productivity and explain how it affects economic growth.

Productivity is output per unit of land/labour. It enables resources to be freed up to potentially be productive and increase output of goods and services overall.

13.   Use the AD/SRAS/LRAS below to explain the effect of rising productivity on short run and long run economic growth.

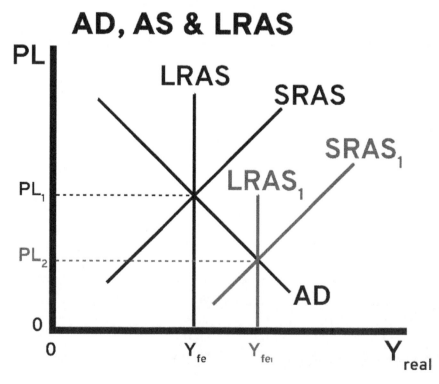

Rising productivity shifts LRAS and SRAS to the right. Examples such as the internet show that the same level of output can be produced using fewer resources and that new services/uses can be found from moving information round the globe instantly and at almost zero marginal cost. With competition prices fall and supply rises. This

leads to greater AD (move down AD1 curve)

14.   Define jobless growth and explain the conditions under which it may occur.

Jobless growth is when growth is coupled with high levels of unemployment. It may occur if the economy is experiencing structural changes (many people have lost jobs) and when producers are introducing new labour-saving technology.

15.   Explain and use the diagram below to show how a rise in economic growth can lead to inflation.

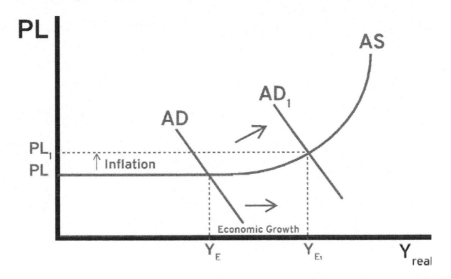

An injection combined with a multiplier effect raises AD to AD1. Here there is economic growth. However some sectors may already be at full employment and shortages of FoPs result in higher costs and higher prices causing inflation PL1 to PL2.

16.   Explain the conditions under which economic growth is sustainable with the environment.
Economic growth is compatible with development if investment is in skills, energy efficiency, renewables, recycling. Rate of use of renewables such as trees, farming, fishing < rate of depletion.

17.   A rise in the quality of worker training on the use of new high technology machinery will affect inflation and economic growth in which one of the following ways:

	Real Economic Growth	Inflation
A	fall	rise
B	rise	rise
C	fall	fall
D	**rise**	**fall**

Explain D *Productivity and hence more can be produced for the same amount of labour. Supply rises and with competition, prices fall.*

18. When the economy is in a deep recession which one of the following is most likely to occur

    A   negative output gap and a rise in exports.

    B   a rise in investment and a rise in unemployment.

    C   **negative output gap with rising unemployment and falling consumption.**

    D   rise in unemployment and inflation and a fall in economic growth.

Explain C.   *In a recession AD is below trend, producers cut output and lay off workers. This leads to further falls in consumption spending.*

19. The change in GDP for Belgium and Switzerland is shown below.

Country	2012	2013	2014	2015
☐ Belgium	–0.3 %	–0.5 %	2.0 %	3.5 %
☐				
☐ Switzerland	0 %	0.1 %	0.2 %	0.1 %
☐				

It can be deduced that:

    A   Switzerland has been growing economically throughout the period.

    B   **Belgium's output at the end of the period is higher than at the beginning of the period.**

    C   Belgium will have a lower level of unemployment than Switzerland.

    D   None of the above.

Explain B   *two years of slight recession followed by two years of even faster expansion.*

20. A rise in productivity of workers may **not** lead to economic growth if

    A   the retirement age is raised.

    B   workers take less vacation time.

    C   raw material prices fall.

    D   **a rise in the school leaving age from 16 to 18 years of age.**

Explain D.   *The gains from productivity rises are offset by loss of workers.*

21.   Economic growth will fall if

   A   **unemployment benefits rise.**

   B   immigration regulations are loosened.

   C   retirement age rises.

   D   none of the above.

Explain A   *unemployment benefits are considered as transfer payments.*

22.   If income tax rates fall along with a fall in unemployment benefits and there is a rise in real disposable income,

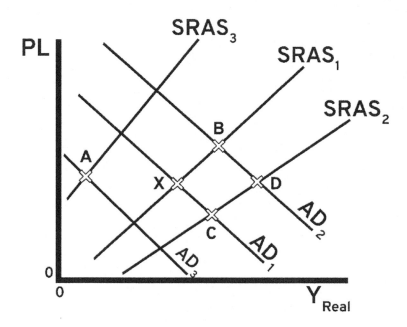

then equilibrium at point X below will shift to new equilibrium point

A   B   C   **D**

Explain_D   *Fall in income tax rate and fall in unemployment benefits strongly incentivizes work. Higher disposable income leads to higher level of spending.*

23.   A rise in real economic growth per capita may not lead to higher standards of living if

   A   population has risen.

   B   there is inflation.

   C   inequality falls.

   D   the level of pollution rises.

Explain_D   *greater production levels may occur at the cost of health.*

24.   Real **potential** economic growth will most likely to rise in the long run if there is

   A   greater government spending.

   B   greater consumer spending.

   C   greater spending on imports.

   D   greater spending on capital investment.

Explain_D   *Capital investment increases the economy's capacity to produce.*

25.   Assume an economy's trend growth rate is 4%. Data on real GDP growth is shown below.

Year	GDP Growth
2012	3.0 %
2013	0.3 %
2014	0.1 %
2015	2.2 %

Between the period 2012 and 2015 (4 years) it can be said that

   A   unemployment increased.

   B   inflation increased.

   C   the economy fell into a recession.

   D   none of the above.

EVALUATION QUESTIONS   **(Macroeconomic Objective: Economic Growth)**

26.   Evaluate the effectiveness of using a loose monetary policy as the main tool to increase economic growth.

- *Define economic growth and loose monetary policy.*
- *Could use Keynesian Transmission Mechanism to show the effectiveness of reducing i% and increasing Ms.*
- *Particularly effective if debts are low, economy well below full employment, current interest rates high(no liquidity trap)and if there is less uncertainty for decisions.*
- *Ineffective if economy has structural problems such as loss of manufacturing base due to say outsourcing.*
- *Long term economic growth driven by technological change and productivity improvements may require supply-side policies.*
- *Loose monetary policy could be inflationary.*

27.   To what extent is economic growth compatible with sustainable development?

- *Define economic growth and measurement (rise in real GDP).*
- *Define sustainable development and measurement (rise in HDI)*
- *Economic growth is compatible with development if investment is in skills, energy efficiency, renewables, recycling.*
- *Rate of use of renewables such as trees, farming, fishing < rate of depletion.*
- *Economic growth is not compatible if output is derived from using up finite and non-renewable resources, or which creates negative externalities.*
- *Currently most economic growth is not sustainable or compatible with sustainable development.*

28.   Since debt is simply a transfer of credit from more patient groups to less patient groups, the net effect on the economy is zero. Discuss this view.

- *Define debt and debt servicing.*
- *With debt the standard explanation is that patient groups are savers who are willing to forgo current spending for a price (i%).*
- *Here we simply have a redistribution of spending of funds. No net change.*
- *In future the two groups reverse their actions (pay back)*
- *However there is a net effect when banks create loans/debt from thin air. Here debt is money and not savings.*
- *If the current impatient groups use the borrowed funds for productive investment then in the future the total real pie will expand. Whole is greater than sum of the parts.*

29.   Evaluate the effectiveness of promoting free market orientated supply-side policies as the main tool of achieving long term economic growth.

- *Define free-market supply-side policies with examples of privatisation, liberalisation, and deregulation, labour market reform, removing zoning regulations, reducing income and profits tax.*
- *Define long term economic growth and measurement (rise in I net)*
- *Here LRAS shifts right through Say's Law (supply creates its own demand)*
- *Effective in that resources are allocated according to market discipline, efficiency argument. Less need for government (tax payer resources) incentives to effort, innovation etc created. Productivity claimed to be higher and rewarded.*
- *Ineffective in that inequalities will worsen. Free market thinking is short-term. The big ideas come from the state (internet). Many socially important projects remain unrealised. Workers' power diluted. Capital favoured over labour. Private sector reluctant to invest in training of population. Debt levels rise. Greater social immobility.*
- *Better off with combination of government intervention free market policies.*

19 MACRO OBJECTIVE IV   (INEQUALITY)

1.   Define inequality of income.

Maldistribution of income between different groups of population

2.   How can inequality of income between different groups be measured?

Using Lorenz curve

3.   Name and label the curve below.

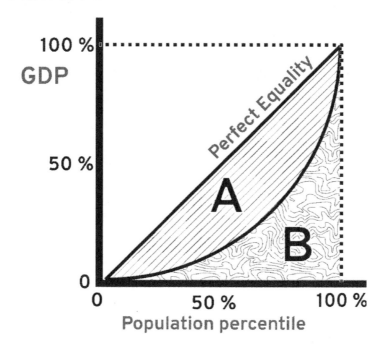

4.   State the formula for the Gini Coefficient using the areas A and B given above.

$$\frac{A}{A + B}$$

5.   What is the value of the Gini Coefficient when there is perfect equality?   *0*

   Explain   *0 = perfect equality.*   *The inequality area does not exist.*

6.   In the case of perfect inequality the Gini Coefficient value is   *1 = perfect inequality.*

7.   List 5 reasons why one country may have more income equality than another.

1. Greater progressivity of income tax system.

2. More job opportunities

3. Less discrimination in the labour market.

4. Lower level of indirect taxes.

5. Greater level of in kind benefits such college grants, housing credits, disability benefits and free child care for the lower income groups.

8   What is the difference between income and wealth?

Income is a flow concept whereas wealth is a stock concept. Wealth is the sum of accumulated income net of spending and taxes over time.

9.   List 5 problems arising from increasing **income** inequalities.

1. Slowdown in economic growth,

2. Greater welfare spending and taxes,

3. Less incentive to spend on R&D and innovation due to lack of markets.

4. Leads to other inequalities in health, housing and education,

5. More spending on crime prevention and dealing with social problems.

10.   List 5 problems arising from increasing **wealth** inequalities.

1. Lack of income in old age.

2. Fall in social mobility,

3. Greater level of discrimination in the labour market,

4. Greater degree of cronyism,

5. More lobbying for privileges for the rich few

6. Hijacking or manipulation of the democratic process to the betterment of a few,

7. Class warfare and feudalism.

11.   Distinguish between inequality and inequity (equality and equity).

Inequality refers to literally unequal shares in wealth or income whereas inequity refers to unfair distribution of resources in line with ethical issues. Some inequality may be desired but inequity is never acceptable.

12. Describe the trade-off between equity and efficiency in the free market system.

The free market is considered efficient, Pareto optimal since the forces of demand and supply are driven by the maximum value the use of FoPs brings to all parties. However, the ownership and distribution of these FoPs and the subsequent goods and services may be considered inequitable/unfair to begin with. The distribution of resources is not necessarily based on needs.

13. List 5 reasons why inequality of income can be considered desirable or necessary.

1. To reflect differences in ability/talent,

2. To reward the differences in the level of effort,

3. To compensate those whose are willing to take higher risks,

4. Creates aspirations and drive and motivation.

5. Acts as a reflection of status and a tool for stratification of an individual's contribution to society.

14. Distinguish between **absolute** and **relative** poverty.

Absolute poverty is when an individual has insufficient resources to reach the threshold of survival (basic needs are not met). Relative poverty is when people are poor (in terms of what they have) compared to others around them even though their basic needs have been met.

15. List 5 possible socio-economic **causes** of poverty.

1. Lack of resources,

2. Lack of know-how and productivity,

3. Lack of opportunities,

4. Indebtedness,

5. Traditions and customs,

6. Discrimination.

16. List 5 possible socio-economic **consequences** of poverty.

1. Low productivity,

2. Low life expectancy and high infant mortality,

3. More domestic violence,

4. More wars,

5. *Low income, savings and investment.*

Inequality of income is one of many types of inequalities. Inequalities in access to education (primary, secondary and tertiary), in access to healthcare, in access to jobs opportunities, as well as the lack of social mobility also contribute significantly to creating an inequitable society. Paul Krugman's view is that currently the statistics from his reading show that dumb rich kids have more opportunities in life than smart poor kids. The long-term effect is a slowdown in progress and the gradual impoverishment of the society.

Since extreme inequality and inequity are considered types of free market failure, government intervention is necessary.

17.   Define direct tax and give 3 examples.

Tax imposed on different forms of income (wages, profit, rent and interest)

18.   Define indirect tax and give 3 examples. *Tax imposed on expenditure (TVA, alcohol tax, import duty)*

19.   Define transfer payments and give 3 examples.

Transfer of money without the corresponding exchange of goods and services. (pension, child benefit, housing credit, food vouchers

20.   Define a progressive tax and illustrate with a numerical example.

as income increases, ART increases. MRT>ART (e.g. Y=100 ART=5%, Y=110, ART=6%)

21.   Define a regressive tax and illustrate with a numerical example.

As income increases, ART decreases. MRT<ART (e.g. Y=100 ART=5%, Y=110 ART=4%)

22.   Define a proportional tax. *ART stays constant even though income rises.*

23.   In the 2 diagrams below draw appropriate lines to illustrate the difference between progressive, regressive and proportional tax. (note the axes)

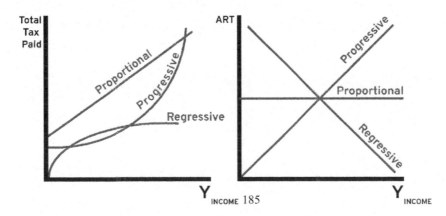

24.   In most countries the **overall** tax system is generally regressive / ***progressive*** / proportional.
      Explain *A state won't raise enough money with other tax systems*

25.   Define marginal rate of tax (**MRT**).   *MRT = change in tax paid/change in income*

26.   Define average rate of tax (**ART**).   *ART = Total tax paid/Total income*

27.   If MRT > ART the tax is considered ***progressive*** / regressive / proportional.

28.   If MRT < ART the tax is considered progressive */ regressive* / proportional.

29.   If MRT = ART the tax is __*Proportional*____.

30 *b*.   Fill in the table below and answer the question.

Worker	Income before tax ($)	Income after tax ($)	ART
A	10 000	8 500	**15 %**
B	50 000	40 000	**20 %**
C	100 000	70 000	**30 %**

a)   Is the above tax system regressive / ***progressive*** / proportional.

      Explain   *As income rises, ART rises*

31.   Define 'in-kind government benefits' and give 3 examples. _

      Targeted benefits given in a medium other than money (eg food vouchers, education grant, housing credits)

32.   List and explain 5 canons of taxation.

      Canons of taxation = what is a good or fair tax (vertical equity, horizontal equity, efficient to collect, should not discourage effort, within EU people or businesses should not move for tax purposes.)

33.   Define and draw the Laffer curve below. _

Relationship between income tax rate and tax revenue collected.

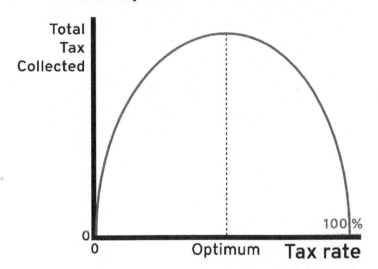

a)   What is the argument behind the Laffer Curve and is there any evidence supporting its existence? *The curve is supposed to show that beyond the optimum tax rate, further rise in the rate of tax will create strong disincentives to effort and hence lead to falls in the total tax collected as workers reduce effort, choose not to work, avoid and even evade taxes. There is very little evidence supporting the existence of this curve. Where the optimum rate is not known. If anything, this curve is used as a political tool to persuade governments to reduce taxes.*

34 *b*. The table below shows yearly income and the MRT. Assume that the rate of tax on sales is 30%.

Annual income ($)	MRT
0 – 20 000	0 %
20 001 – 40 000	15 %
40 001 – 60 000	25 %
60 001 – 90 000	30 %
≥ 90 001	35 %

a)   Work out the amount of income tax each of the following pays for the year and the ART for each worker W, X, Y, Zj.

i   Worker W works part time and earns $ 18000 for the year. _*Tax paid = 0, ART = 0%.*

ii.   Worker X earns $ 38 000 for the year. *20 000 @ 0% + 18 000 @ 15% = $2700 Total tax paid.*

        ART = 2700/38 000 = 7.1% = ART

iii.　　Worker Y earns $ 58 000 for the year.　*20 000@0% + 20 000@15% + 18 000@25% = $ 7500 = Total tax paid.*　　*ART = 7500/58 000 = 12.93% = ART*

iv.　　Worker Z earns $ 98 000 for the year.

20 000@0% + 20 000@15% + 20 000@25% + 30 000@30% + 8000@35% = $19 800 = Total tax paid. ART = 19 800/98 000 = 20.20% = ART

b)　　Work out the **total** tax paid (direct and indirect) by each individual if:

i.　　Worker W saves no income.　*(direct tax = 0) + (indirect tax = 18 000 @ 30% = 5400).*

　Total tax paid (direct and indirect) = $5400

ii.　　Worker X has a savings rate of 10% of disposable income.

Y_D = 38 000 – 2700 = $35 300 (savings = 35 300 @ 10% = 3530)

Income to spend = $31 770　(direct tax =2700) + (indirect tax = 31 770 @ 30% = 9531).

Total tax paid (direct and indirect) = 2700 + 9531 = $12 231

iii.　　Worker Y has a savings rate of 20% of disposable income.

Y_D = 58000 – 7500 = $50500 (savings = 50500% 20% = $10100)

　Income to spend = $40400　(direct tax =7500) + (indirect tax = 40400@30% = 12120).

Total tax paid (direct and indirect) = 7500 + 12120 = $ 19620

iv.　　Worker Z has a savings rate of 30% of disposable income.

Y_D = 98 000 – 19 800 = $78 200 (savings = 78 200 @ 30% = $23 460)

Income to spend = $54 740　(direct tax = 9800) + (indirect tax = $54 800 @ 30% = 16 422).

Total tax paid (direct and indirect) = $19 800 + $16 440 = $36 222 = Total direct and indirect tax bill.

35. Use the Gini Coefficient to decide which of the 4 Lorenz curves in the diagram below depicts the highest level of income inequality.

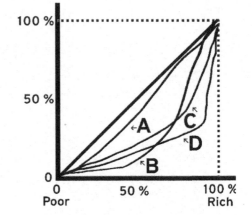

A   **B**   C   D

Explain *The poorest have the lowest share of the GDP. However, for an overall more precise answer we need to work out the Gini Coefficient.*

36. Decide which of the following policy combination could have moved Lorenz Curve P to Lorenz Curve Q below.

MRT on richer households | State pensions/social security

	MRT on richer households	State pensions/social security
A	increase	decrease
B	decrease	increase
C	*increase*	*increase*
D	decrease	decrease

Explain *C State pensions tend to be biased towards the lower incomes group. They act as a great equaliser. A high MRT on richer households implies a more progressive tax system focused on reducing inequalities.*

37. The diagram below illustrates which of the following combinations

	Type of Tax	Example
A	flat rate	sales tax 10%
B	*regressive*	*sales tax 15%*
C	progressive	income tax
D	regressive	wealth tax

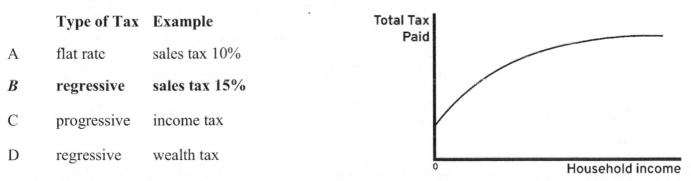

Explain B The *ART rate falls as income rises. Sales taxes take up a greater % of income of poor families than for the rich households.*

EVALUATION QUESTIONS (Inequality)

38.   Evaluate the view that a wealth tax is more equitable than a tax on income for a country.

- *Distinguish between wealth and income. Wealth is the accumulated value of assets owned. Income the annual change in the value of the assets or the annual returns to the assets (wealth: stock, income: flow)*
- *Inequalities of wealth are much greater than inequalities of income*
- *Inequalities with grow to be problematic if left uncorrected (Piketty's rate of return from assets > rate of growth of income)*
- *Most of wealth in families is inherited and not earned. This causes problems arising from social immobility, cronyism. Society resembles feudalism that is neither merit nor ability based.*
- *The very rich receive a much bigger portion of their income from ownership of capital rather than labour. A more progressive wealth tax rather than a progressive income tax will reduce inequities to much greater degree.*
- *The level of AD will rise along with economic growth and job creation as MPC and multiplier effect for low income groups is higher than the well off.*
- *Alternative view: I and entrepreneur rewards to new ideas fall with higher wealth tax. The wealthy may leave to more rich friendly countries. Greater tax evasion for those remaining. Less incentive to save for an uncertain future, for education for children, for accumulating funds for opening businesses and buying a house. The tax revenue raised may not be sufficient for government services.*

39.   Evaluate the view that a single flat rate of income tax is easy to implement and fair.

- *Define flat tax with diagram.*
- *Explain why proportional income tax is considered equitable. Argument that since we all use services provided by the government, we should all pay an equal share (equal %).*
- *Simplicity results in easily understood and calculated tax as well as less desire to evade tax and cost savings in collection.*
- *Problem is that some low-income earners are already paid below living wage and paying tax is unbearable. Flat tax needs to be much higher to rise to same level of funds as before. Tax evasion may not stop. The rich create and exploit loop holes. The overall mpc and multiplier will fall. Government's ability to help the poor and provide a safety net weakens.*

40.   To what extent do you agree with the view that since tax on income is a tax on effort, governments should finance their spending chiefly through indirect taxes?

- *Define direct tax and indirect tax illustrated with examples.*
- *Diagram to explain the difference between progressive and regressive tax.*
- *Disagree with view since: progressive income is fair in terms of canons of taxation. Creates equity and is needed in order to collect sufficient funds for governments to pay for services. Less burdensome on the poor. The well-off can afford to contribute more after all we are a community. Feudalism is not a welcoming proposition. Indirect taxes are regressive and must be set at a very high rate to raise enough money for government. Uncompetitive sales taxes encourage consumers to shop abroad, deprive local spending affecting AD adversely. Firms contract and jobs are lost. End up with too high savings rate and not enough investment projects which bring in returns.*
- *Agree with the view since firms which produce products which last gain over firms which produce low quality products. Could have a positive environmental affect where conservation and recycling is promoted. Effort is rewarded. Jobs created in areas where products can be fixed/serviced and well looked after. Less dependence on factory employment.*

41. Examine the merits of a government replacing the minimum wage rate with a citizen income for all citizen adults to address the effects of new technology replacing labour with machines on a wide scale.

- *Define minimum wage.*
- *Point out the difference between minimum wage and living wage.*
- *Show how it is supposed to work.*
- *Most of the time minimum wage is significantly below living wage. The gains from globalisation are not equitably shared.*
- *Firms offering only min wage to workers will gain at the expense of the taxpayer who has to finance the higher welfare bill. (the US has around 50m users receiving food stamps)*
- *Machines replacing is another gain for society and results in higher productivity. This gain has to lead to higher wages and greater job creation. If this mechanism fails in capitalism, then we have to correct market failure via government intervention.*
- *A basic citizen income fulfils many of these roles. Can be more efficient than current plethora of means tested benefits.*
- *Arguments against include: where to set the amount, who qualifies, direct taxes may rise if more money is needed, aggressive lobbying from the potential losers, distortion on the incentives to effort, what historical evidence is there, distortions in the desire to work, gaming the new system, employers find it more difficult to retain workers, worker-employer power changes.*

20 MACROECONOMIC POLICIES I

The enlargement of the circular flow of income in real terms means more final goods and services are being produced (real economic growth), generally more jobs are being created (fall in unemployment) without the pressure on prices (low inflation) and hopefully the fruits of efforts will be shared by all (more equitable distribution). The government, at the macro level uses demand-side and supply-side policies to manage the circular flow of income to attain these macroeconomic objectives.

The demand-side/demand management policies comprise of using fiscal and monetary policy to maintain the level of aggregate demand at or near full employment level of real GDP.

Fiscal Policy

1.   Define fiscal policy.

    This is a policy where government manages the economic activity in the economy by changing government spending (G) and taxation (T)

2.   List 5 examples of **expansionary** fiscal policy.   *This is when the government lowers taxes and increases government spending to promote increase in aggregate demand (AD). Government typically adopts this policy when the economy is in a recession and unemployment is high.*

    - Cutting direct taxes

    - Cutting indirect taxes (i.e. TVA)

    - Government creating new projects (ex: CEVA, the new metro system in Geneva, Switzerland))

    - Government increasing unemployment benefits

    - More/new transfer payment schemes such as housing credits and higher state pensions.

    - Government subsidies on energy

3.   List 5 examples of **contractionary** fiscal policy.   *This is when the government increases taxes and lowers government spending to lower aggregate demand (AD). Government typically adopts this policy when the economy is going through a boom and inflation rates are going up.*

    - Increasing direct and indirect taxes

    - Reducing child benefits and/or increasing workers state health insurance premiums

    - Government shelving new projects

    - Reduction of unemployment benefits.   - Reducing transfer payments

4.   An expansionary fiscal policy, ceteris paribus, will shift the AD curve to the left / ***right*** whereas a contractionary fiscal policy will shift AD to the ***left*** / right.

5.   Distinguish between a government budget surplus, budget deficit and a balanced budget.

A balanced budget is when government spending is equal to the revenue it gets from taxes (G=T), meaning that the government is spending as much as it is receiving from the taxpayer. A budget deficit occurs when government is spending more than what it is receiving from taxes paid by the taxpayer and profits from state owned companies (G>T). A budget surplus occurs when government is spending less than what it is receiving from the taxes and profits from state owned companies (G<T).

6.   Distinguish between discretionary fiscal policy and automatic stabilisers giving 5 examples of each.

Discretionary fiscal policy – This is when government spending and taxation changes <u>require</u> changes in the law. Here, changes in G and T need to be discussed in parliament - votes have to be cast. There is a lot more negotiation going on; significant time lags and uncertainty are present as government may not have enough votes.

Ex:

- *Recent financial crisis: economy suffered severe fall in AD, so on top of Automatic stabilizers, EU governments and US brought in a "Cash for Clunkers" scheme = to support jobs in car industry, government offered 3000Euros to anyone removing old cars and replacing them with new cars.*
- *Similar subsidies given to households installing solar panels, new insulation.*
- *In the US, unemployment benefits were extended for an additional period of time.*
- *Employers were given subsidies to hire new workers.*
- *Decreasing VAT*

Automatic Stabilizers – This is government spending rising and falling in accordance to the level of economic activity. This spending is already built into the system, hence, requires no change in the law system.
Ex:

- *Unemployment benefit spending rises without a change in the law when economy enters a recession.*
- *Progressive taxation = when the economy is booming, and lots of new jobs are created, there is a rise in income and, automatically, government spending falls below the level of tax collected as tax revenues rise.*
- *Corporate profits = taxes on corporate profits go up substantially during boom times, and decline rapidly during times of recession.*
- *Unemployment benefits / child benefit / state health insurance / housing benefits*

7.   Changes in discretionary fiscal policy (autonomous government spending) will have a larger multiplier effect than automatic stabilisers (induced government spending). ***True*** / False. **Explain** *discretionary spending such as a stimulus package has a multiplier effect which is clearly measurable and can be directed more so than automatic stabilizers in terms of reducing the level of leakages.*

8.   Distinguish between a government's capital budget and its current/operating budget.

- A government's budget consists of two budgets:

- Operational budget = used to cover the day to day costs of providing services (about 90% of the whole budget)

- Capital budget = expenditure on new projects (about 10% of the whole budget)

9.   List 3 examples of the likely items in the capital budget account and 3 items in the operating budget account.

Items in an operating budget account:
- *Fixing potholes in the roads*
- *Traffic lights*
- *Health care funding and paying teachers to keep schools running*

Items in the capital budget account:

- CEVA cost incurred in building a new metro system in Geneva, Switzerland

- New Hospital

- New public school

10.   List 5 ways in which a government can finance a budget deficit.

- Sell government owned assets

- Increase taxes   *- Printing money*

- Borrowing money   *- Attract new companies from outside to set up operations.*

11.   List 5 reasons for a government to run a budget deficit.

- Demographic pressure (if a government has a high level of ageing population)

- High levels of government subsidy and financial support (ex: farming sector in Switzerland)

- Borrowing to make repayments on previous loans

- Cyclical reasons: for many countries a government deficit is unavoidable during a recession or sustained period of slow growth.

- Keynesian Fiscal Deficits: a large (and rising) fiscal deficit might also be the deliberate effect of a government choosing to use expansionary fiscal policy to boost aggregate demand, output and employment at a time when private sector demand (C+I+X) is stagnant or falling.

-Going to war

-Dealing with a natural disaster

12.   List and **explain** 5 strengths of fiscal policy.

- It can significantly impact the national income (and increase/decrease in taxes and/or increase/decrease in government spending to easily manipulate the economy) and therefore have immediate effect on the economy. Fiscal policy therefore may be very effective in reducing demand-deficient unemployment.

- Taxes on negative externalities of consumption and production and decreasing taxes on positive externalities can help divert the consumers' and producers' attention to products that have positive externalities.

- Tax cuts on wages can encourage people to work and therefore shift the SRAS to the right.

- Different rates of tax on different levels of income groups can help reduce disparities and inequalities between rich and poor.

- Can dampen the trade cycle considerably using automatic stabilizers and can address fundamental economic discrepancies using discretionary fiscal policy

- To fund research in fundamental science e.g. the internet, Ebola vaccine.

13.   List and **explain** 5 weaknesses of fiscal policy.

- Inflexibility - changes in direct taxes may take considerable time to implement and government spending is often inflexible in a downwards direction; e.g. for political or moral reasons, it is usually difficult to reduce government spending on pensions and benefits and once a capital project such as a motorway has been started, it is difficult, if not impossible, to stop it in mid-stream.

- Conflicts between objectives - fiscal policy designed to achieve one goal may adversely impact on another. Eg: reflationary fiscal policy designed to stimulate AD and reduce unemployment may worsen inflation

- Supply side economists believe that certain fiscal measures will have a disincentive effect. For example, an increase in income tax may adversely affect the supply of labour, an increase in profits tax may adversely affect the incentives of firms to invest and an increase in welfare benefits may adversely affect incentives to seek employment.

- If it's a discretionary policy, the votes needed in parliament to implement the package may not be sufficient and hence the policy many never occur even though it is needed.

- Tax evasion, avoidance and bribing often increase when taxes increase (especially for big firms) and hence the government may start running a budget deficit.

- Fiscal policy puts pressure on government resources. Deficits and debts rise putting pressure on future generations.

- Distort free market and may conflict with other policies and objectives (especially with automatic stabilizers)

14.   Define **crowding out effect** and explain why it is most likely to occur at full employment.

The crowding out effect is an economic theory suggesting that rises in public sector spending will reduce or even eliminate private sector spending as society's limited resources are directed towards the state sector. It is more likely to occur at full employment since at that rate when there is little or slack in capacity. Interest rates may rise as both sectors are competing for limited funds.

Monetary Policy

15.   Define monetary policy. *This is a policy set by the "independent" central bank (ex: Fed, BoE, SNB, BoJ,) on the cost of credit (i%) and the availability of credit (Ms) in the economy.*

16.   Explain **loose** monetary policy and list 3 reasons for implementing this.

Loose monetary policy is when the central bank decreases interest rates and increases the amount of credit available in the economy. This is used to encourage economic growth and consumer spending (i.e. economy is in a recession), to decrease the value of the currency, and to promote investment and build business confidence. In addition it helps governments to pay back or finance their loans.

17.   Define **tight** monetary policy and list 3 reasons for implementing this.

Tight monetary policy is when the central bank increases interest rates and reduces the amount of credit available in the economy. This is used when spending in an economy is seen to be growing too quickly (economy is in a boom), when inflation is climbing too fast, and to increase the value of its currency.

18.   List 5 functions/roles of a central bank.

- Principal authority for the nation's financial matters and decisions

- Help manage macro-economic objectives (inflation target, unemployment target, economic growth rate)

- Promote stability of the country's financial system

- Manage the production and distribution of the nation's currency

- Inform the public of the general state of the economy by publishing statistics and data regularly

- buyer of last resort of government bonds, as is the case with the Bank of Japan.

19.   A loose monetary policy will generally *increase* consumer spending. **Explain**

Since i% fall and the availability of credit (Ms) rises, consumers will find borrowing much more affordable and will hence start spending more while the interest rates are still low.

20.   A tight monetary policy will generally *decrease* investment spending. **Explain**

With high i% and little credit available on the market, businesses and businessmen will refrain from borrowing as their costs of production will rise. Hence, they will invest less in new projects or already existing projects due to the rise in cost.

21.   A loose monetary policy can *decrease* government spending. **Explain**
An decrease in i% will encourage consumer spending. Hence, the need for government spending will decrease and may indirectly decrease it. A booming economy may mean less spending needed on social security.

22.   A tight monetary policy can *decrease* demand for exports. **Explain**

As i% rise, the value of the currency rises accordingly. Hence, the price of exports will rise compared to prices of goods abroad, which will decrease the demand for exports by other countries, ceteris paribus.

23.   A loose monetary policy can *decrease* spending on imports. **Explain**

As i% falls, the value of the currency weakens and hence the price of imports rise. Consumers may switch to buying more domestic alternative goods which are now cheaper than foreign goods. More likely to occur in services such as tourism.

24.   A tight monetary policy, ceteris paribus, will shift the AD curve to the *left* causing a *contraction* aggregate demand whereas a loose monetary policy will shift AD to the *right* causing an *expansion* of aggregate demand.

25.   List and **explain** 5 strengths of monetary policy.

- Stable prices: it enables the central bank to play around with the credit to stabilize prices in the economy (ex: in case of inflation, the Fed may sell bonds to remove Ms or increase i%)

- Long-term perspective: short-run action enables policy makers to assess economic conditions and promote sustainable growth and low inflation over the long term.

- Requires no resources

- Shorter time lags than Fiscal Policies

- No crowding out effect (unlike Fiscal Policy)

- No government stop-go policy problem creating uncertainty which adversely affects investment decisions

26.   List and **explain** 5 weaknesses of monetary policy.

- Conflicting goals: the objectives of sustainable economic growth and inflation often conflict as, in a growing economy, a fall in the interest rate may increase AD to rise faster than AS can accommodate resulting in inflation . Economic growth objective conflicting with stable prices objective.

- Monetarist vs Keynesian: the relationship between i% and I may be elastic (monetarist) or inelastic (Keynesian).

- Problem stemming from law of diminishing marginal returns of investment (ex: China mal-investment in shopping malls which do not generate the returns required to cover the costs)

- Commercial banks and hedge funds get first access to cheap money. They leverage themselves up and gamble on financial assets. Very little of the credit gets down to small businesses and households and hence the real economy is not affected (greater disparities between rich and poor).

- Problem of NINJAs – lending money to consumers who have No Income No Jobs or Assets (i.e. subprime loans, reason for 2008 crisis)

- Can encourage over-borrowing from too low i% and debts may rise for Households (consumption may become unsustainable), private sector corps, and the public sector.

- Higher risk of defaults if i% rise too quickly

-In an environment of Stagflation, monetary policy becomes ineffective.

27.   Define **liquidity trap** and explain why a further easy money policy in a liquidity trap is ineffective.

This is when i% are already extremely low and borrowing is still not occurring, lowering the i% further will not have an effect on the real economy. The only effect is on the asset prices (stock markets, real estate prices rise on borrowed money).

28.   Define **'stagflation'** and explain why monetary policy is usually ineffective during a period of stagflation.

Stagflation is a term used to describe when the economy is experiencing a falling economic growth, rising inflation and rising unemployment. Economist Phillips suggested that there was an inverse relationship between the rise in prices and the rise in unemployment. Hence, since monetary policy can only target one area, the central bank has to choose which to target, which may relieve pressure off one, but will worsen the other. Government is better off promoting supply-side policies in this case.

29.   Draw the Keynesian Transmission Mechanism below to explain how a loose monetary policy can lead to economic growth, a fall in unemployment and possibly inflation.

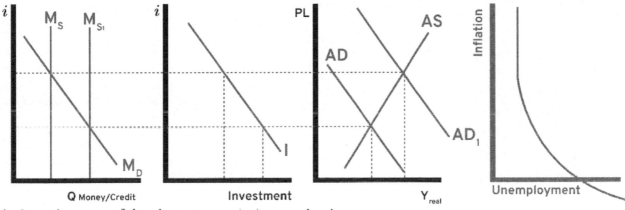

Explain 3 weaknesses of the above transmission mechanism.

- The relationship between the i% and I may not be as elastic as we think due to the issue of liquidity trap: the i% may be historically low but I is not picking up due to uncertainties in business decisions.

- The relationship between i% and AD may not be as elastic either since a fall in i% may only benefit big businesses, hedge funds, and commercial banks as the benefits may not trickle down to the consumers.

-In a liquidity trap further loosening of credit will not raise AD components.

Supply Side Policy.

30   Define and explain 2 objectives of supply side policy.

Defined as policies designed to increase the productivity of Fops and efficiency of markets.

Supply-side policies aim to increase LRAS in the economy to achieve the macro-economic objectives (low inflation, low unemployment, and steady economy growth).

It aims to improve incentives to work and invest in people's skills, increase labour and capital productivity, increase occupational and geographical mobility of labour to help reduce the rate of unemployment, increase research and development, promote competition and stimulate a faster rate of innovation to promote competition, provide a platform for sustained non-inflationary growth, encourage start-ups and expansion of businesses, and improve the trend-rate of real GDP growth.

31.   Say's Law provides the basis for supply-side policy. State and explain using a diagram, Say's Law.

Say's Law suggests that supply creates its own demand. According to this law, when an individual produces a product or a service, he or she gets paid for that work, and is then able to use that income on other goods and services.

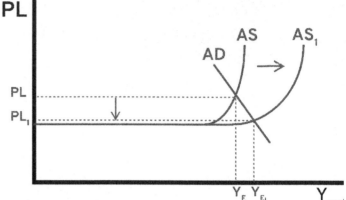

The goals of supply-side can be achieved in 2 ways, interventionist approach or a free market approach.

32.   Define interventionist supply-side approach.

These are government-directed supply-side policies based on investment.

33.   List 5 interventionist supply-side policies and explain how they are supposed to work.

- Investment in human capital: by increasing the skills base of labour, decreasing the search costs of both employers and job searchers and creating incentives for increased labour mobility, AS of labour will increase (ex: government training programs, soft loans and subsidized rents for startups, regional support and outsourcing of government agencies to depressed areas).

- Policies encouraging investment (physical capital): these aim to encourage investment and startup firms to flourish (ex: subsidies to start-ups, tax breaks for firms investing in physical capital, tax holidays for FDIs, soft loans for firms needing to invest). An increasing in SRAS due to these policies increases productivity which in turn shifts LRAS outwards.

- Infrastructure: by investing in infrastructure, governments enable workers to get to their jobs, produce being transported from rural to urban areas, power, water and electricity becomes available for businesses, and enhanced market accessibility increases the level of competition in an economy. By facilitating the job for business, governments hope to achieve increases in both SRAS and LRAS due to increased productivity and incentive to work.

- Industrial policies: governments take an active role in helping industries via government legislation and allocation of funds, which increases long run potential (ex: R&D grants to firms together with government support for R&D units linked to state universities, regional support for failing industries, relocation subsidies for workers to seek and take jobs in other regions)

34.   Define free market based supply-side approach.

Free-market based supply-side policies aim to increase LRAS and productivity which include policies to encourage competition, labour market reforms and incentive-related policies.

35.   List 5 free market based supply-side policies and explain how they are intended to work.

- Privatization: transfer of public sector assets to the private sector. It aims to collect revenue to pay for deficits, to inject private sector motive, to increase competition, bring consumer choice, encouraging new I and rising productivity and LRAS.

- Liberalization: country lowers/removes protectionist barriers and allows foreign companies to set up operations and sells in that country. This increases output, consumer choice, and competition, bringing down prices, creating new jobs (increase in LRAS), and new ideas and skills increase.

- Deregulation: this is changing current laws such that the free market can decide how to use its FOPs (ex: changing land use zoning regulations such that apartments can be built upon agricultural land or in villa zones, supermarkets offering banking services, make it easy to startup in terms of bureaucracy). This increases capacity, competition, and choice, shifting LRAS outwards.

- Labour Market Reforms: these aim to decrease the cost of hiring labour (SRAS shifts to the right) and increases productivity of workers (LRAS increases).

- Incentive related policies: policies such as lowering personal income tax rates, where the argument is that since labour is rewarded more, workers will put in more effort, increasing the opportunity cost of unemployment and productivity; lowering taxes on capital gains and interest income; and lowering business taxes, since after tax, profits rise and hence there will be more incentive to make investments and create jobs.

36.   Explain why labour market reforms are considered part of supply-side policies.

Supply-side policies aim to increase productivity and LRAS, and so do Labour Market Reforms: by reducing the cost of hiring labour it provides an incentive for businesses to hire more and by decreasing security for workers, it makes them more willing to work hard to keep their jobs, shifting SRAS and eventually LRAS to the right and increasing worker productivity.

37.   List 5 labour market reforms.

- Abolishing minimum wage legislation

- Weakening the power of worker's unions

- Reducing unemployment benefits

- Reducing job security

- Introducing "easy to hire easy to fire" regulations

38.   List 5 strengths of supply-side policies.

- Dual role of I under both interventionist and market based creates new jobs, rises in productivity as new technology is employed. Increases actual growth (AD) during the building for the project and potential growth for the jobs that will be created when the project is complete.

- ppf1 rises to ppf2, which indicates a rise in potential growth while point X rising to point Y closer to the ppfs indicating actual growth and fall in unemployment.

- Long-run global competitiveness rises due to higher productivity as do standards of living.

-Addresses the long term structural issues by promoting technological progress and innovation.

39.   List 5 weaknesses of supply-side policies.

- Time lags are long both for interventionist and free market policies

- Government resources needed especially for interventionist policies

- Government training programs may not be industry specific

- Stop-go policies

- Effects on environment (ex: new airports)

- Effects on equity: tax incentives may end up favouring already well-off

40.   List 3 arguments favouring interventionist policies.

- Government supporting SMEs may help create new industries and source of growth.

-Spending on fundamental science eg. Internet and fibre optics result in benefits to all and not just limited to patent owning companies.

-Fundamental science can be cost effective when it is shared among countries eg CERN.

41.   List 3 arguments favouring market-based policies.

- Do not require the resources from the government and hence may not affect the government's budget

- Deregulation allows new start-ups as well as allows established firms to diversify

-Allocative efficiency is achieved since resources used where they are valued the most.

42. An expansionary fiscal policy is most likely to lead to **crowding-out** private sector investment when:

    A   the savings ratio is high.

    B   the output gap is high and increasing.

    C   capacity utilization is low.

    D   none of the above.

Explain *D* – *the economy is close to full employment of FOPs and both state and private sector are competing*

43. Ceteris paribus, which one of the following is most likely to lead to a fall in both investment and savings.

    A   A loose monetary policy.

    B   An increase in the government budget surplus.

    C   An appreciating exchange rate.

    D   Nine of the above.

Explain *B* *Spending power leaks out of the circular flow of income, leading to contraction in Y, S, I*

44. Which one of the following is an example of monetary policy?

    A   The decision by the government to lower the interest rate.

    B   The decision by the government to weaken the exchange rate.

    C   The decision by the central bank to raise the base interest rate.

    D   None of the above.

Explain *C* – *Monetary policy is conducted by the central bank, not the government*

45. A fall in structural unemployment may be best possible through which one of the following:

    A   Central bank tightening monetary policy.

    B   Government introducing expansionary policies whereby increasing public sector services.

    C   A fall in consumer and producer confidence.

    D   A rise in international competitiveness.

Explain *B* – *this is the only supply-side policy likely to address the problem of structural unemployment. Least*

worst solution.

46. *h.*   Which of the following combinations describes an economy with natural rate of unemployment in the long run.

	unemployment rate	inflation rate
A	**constant**	**variable**
B	constant	constant
C	zero	zero
D	variable	constant

Explain A   *this refers to the Long Run Phillips Curve (LRPC) which is vertical.*

47.   After a significant cut in the personal income tax rate which of the following problems is most likely to occur?

A   The exchange rate is most likely to appreciate.

B   The budget deficit is bound to fall.

C   A rise in unemployment as employers cut the number of workers.

D   Demand inflation if the output gap is small.

Explain *D – consumers have more disposable income now, and with AD rising faster than AS can keep up, inflation will rise, ceteris paribus.*

EVALUATION QUESTIONS   (Macroeconomic Policies I)

48.   Discuss the effectiveness of using **only** supply-side policy to reduce inflation and unemployment simultaneously.

- *Define supply-side policies. State Say's Law. Give 3 examples.*
- *It is probably best to employ a mixture of both demand-side and supply-side policy.*
- *Supply side can address deep structural issues in the economy like productivity, moving from manufacturing to a service-based economy. Supply side policies can improve the productivity of FoPs and the efficiency of the markets through privatisation, liberalisation and deregulation as well as taxation policies and labour market reform.*
- *However, problems of time-lags, inequities, exploitation from private monopolies, job insecurity, gig economy and zero hour contracts. Loss of tax revenue and government services. Social implications.*

49 *b*.   Explain the concept of natural rate of unemployment using the Phillips Curve and evaluate policies to reduce this rate.

- *Define NAIRU, diagram: SRPC (Short-Run Phillips Curve)*
- *Go through process where government expansionary fiscal policy (increasing G) in a tight labour market can increase wage demands and leads to fall in unemployment but a rise in inflation.*
- *Point out that in the long run according to Monetarist government demand side policies only raise inflation. There is no trade-off. (diagram: LRPC, Long-Run Phillips Curve).*
- *However, if government policy is focused towards increasing the long run capacity to produce then there is less inflationary pressure. In addition, if government supply-side expansion occurs in a deep recession then there is little crowding out effect and less inflationary pressure caused by shortages of resources.*

50 *b*.   Evaluate the view that unemployment can only fall if inflation is permitted to rise.

- *Define unemployment, inflation.*
- *Support the view using the SRPC (trade-off)*
- *Support opposite view by using the LRPC (no trade-off in the long run) Here short run policies to reduce unemployment completely fail, leaving the economy with only higher inflation and unemployment back to being high.*
- *Alternatively show that with supply-side policies both unemployment can fall in the short run when I am spending is taking place (multiplier effect causing actual growth to rise and jobs created) and in the long run prices fall when additional capacity is created (potential growth). Use PPF or AD/AS diagram. Policy particularly effective in deep recession.*

51.   Do strong labour unions increase the demand for goods and services through higher wages or do they simply increase costs of production and drive prices higher?

- *Strong labour unions keep wages and conditions up for their members. They insure that the essential balance is kept between capital and labour share of the output gains. This results in higher demand for goods/services that is produced.*
- *Higher wages without productivity gains can be inflationary as producers raise prices to compensate. Some employers lay off workers to keep the wage bill the same. Some companies substitute workers for machinery.*

- *The gains from higher productivity have to be equitably shared to resolve the problem.*
- *Labour union, firms function myopically. Only focused on micro-issues and self-interest.*
- *In the macro-sense capitalism still needs to solve the conundrum "workers are consumers, and consumers are workers'. The role of the state is crucial here.*
-

52.   If profits take an increasing share of national income, evaluate the effects of this outcome.

- *If profits are kept with the few rich then trickle down is usually weak and the economy will slow down especially in the long run as incomes for the majority remain stagnant and new ideas less likely to be realised due to stagnant markets. Inequality will worsen.*
- *The MPC for poor is greater than MPC for the rich.*
- *Rising profit share may bring more funds for new ideas but hard to find new customers unless the new ideas are technological breakthroughs which result in lower costs and prices (internet). This is not as common as many think.*

53.   Evaluate the economic policies which government can use to fight accelerating deflation.

- *Very important to distinguish between demand deflation and price deflation.*
- *Demand deflation results in shrinking circular flow of income (diagram), or AD/AS diagram. Government can use demand-side policies of expansionary fiscal and the central bank can use loose monetary policy.*
- *Dangers of national debt exploding, rising debt to income ratio, 'white elephant' projects, falling interest rates only blowing up asset bubbles, liquidity trap, time-lags, firms focused on replacing workers with machinery, unbalanced recovery.*
- *Price deflation may be caused by greater competition (globalisation benefits), technological breakthroughs (internet leading to costs savings in the digital economy)*
- *Misdiagnosing the type of deflation may lead to employing wrong policy and worsening the problem.*

54.   Evaluate government policies that can be used to increase full employment level of real GDP.

- *Define full employment.*
- *Explain how expansionary fiscal and loose monetary policy increase AD (via rise in C, I, G and X) creates more jobs. Government interventionist supply-side policies create more jobs. Promotion of R&D and the long term gains created.(internet technology)*
- *However, dangers of stoking inflation especially near full employment. Phillips curve trade-off. Loss of international competitiveness.*
- *Problems of time-lags, liquidity trap, QE leading to asset bubbles with no wealth and real spending effect but simply pushing up debt-burden, national debt becoming unmanageable, 'white elephant' projects resulting in poor returns, jobless-growth, over-manning.*

55.   Evaluate the proposition that policies to achieve greater income equality should be given priority over other macroeconomic objectives.

- *Define income inequality and measurement.*
- *Income inequality force for good because it rewards the productive, the risk takers, encourages new ideas but income inequity is a problem.*
- *Income inequity given priority because of following reasons. Income inequity highly correlated with health, opportunity and education inequity.*
- *Adverse effects of social immobility.*

- *Long term negative effects will be low economic growth, social problems and lack of innovation as education affordable only to a narrow group. Unmanageable debt burdens. Market shrinks with poor consumers.*
- *Policies to promote equity have their own pros and cons. (see next question)*

56.   Evaluate the policies a government can use to reduce wealth inequality, income inequality, education inequality, health inequality and inequality of opportunities.

- *Discussion essentially revolves around the merits of government interventionist-based supply side policies of progressive taxation (Robin Hood approach), skills and training, education to increasing productivity (Learning to Fish approach) and provision of job opportunities and removing all types of discrimination in the work place (Equality for All approach)*
- *List the merits and demerits of policies of each approach. (diagrams: Lorenz curve, AD/AS, ppf, labour market)*

21 MACROECONOMIC POLICIES II

Governments tend to use a combination of fiscal, monetary, supply-side and exchange rate policies to achieve the macroeconomic objectives full employment, price stability, steady stable sustainable economic growth, equitable distribution of income and a favourable balance of payments situation. However differences between Keynesians and Monetarists and many others lay not so much in which medicine/policy to apply to employ but rather which policy to lead with and dosage to administer. This chapter is aimed at discussing the policy mix available to governments.

Macroeconomic Objective I Inflation

1. List 3 possible problems resulting from **demand pull** inflation.

   - loss of purchasing power

   - lower <u>real</u> interest rates for savers   (i real = i-nominal – rate of inflation)

   - creates uncertainty for investors as their investment decisions become difficult to compute

2. Explain short term and long-term policy mix that can be used to reduce **demand pull** inflation.

To reduce demand pulled inflation, government can employ contractionary fiscal policy which will increase taxes and decrease government spending to control the growth of the economy in the short term. In addition, use a tight monetary policy where the central bank can aid the government by increasing interest rates and decreasing money supply to limit rises in AD. Use Supply-side policies to promote rise in AS via deregulation, liberalisation, lowering barriers to entry.

3. List 10 problems associated with any policy mix employed to combat **demand pull** inflation.

   - Government may not want to increase taxes for political reasons

   - crowding-out effect

   - relationship between I, AD and i% may not be elastic

   - higher risk of defaults if interest rates rise too quickly as highly indebted firms are unable to make their payments.

   - If in a period of stagflation, monetary policy does not work well (do you raise or lower i%?)

   - Tax evasion and loop holes

- black market and illegal activity rise

- Distortion of market (fiscal policy mostly)

- conflicts between policies can have adverse effects on macro policies

- effects on jobs (public sector trade union reactions)

4. List 5 possible problems resulting from **cost push** inflation.

    - unemployment rises due to firms' costs of production rising

    - less incentive to produce in that area

    - loss of purchasing power

    - reduction of international competitiveness

    - inflation acts as a stealth tax

5. Explain short term and long-term policy mix that can be used to reduce **cost push** inflation.

Policies to reduce cost push inflation are essentially the same as policies to reduce demand pull inflation.

The government could pursue deflationary fiscal policy (higher taxes, lower spending) or monetary authorities could increase interest rates. This would increase cost of borrowing and reduce consumer spending and investment.

The long-term solution to cost push inflation could be better supply side policies which help to increase productivity and shift the AS curve to the right. But, these policies would take a long time to have an effect.

6. List 10 problems associated with any policy mix employed to combat **cost push** inflation.

    Same as question 3 since the policies are the same.

7. List 5 possible problems resulting from **hyperinflation**.

    Same as inflation except more serious

    - fixed income recipients will be hurt

    - creates uncertainty

    - money illusion problems

    - acts as a stealth tax

    - loss of competitiveness for a country

8. Explain short term and long-term policy mix that can be used to stop **hyperinflation**.

Drastic measure of first stop printing money which is not linked with a productive asset. Link currency with another currency which is stable. Aim is to restore faith in the fiat currency. Money has to reflect the value of effort. (1920s German hyperinflation came under control after the currency was backed by a unit of land)

9.   List 10 problems associated with any policy mix employed to combat **hyperinflation**.

- *Government may not want to increase taxes for political reasons*

- *crowding-out effect*

- *relationship between I, AD and i% may not be elastic*

- *higher risk of defaults if interest rates rise too quickly*

- *If in a period of stagflation, monetary policy does not work well (do you raise or lower i%?)*

- *Tax evasions and loop holes*

- *black market and illegal activity rises*

- *Distortion of market (fiscal policy mostly)*

- *conflicts between policies can have adverse effects on macro policies*

- *effects on jobs (public sector trade union reactions)*

10.   List 5 possible problems resulting from **stagflation**.

- *Not possible to use monetary policy as while focusing on one objective, government/central bank may end up ruining another.*

- *the economy shrinks*

- *uncertainty rises*

- *AD falls*

- *wage-price spiral (workers react and demand higher wages)*

11.   Explain short term and long-term policy mix that can be used to stop **stagflation**.

For example, the Central Bank could use Monetary policy to try and reduce inflation. Higher Interest rates increase the cost of borrowing and this will reduce AD. This will be effective for reducing inflation, but, it will cause a bigger fall in GDP. Therefore, the Central Bank may be reluctant to target inflation when growth is already low.

If the Central Bank cut interest rates to try and increase GDP, they could make inflation worse. Therefore, demand side policies cannot solve stagflation they can only solve one particular aspect.

One solution to stagflation is to increase AS through supply side policies, for example privatisation and deregulation to increase efficiency. However, these will take a long time. Also if the cost push inflation occurs because of a global increase in the price of oil and food, there is little that the government can do about it.

12.   List 10 problems associated with any policy mix employed to combat **stagflation**.

- *time lags are long for both interventionist and free market policies*

- *require government funding*

- *government training programs may not be specific*

- *stop-go policies create uncertainty*

- *effects on environment*

- *exploitation of workers may occur due to deregulation*

- *weak domestic producers and workers may suffer due to liberalization*

- *privatization may cause state monopolies to become private monopolies*

13.   List 5 possible problems resulting from **deflation**.

- *increase in real amount of debt owed by borrowers*

- *fall in incomes and hence consumption*

- *economy goes into recession*

- *firms shelving new projects and postponing investment*

- *fall in AD leads to rising unemployment*

14. Explain short term and long-term policy mix that can be used to stop **deflation**.

Loose monetary policy accompanied by expansionary fiscal policy for the short term and supply-side policies for the long term to promote structural change.

15. List 10 problems associated with any policy mix employed to combat **deflation**.

- size of stimulus unknown

- distortion of markets, may create stock market bubbles

- government requires resources and this may add to the national debt.

- time lags

- problem of NINJAs (lending credit to sub-prime groups who have No Income No Jobs or Assets)

- can encourage over-borrowing

- commercial banks and hedge funds get first access to cheap money and the benefits may not trickle down to the consumers

- crowding out effects (for fiscal policy) depending on the type of government expansion

- stop-go policies creating uncertainties

- misdiagnosis of the type of deflation. Is it demand deflation of price deflation due to technological progress.

Macroeconomic Objective II   Unemployment.

16.. List 5 possible problems resulting from **equilibrium unemployment**.

- waste of resources

- tax revenue falls

- erosion of human capital as skills unused, wither away.

- lower incomes and hence lower consumption (fall in AD)
- opportunity cost. Regions lose identity and more trade as the main industry shuts down.

17. Explain short term and long-term micro and macro policy mix that can be used to reduce **equilibrium unemployment**.

Short run: policies directed towards reducing unemployment: these could be better job information, training for the unemployed, lower unemployment benefits, employment subsidies and relocation grants.

Long term. increased labour market flexibility, greater emphasis on role of education in raising productivity and improvements in infrastructure.

18. List 10 problems associated with any policy mix employed to combat **equilibrium unemployment**.

- time lags

- can encourage exploitation

- stop-go policies

- training programs may not be specific

- requires government resources

- LDCs may not be able to afford it

- may increase budget deficit

- weakens currency (which can be a disadvantage in some cases)

- unemployment may be regional or cyclical rather than structural (training won't work)

19. List 5 possible problems resulting from high levels of **disequilibrium unemployment**.

- real wage rate higher than foreign competitors and it refuses to fall.

- sticky wages leads to distortion in the labour market.

-sticky prices mean markets for real goods and services do not clear.

- less well-off workers and those with poor education suffer disproportionately the more education the job requires

- exploitation of human capital and workers as newly qualified workers have fewer job opportunites

- costs of production rises for businesses

20.   Explain short term and long-term policy mix that can be used to reduce **disequilibrium unemployment**.

Government can provide businesses with subsidies. Along with that, they can increase direct tax on income so they can take in some revenue to pay for the subsidies. Hence the fiscal policy may or may not be neutral.

The government can also use expansionary fiscal policy.

Central bank can use monetary policy to encourage greater spending and raise AD for labour.

Supply-side policies towards reducing benefits and lowering minimum wage rate, zero contract hours and easy to hire and easy to fire policies to create a greater willingness to hire.

21.   List 10 problems associated with any policy mix employed to reduce **disequilibrium unemployment**.

- time lags

- requires government resources

- multiplier effect may be too small or its size unknown

- businesses may revolt and bribe political leaders for their benefits

- stop-go policies

- may increase budget deficit

- LDCs may not be able to afford the resources with which come the policies.

- LDCs may have to kowtow to MNCs to attract the FDIs for job creation.

- size of stimulus necessary is not always known.

Workers may lose out due to labour market changes.

Macroeconomic Objective III   Economic Growth.

22.   List 5 possible problems resulting from a lack of **economic growth**.

- unemployment

- quality of life may not be improving. Government tax receipts fall and subsequently services are cut.

- foreign investment may not come.   - AD shrinking and poor job creation

- no business confidence/incentive

23. Explain short term and long-term policy mix that can be used to promote **economic growth**.

Government can implement expansionary fiscal policy and central bank can accompany it with a loose monetary policy to boost AD in the short/mid-term.

Supply side policies like labour market reforms, privatization, liberalization, deregulation and promotion of R&D and infrastructure improvements can be implemented for the long-term. Rise in productivity through technological progress can form the basis of long term growth.

24. List 10 problems associated with any policy mix employed to promote faster **economic growth**.

- *time lags*

- *relationship between I, AD, and i% may not be elastic*

- *multiplier may be insufficient*

- *requires government resource (supply side and fiscal policy)*

- *corruption and market distortions as governments may favour certain groups over others.*

- *workers' unions may not be satisfied if economic growth does not filter to their members.*

- *may increase budget deficit if governments go on a spending binge instead of reducing debt.*

- *LDCs may not have enough resources*

- *The problem may only be cyclical, so there may be no returns on these policies*

- *policies may be 'trickle up' rather than 'trickle down' and hence inequalities worsen*

- *policies towards increasing automation and hence productivity may lead to jobless growth*

- *inflation may rise*

Macroeconomic Objective IV   Equitable distribution of income.

25. List 5 possible problems resulting from poor **distribution of income**.

- *no development of middle class.*   - *poor become poorer and rich become richer*

- *benefits may not trickle down to the poor.*   - *jobless growth.*   *-danger of social unrest*

 AD may not rise due to fall in incomes and standards of living

-results in poor distribution of healthcare resources, education resources and job opportunities.

26.   Explain short term and long-term policy mix that can be used to reduce **inequalities.**

Government should install a progressive taxation system or make it more efficient if it is already existent. In addition, it can add welfare benefits, amongst other supply-side policies (ex: income support, health benefit, unemployment benefits, …). This can potentially be topped by loose monetary policy by the central bank to provide greater access to credit for small businesses. Longer term is the promotion of equity where the gains from economic growth and productivity are passed on to workers equitably.

27.   List 10 problems associated with any policy mix employed in reducing **inequalities.**

- requires government resources

- may push inflation

- growth too rapid and haphazard

- multiplier may not be sufficient

- benefit only available for higher class

- reduce incentive to work since state provides all the benefits.

- progressive tax system may be ill-designed and ends up penalising all except the very rich. This can encourage the brain drain.

- loopholes and tax evasions are found

- monetary policy simply too loose for too long resulting higher household debt.

- progressive tax system is too complex to calculate

28.   Which one of the following combinations is most likely to lead to **disinflation?**

	Indirect Taxes	Exchange Rate	Interest Rate
A	*rise*	*rise*	*rise*
B	fall	fall	rise
C	fall	rise	fall
D	rise	fall	fall

Explain   A   *A rise in all three will have the effect of reducing real AD and thus reducing the pressure on price rises. (inflation rising at a slower rate = disinflation)*

29 *b.* In the Phillips Curve below which of the following would shift Phillips Curve 1 (PC1) to Phillips Curve 2 (PC2)?

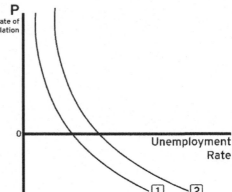

A Fall in the natural rate of unemployment (fall in NAIRU).

B Improvement in labour productivity.

C Tightening monetary and contractionary fiscal policy.

D *Rise in the expectation of faster inflation.*

Explain D *workers and employers adjust their wage claims and price rise such the economy ends up with higher rates of inflation for any given level on unemployment.*

30. If the inflation rate unexpectedly rises and the central bank reacts by raising interest rates the 3 to 6 month effect will be

A that the exchange rate will depreciate.

B that investment will fall.

C *little or no effect due to time lags.*

D that unemployment will rise significantly.

Explain C *Current contracts are all set and binding. It is only over time when new contracts come to be renegotiated that the data picks up the changes.*

31. An example of a supply-side policy is:

A a lowering of the interest rate to increase consumer borrowing.

B government increasing child benefit to boost household spending.

C government weakening the exchange rate.

D *government cutting income tax rates to boost the incentives to effort.*

Explain D *The other policies tend to affect the demand side more that supply-side. Income tax rate affects the supply of FoPs which in this case is labour.*

32.   The AD/SRAS diagram below shows a fall in prices and real output. This could have been the result of which of the following?

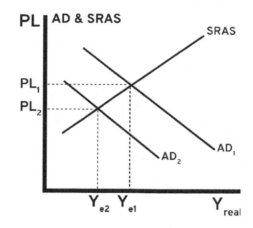

A   A fall in the price of raw materials.

B   A rise in the wage bill or (total cost of labour).

C   A fall in the interest rate.

D   *None of the above.*

Explain D   *A and B affect the SRAS, answer C promotes greater spending and I and hence AD.*

33.   A tight monetary policy aimed at reducing demand pull inflation is likely to be unsuccessful if:

A   the government uses interventionist supply-side policy to reduce long run aggregate supply (LRAS).

B   *the government introduces an expansionary fiscal policy.*

C   the government increases its spending on the military.

D   none of the above.

Explain B   *An expansionary fiscal policy contradicts a tight monetary policy by increasing AD instead.*

34.   The central bank introduces a loose monetary policy while at the same time the government introduces an expansionary fiscal policy. This combination is most likely to lead to:

    A   a rise in AD and a fall in SRAS.

    B   a rise in AD and a fall in LRAS.

    C   a rise in inflation and a fall in unemployment.

    D   a rise in inflation and a rise in unemployment.

Explain C   *Ceteris paribus AD rises rapidly and SRAS may not be able to accommodate fully with shortages of FoPs in some sectors which consequently manifest themselves in higher prices and inflation. The higher demand in other sectors result in more jobs being created.*

35.   A **Monetarist** would agree with which of the following:

    A   A reduction in wages will increase unemployment.

    B   Free-market does not have a self-adjusting price mechanism.

    C   Wage and price rigidity is an inherent feature of the free market.

    D   A rise in the money supply will be inflationary in the long run unless it is compensated by a fall in the velocity of money (spending).

Explain D   *This comes from the Fisher equation for the quantity theory of money MV = PT*

36.   Keynesians are likely to believe that:

    A   prices and wages are flexible to achieve full employment in the long run.

    B   government budget deficits are always inflationary.

    C   governments can budget for a deficit and manage the AD.

    D   None of the above.

Explain C   *When private sector is contracting and hence AD is falling the government can intervene and maintain AD by increasing its spending in the circular flow of income.*

37 *b*. If unemployment is at NAIRU or at 'natural rate', in the long run, then what is the likely effect of an increase in state pensions and other transfer payments.

	Unemployment	Inflation
A	zero	constant
B	**constant**	**rise**
C	fall	constant
D	fall	fall

Explain B   *The economy is operating on the vertical LRPC and hence any increase in AD will simply increase inflation in the long run as FoPs are fully employed already and that there is no money illusion.*

38.   If the government's budget deficit rises and private sector reduces its borrowing as a result of higher interest rates, then this is an example of:

A   Liquidity trap.

B   the crowding-out effect.

C   a negative multiplier effect.

D   a positive multiplier effect.

Explain B   *Assuming the economy is already at full employment then if the public sector expands, it will raise the demand for the limited FoPs that are available. This is done through the money markets and the interest rate will rise and deter private sector borrowing for investment and consumption.*

39.   Ceteris paribus, the government reduces its budget deficit. Which of the following must be true?

A   unemployment must rise.

B   taxes must fall.

C   national debt must rise.

D   inflation must fall.

Explain A   *Most of government spending goes on workers providing services. Cuts in public sectors usually involve laying off workers. Answer A is more correct than the others.*

EVALUATION QUESTIONS   **(Macroeconomic Policies II)**

40.   To what extent does the government policy of austerity and labour market reforms help achieve the macroeconomic goals of sustainable economic growth and full employment?

- *Define austerity (reduce G, balance the budget)*
- *Define labour market reforms (reduce the cost of workers, increase productivity through wage decreases and worsening conditions for workers)*
- *Empower private sector to take on the slack/released resources from the public sector.*
- *Neo-Liberals believe that greater power to capitalists nationally and globally will lead to investments and job creation using free market discipline.*
- *Alternative view is that inequalities will rise within each country even though globally inequality falls. Decimation of middle-class. Surplus of unemployment labour leads to social chaos will result in increasing cost for the government.*
- *Conundrum to resolve "consumers are workers, workers are consumers".*

41.   Comment to what extent quantitative easing (expansion of cheap credit) leads to improving the economic performance of an economy.

- *QE allows commercial banks to borrow cheaply.*
- *Commercial banks are supposed to complete with each other for customers by passing on the lower interest rates to businesses and households. AD will increase as I, C, and even G rises. Result is economic growth, more job creation but be vigilant on inflation.*
- *Alternative view is that banks lend out little in a severe recession, households already carry high debts and hence less willing to borrow and many have poor credit histories. So banks lend to narrow group (very rich), assets prices rise, (financial or physical), wealth effect on for the rich and no trickledown effect. Economy does not grow or create jobs with a living wage. Economy stuck in Liquidity Trap.*

42.   Assume the economy is in a deep recession. Evaluate the differences between Keynesians and New Classical approaches in dealing with this situation.

- *Keynesian approach is that government must actively raise AD by increasing G and reducing T for the low-income groups which have higher mpc and hence multiplier effect. The focus is on I projects which create lots of jobs. Here actual and potential growth will rise. Budget deficits and national*
- *debts will rise but this is acceptable since in recovery or boom period government focuses on paying off the debts using the newly acquires gains in revenues.*
- *Neo Classical believe in automatic mechanism of the market where prices and wages adjust to restore equilibrium. Economy will grow in the long term through new ideas and entrepreneurship. Government's role is as a facilitator and run a balanced budget.*

43.   "The government like any household cannot spend beyond its means. The government is not a household and hence must be open to spending beyond its revenues." Evaluate the economic thinking behind each of the above statements. Which statement do you agree with?

- *$AD = C + I + G + X - M$ In a recession with C, I, down then if G=T as in a household, where is the growth on the economy going to come from.*
- *Here the role of the government is no longer as a manager by rather only as a basic service provider. Government's spending can be counter-cyclical.*
- *High tax revenues in a boom period can be used to keep debts down such that borrowing at low interest rates can be easily done in the recession.*

44 b.   Discuss the following view, "policy makers must accept the trade-off between the rate of inflation and the rate of unemployment and make a choice."

- *Explain Phillips Curve trade-off (SRPC), and no trade off in (LRPC)*
- *Short run implications that unemployment can be reduced by government spending policies, especially in a deep recession and on investment projects which bring long term market rates of return. Here no trade-off.*
- *Monetarists begged to differ.*
- *Jury is out whether Phillips empirical relationship has now broken down or even applicable.*

22 INTERNATIONAL TRADE AND DEVELOPMENT

GAINS FROM TRADE

1 *b.*   Suppose two countries have the following prices for things (in ounces of silver)

	Salt (NaCl)	Pepper	Amber
Rome	10	20	40
Indies	10	10	60

A merchant seeking to make a profit would carry **_pepper_** from the Indies to Rome, and return with **_amber._**

2*b* .   A commodity might be produced more cheaply in one area for any of the following reasons except:

     A.   The climate is more favourable in that area

     B.   **Labour is in high demand in that area**

     C.   Key natural resources are available in that area

     D.   Technical knowledge is available in that area

Explain B   *high demand for labour often leads to higher wage/ higher cost of productions, discouraging production*

3*b* .   State the meaning of "absolute advantage (AA)".
    The ability to produce a product using fewer resources

4*b* .   Country A has a comparative advantage (CA) over Country B, in producing some good, if the **_opportunity cost_** of producing the good is lower in Country A.

5*b.*   Each of the arrays below shows the amount of output that can be produced by a unit of labour in two areas which trade with each other. Assume in each case that they are the only countries, and that the goods shown are the only goods. Tell, for each array, which country has the absolute advantage (AA) in each good and which has the comparative advantage (CA) in each. Label which PPC diagram goes for which country, and label quantities on the intercepts of the PPCs (given that there are 2 units of L in each country: the first intercept is done for you).

	Eggs	Apples		AA	CA
France	4	6	Eggs	Italy	Italy
Italy	8	4	Apples	France	France

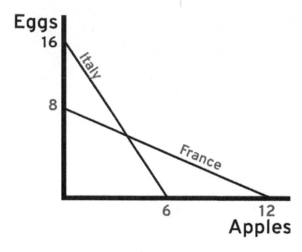

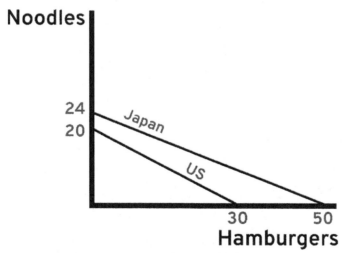

	Noodles	Burgers		AA	CA
US	10	15	Noodles	Japan	China
Japan	12	25	Burgers	Japan	Japan

	Yogurt	Beer		AA	CA
Bohemia	10	15	Yogurt		

Mora via	12	25	Beer

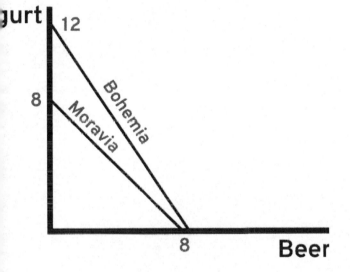

	Sugar	Salt			AA	CA			
				India	20	30	**Sugar**	India	India
				Thailand	12	20	**Salt**	India	Thailand

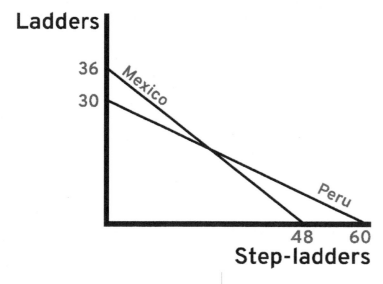

	Step-ladders	Ladders			AA	CA
Mexico	24	18	**Step-ladders**		Peru	Peru
Peru	30	15	**Ladders**		Mexico	Mexico

6 *b*.   If the opportunity cost of producing 100 kilograms (kg) of figs per year is 2 bicycles, and the nation can import 100 kg of figs for the price of 1.5 bicycles, the implication is:

  A.   **bicycles produced are worth 66.6 kg figs, though 50 kg figs would be given up to make them**

  B.   it should produce more figs because they are worth more bicycles than on the world market

  C.   it is cheaper to produce figs than to import them

  D.   it has a comparative advantage in fig production

Explain A   *A domestic "opportunity cost" exchange rate: 1bicycle = 50kg figs*
      International exchange rate: 1 bicycle = 66.7kg

7 *b.*   On the PPC's below, calculate the opportunity cost of Kayaks using the intercepts.

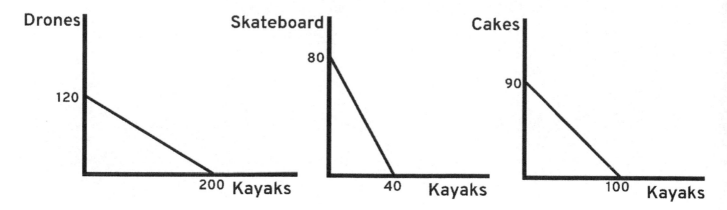

8 *b.*   In order for both countries to benefit from trade with each other, the ratio of how much of one good trades for how much of the other (called the Terms of Trade) must be in a certain range. What is the requirement for the range of values of the Terms of Trade? *in between the domestic opportunity costs (exchange rates)*

Protectionism.

9.   Suppose that imports of cherries suddenly become available in a country at a price below the previous market-clearing price within the country. Suppose further that it is a small country, so that its import amounts do not affect the world price.

a)   On the diagram below, show the changes in price, Qd and Qs (domestically) due to allowing the imports.

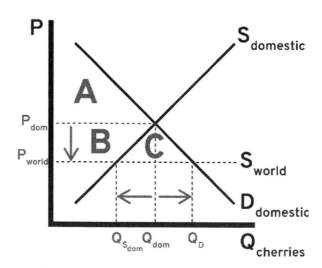

b) Indicate the change in producer surplus (earned by domestic producers) above. *B lost*

c) How can we tell that the country is better off? *Gain B + C (consumers) larger than loss B (producers.)*

10.   Using the diagram below, show the domestic effect (in its market) of applying a tariff on imports of melons:

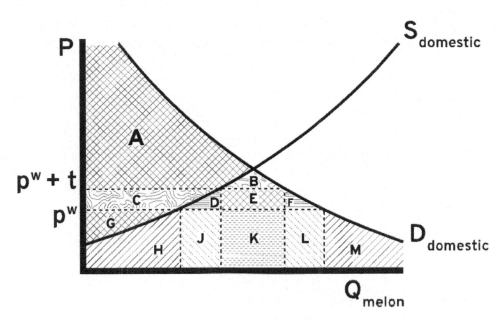

a)   Which areas show consumer surplus before the tariff, and which show it after?

before; a +b + c + d + e +f   *after: a + b only*

b)   Which areas show producer surplus before the tariff, and which show it after?

before: g only   *after: g + c*

c)   Which area shows the revenue from the tariff, going to the government?   *area e*

d)   Compare the areas showing net gains and losses to each of the groups. Is the country better or worse off overall? Interpret this result.   *losses to CS are larger than gains to PS and G combined. Difference is Deadweight loss d + f*

11.   Why are imports less with a tariff? (Explain both of the changes which cause this reduction).

    higher P leads to less Qd and more Qs domestically the difference Qd – Qs is imported

12.   What areas show the loss of sales revenue to the foreign producers of the imports? *area j + area l*

13.   True **T** or False **F**

a)   The gain in producer surplus from adding a tariff is always greater than the gain in revenue going to the government. T / **F**

b)   The loss in consumer surplus from a tariff is always greater than the gains to producers and government combined. **T** / F

c)   If a tariff increase causes government revenue to decrease, it will also cause producer surplus to decrease. T / **F**

d)   For tariffs getting higher and higher, once they have eliminated imports of a product, there is no effect of a further increase in the tariff. **T** / F

14.   A tariff on hardwood is reduced by half. On a market diagram:

a)   show the effect on domestic price;

b)   show the effect on imports.

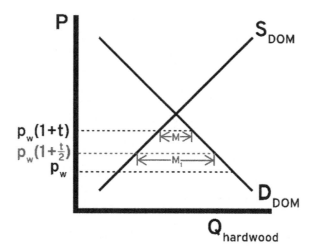

15.   What is the difference between a tariff and a quota?

   a tariff is a tax on imports, a quota limits the quantity of imports numerically

16.   How is the effect of a quota different from the effect of a tariff? Illustrate the effect of a quota on a diagram showing the domestic market with a quota imposed on imports. If the price changed by the same amount as for a tariff, how would the effects on consumer surplus, producer surplus, and government revenue be different from the case of the tariff?

all is the same except that there is no revenue from a quota, (some countries auction the quota licenses for about the same amount of income)

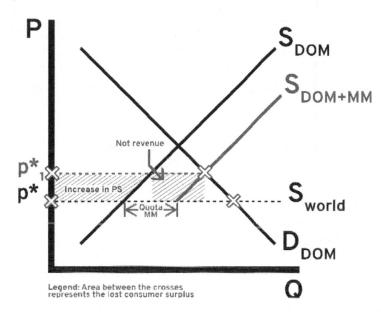

17.   Suppose the government increased the amount of imports allowed under a quota.

a)   Show the effect on a diagram.

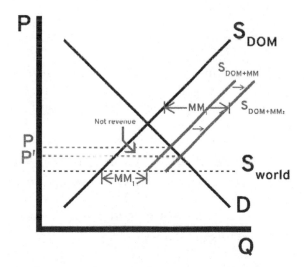

b)   What happens to the price of the good inside the importing country?

the price falls due to greater effective supply

18. On a diagram for the market for an imported good, show the result of the government subsidising domestic producers.

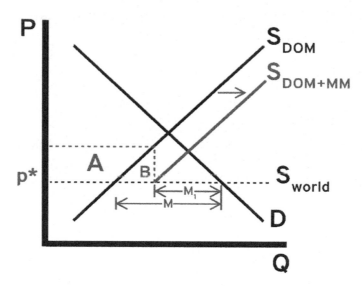

a) What happens to price? *nothing: the country is small (S_{world} is horizontal)*

b) What happens to the amount consumed? *nothing*

c) What happens to the amount imported? *imports fall since Sdom increased*

d) Show the welfare loss (deadweight loss)? *area B*

e) Why is there no welfare loss under the demand curve?

   there is no distortion to consumption decisions – only production

f) Compare the cost of the subsidy to the total of all benefits within the country.

   subsidy cost is PS gained (A) plus deadweight loss (B): always greater than + PS

19. What is "dumping," and why might it be a good justification for protectionism, allowing the responding country to be better off as a result?

   selling abroad below cost if domestic producers are driven out of business, the foreign producer can raise price and make excess profits at consumers' expense, so anti-dumping tariff is justified

20. What is the infant industry argument for protectionism? What assumption about future production is necessary for it to justify current losses in welfare?

   the extra cost to consumers is only justified if costs will fall with scale and experience, enough for the country to have a comparative advantage

21.   List **five** arguments against the use of protectionism.

-     *inefficiency as measured by welfare loss;*

-     *harm to consumers in higher price and loss of variety;*

-     *may lead to lower quality;*

-     *higher price of inputs may harm competitiveness;*

-     *may lead to retaliation and reduce motivation for peace;*

-     *may encourage corruption as producers give bribes to be protected*

EVALUATION QUESTIONS   (International Trade)

22.   Evaluate the effect of a tariff, counting only domestic costs and benefits, using the comparison structure provided by "winners and losers". On what basis can you come to a conclusion?

Use diagram and loss of CS, compared to gain of PS and tariff revenue. Consumer losses are always larger. Downstream industries may be hurt also if intermediate inputs are protected. Unless one of the motivations for protectionism is substantial, such as dumping, on the industry is an infant industry, (just starting out against experienced foreign producers, the country is better off without the tariff.)

23.   Evaluate the use of protectionism as policy for a less developed country and a more developed country. **LDC much more likely to need infant industry protection.**

24.   Evaluate the use of a subsidy to address the infant industry problem, by contrast with the use of a tariff. (For the same benefit to the infant industry, which creates more welfare loss in this market? Why? What other issues should be addressed?)

    Two diagrams, with the same increase in domestic supply and PS.

    The subsidy diagram has a cost to government/taxpayers, while the tariff case has tax revenue coming to

    the government.

    The welfare loss on the diagram is larger for the case of the tariff, but if we knew how much it distorted the economy to pay for the subsidy, the subsidy case might be the more costly to economic efficiency.

Subsidies are explicit budget items and thus much easier to get rid of politically, so if the infant industry never seems ready to be competitive, subsidy approach will probably be cut off first.

23 EXCHANGE RATES.

1.   Which is the least accurate definition a country's exchange rate?

    A   The number of units of another currency which will exchange for a unit of that currency.

    B   The value of that currency.

    C   How much of that currency a US dollar will buy.

    D   The price of the country's currency in units of foreign currency.

Explain B_ *The currency value is defined in terms of goods it will buy more than in terms of other currencies*

2.   An "appreciation" means a currency will buy (*more* / fewer) units of foreign exchange. A "depreciation" means the opposite.

3.   Which of the following is NOT a method of setting exchange rates?

    A   The International Monetary Fund, based on total currency amounts.

    B   Government declaration of a specific legal exchange rate.

    C   Market supply and demand by those wishing to exchange currencies.

    D   Central banks buying and selling in private markets to target a certain rate.

Explain_A   *Markets or governments set exchange rates, not the IMF*

4.   Which of the following does NOT create demand for the Swiss Franc on foreign exchange markets?

    A   More Swiss citizens travelling abroad

    B   World demand for the exports of the country

    C   Foreign investment into the country

    D   Borrowing from foreign countries

Explain_A *Greater supply of imports would be most likely to affect supply of the country's currency.*

5.　　　Which of the following does NOT increase the supply of the Indian rupee on foreign exchange markets?

　　　　A　　　**Indian workers going to other countries to find work and sending remittances**

　　　　B　　　India's imports of foreign goods

　　　　C　　　India lending funds to other countries

　　　　D　　　Indians repaying earlier loans borrowed from foreigners

Explain　　　　　*A is neutral, the others create supply.*

6.　　　On the diagram below, what is the effect of an increase in world demand for the country's exports?

a)　　　On the diagram, which curve shifts and in which direction (left or right)? *D right*

b)　　　Show the result for the exchange rate. *e. r. rises*

c)　　　Show the result for the amount of the currency transacting in foreign exchange markets. *£ increases*

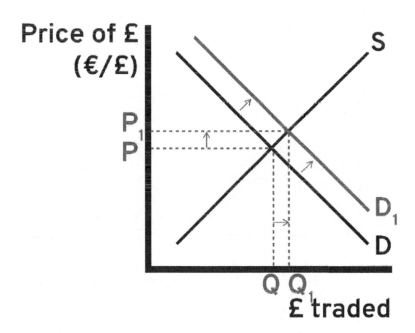

7.   Shift the correct curve and show the results for exchange rate and amount of currency trading, in each of the following cases.

A. An increase in demand for imports   B.   A fall in interest rates   *D left*

S right

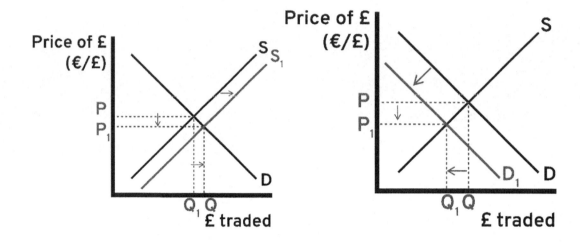

C.   A financial inflow *D right*   D.   A loss of exports *D left*

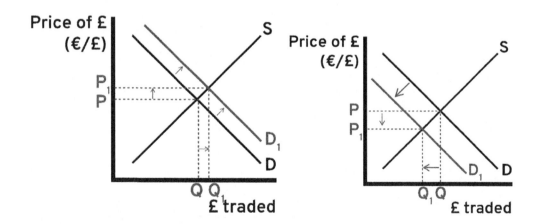

8.   Draw below on a currency exchange diagram the effect of inflation (domestic goods have higher prices, and all other things are held constant) on exports. What is the effect on a country's currency if the country experiences inflation?   *D left, e falls*

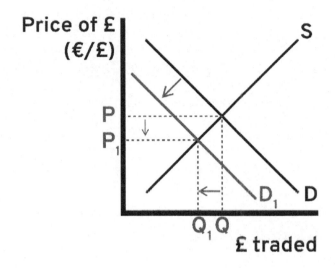

9.   What (international) category of aggregate expenditure (e.g. C, I, etc.) is immediately increased when GDP is increased? As a result, what is the effect on a country's exchange rate if GDP rises?

M increases, e falls.

10.   List five factors that could cause an appreciation of a country's currency: *increase in sales of exports; decrease in expenditure on imports; increase in interest rate; increase in foreign direct investment inward; stop lending abroad.*

11 *b*.   Suppose the Euro appreciates, from 1.0 USD per Euro to 1.2 USD per Euro.

a)   What happens to the price in the U.S. of a European tin of foie gras costing 20 Euros to manufacture?   *It rises from 20 dollars to 24 dollars*

b)   Based on this example, what is the effect of appreciation of the Euro on European exports?

   exports will fall.

12.   For the same appreciation as in the previous question,

a)   What happens to the price in Europe of a U.S. roll of cotton cloth costing 40 USD to manufacture?

   changes from 40 Euros to 33.67 Euros_ (40/1.2)

b)   Based on this example, what is the effect of appreciation of the Euro on European imports?

   Europe will buy more imports (move along S line up and outward)

Challenging Questions

13*.   Investment into a country can be thought of as providing funds to pay current resources to create fixed capital.

a)   Explain why, normally, building a building in the Philippines, by borrowing foreign funds for finance, will create a demand for Philippine pesos on the foreign exchange market.   Who is trying to change their currency into a different one?

Lender providing their currency, changing into pesos to pay Philippine workers

b)   What happens to the market for pesos when the loan is repaid?

Repayment will increase supply of pesos, converting back to the lenders' currency

14*.   If interest rates in a country rise because the economy is expanding, why would foreigners be more interested in lending their funds within that country?   *Compared to other currencies, they can now earn more on this investment. Other factors could interfere, but this proves to be a reliable relationship.   The growing economy is more able to repay*

15*.   Suppose the interest rates are rising because the Central Bank is slowing the economy to fight inflation. Would foreigners still be more interested in lending their funds within that country? Explain. *In general, yes. Lower future inflation tends to improve the value of the repayment. Only if serious economic damage is done would this fail.*

16*.   (Relative Purchasing Power Parity) Explain why it makes sense that the value of a country's currency would depreciate just enough to exactly offset inflation. With both inflation and the offsetting devaluation, what crucial comparison is restored to being exactly the same as before either effect happened?   *Cost of local and foreign goods, translated into the same currency such as US dollars, is restored to previous relative levels.*

17*.   The Big Mac Index translates the cost of a MacDonald's Big Mac hamburger from a country's local currency into US dollars. If the cost in a country is relatively high, compared to the equivalent in many other countries, the index forecasts a fall in the currency value.

a)   why does it make sense that the currency value is too high if a "typical product" costs more dollars than in other countries? *Then manufactures will also cost more, and the country will suffer loss of exports*

b)   some countries, such as Switzerland, continually have a high cost of Big Macs without any devaluation resulting. What does that tell you about the cost of factors of production in those countries? What does it tell you about demand for those factors of production? *Factors of production specific to Switzerland are costly. This is only sustainable if they are continually in high demand, presumably for goods and services not facing strong competition*

EVALUATION QUESTIONS.   (Exchange Rates)

18.   What is helpful about the appreciation of a country's currency (i.e. good for that country)? If you can name three things that are helpful, which is the most important?

1) easier to afford imports - most important   2) keeps inflation down

3) makes low productivity industries contract and free resources for strong industries

19.   Name three things which could cause a country's currency to appreciate. Which of these are clearly good things? Are any clearly bad things? Discuss.

1) More demand for exports – good   *2) Increased efficiency in exporting – good*

3) Increased efficiency in producing goods which compete with imports – good

4) Borrowing due to fiscal laxity – bad

5) Borrowing due to good prospects in the private sector – usually good

20.   How might the overall benefit or harm of an appreciation depend on the cause of the appreciation? *Temporary source of higher exchange rate, such as tighter money, or source with no lasting beneficial experience, such as sale of minerals, can mean country is less competitive and standard of living lower in long term*

21.   What is bad about the appreciation of a country's currency (for that country)?

Causes manufactured exports to face tougher price competition

This can create unemployment

22.   Under what economic conditions would the problems of an appreciation be more important than the benefits? Under what economic conditions would the benefits be more important than the problems? *In a recession, the unemployment (harm) is more important than the lower import prices. In times of high aggregate demand, the lower import prices (benefit) are more important than the unemployment.*

23   Use a "stakeholders" approach ("winners and losers") to evaluate the effects of a currency appreciation. Is there any reason to be more concerned about winners than losers, or vice-versa?

1) Workers and owners in industries facing loss of competitiveness are worse off. They may not be able to match the former earnings in new sectors.

2) Consumers are better off. Industries using imported inputs are better off.

Which matters more depends on economic conditions and ease of transition of factors of production.

24 BALANCE OF PAYMENTS

1.   Match these terms to their definitions at right.

___c___Imports   a. external transactions for immediate purposes

___d___Depreciation   b. payments sent back home by workers abroad

___g___Devaluation   c. goods purchased from foreign countries

___i___Invisibles   d. a fall in the value of the currency on exchange markets

___a___Current Account   e. money paid without getting something in return

___h___Trade surplus   f. sales of financial assets to foreign countries

___e___Transfers   g. a fall in the official value of a currency, set by government

___b___Remittances   h. an excess of export earnings over import expenditure

                            i. services, such as banking or education

2.   A trade deficit means that the value of exports is greater / *less* than the value of imports. A trade surplus means the opposite.

3 *b*.   Which of the following is not one of the items added to the Merchandise Balance of Trade, to arrive at the Current Account Balance?

        A   The balance on invisibles

        B   *Net financial capital investment*

        C   Net unilateral transfers from abroad

        D   Net factor income from abroad

4 *h.*   Both the US and the UK typically run deficits on their Current Account Balance, but much larger deficits on their Merchandise (visible) Balance of Trade. This could be because:

   A   ***they are exporting more services than they are importing****.*

   B   they are lending money to foreign countries.

   C   the value of their exports is greater than the value of their imports.

   D   large profits are leaving the country from Japanese and other foreign investments.

5 *h.*   Which of the following is not a service on which some countries earn foreign income?

   A   Tourism

   B   Education

   C   Insurance

   D   ***Books***

6 *h.*   Remittances are

   A   Amounts paid for internet purchases in foreign countries

   B   Income from government transfers to retired people in foreign countries

   C   Amounts of money paid for any international transaction

   D   ***Amounts of money sent by workers back to their home countries***

7 *h.*   Unilateral transfers refer to

   A   ***payments made without compensating value returned***

   B   foreign investments, either portfolio or direct

   C   pension fund payments, private or public

   D   monetary flows to repay debts

8 *b.*   The difference between portfolio investment and direct investment is

    A   portfolio investment is by households, direct investment is by companies

    B   portfolio investment is by companies, direct investment is by households

    C   ***portfolio investment is in paper, such as shares, direct investment is in production***

    D   portfolio investment is in production, direct investment is in paper, such as shares

9 *b.*   If Italy has exports worth €207 billion and imports worth €240 billion, (and all other Current Account transactions net to zero), its balance will be a __(surplus_/ ***deficit***)   of _____*33*_____ billion Euros on the Current Account.

10 *b.*   In the Balance of Payments tables, export values are entered as positive amounts (credits) thinking of them as earnings which can be spent. Import expenditure is entered as negative amounts (debits). "Net" implies that some adjustment has been made to the initial amount, In the Balance of Payments this is usually done by subtracting the funds moving in the opposite direction for the same purpose.

    a) Explain the meaning of a positive amount for the Merchandise Trade Balance. __***value of exports exceeds cost of imports, for goods (but not services)***
    b) Is the Merchandise Trade Balance the same as "Net Exports" in the national income accounts?
        close but it omits services
    c) Explain the meaning of a positive total for Net Property Income from Abroad. Explain why this functions like a positive amount in the Merchandise Trade Balance.__***earnings from foreign profits, rent and interest is greater than that paid abroad; a country can buy imports with it***
    d) Explain the meaning of a <u>negative</u> total for Net Direct Foreign Investment from Abroad. ***more foreign investment by domestic companies occurred than the reverse***

11 *b*. Arrange the sums below within a Balance of Payments accounting structure here, and find the sums needed to fill in the box.   All amounts are in billions of pesos.

Merchandise import expenditure	*- 375*
Net direct investment from abroad	*43*
Net transfers from abroad	*12*
Merchandise export earnings	*410*
Invisible export earnings	*65*
Net remittances from abroad	*- 4*
Net portfolio investment from abroad	*- 75*
Capital account balance	*5*
(= debt forgiveness, land sales, etc)	
Invisible import expenditure	*- 90*

Category	**Amount**
__Exports__	*410*
__Imports__	*-375*

Merchandise/visible Trade

Invisible export earnings	*65*
Invisible import expenditure	*-90*
Net property income from abroad	*0*
Net remittances from abroad	*- 4*
Net transfers from abroad	*12*

Current Account Balance

Net direct investment from abroad	*43*
Net portfolio investment from abroad	*-75*
Other financial transactions	*0*

Financial Account Balance

12.   A depreciation will normally cause a Current Account deficit to be eliminated (a process known as "adjustment" to equilibrium) because

  A   *imports fall and exports rise*

  B   imports rise and exports fall

  C   imports and exports both fall, but imports fall by more

  D   imports and exports both rise, but exports rise by more

13 *b*.   The Marshall-Lerner condition says that _*a currency depreciation*_ will lead to a (*fall* / *rise*) in a Current Account deficit, as long as __*PEDx + PEDm > 1*.

14 *b*.   Give three examples of imports which are likely to be price inelastic (PEDm < 1). *Oil, ore, spare parts*

15 *b*.   Explain in general, using examples to illustrate your explanation, why demand for imports might be more elastic in the long run than in the short run.   *the local market finds substitutes, including domestic production, which take time to replace the imports*

16 *b*.   Imports cost 10 Euros per unit. The currency of Peru, the peso, devalues from 0.25 Euros per peso to 0.2 Euros per peso.

a)   Fill in the missing values. Demonstrate that the responses by import quantity are inelastic in the short run (SR), but elastic in the long run (LR).

Exchange rate (€/S/)	Import price Euros	Import price Sols	Import Quantity	Import expenditure in sols (V_M)	PED_M
0.25	10	40	200	8000	N/ A
(SR) 0.20	10	**50**	180	**9000**	**−0.4**
(LR) 0.20	10	**50**	120	**6000**	**−1.6**

b)   Suppose that export earnings Vx were 6000 pesos before the devaluation, and increased to 6500 after the devaluation, then stayed constant. Compute and plot the Current Account Balance (C.A.B.) at three points in time: at first, after the devaluation in the SR, and in the LR.

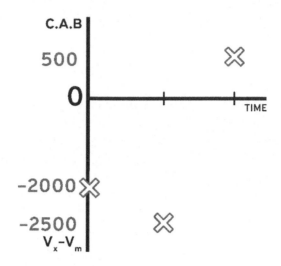

17 *b*.   Explain why the Marshall-Lerner condition might fail in the short run (SR) and yet be satisfied in the long run (LR).   Why would this pattern create a J-curve?   *__imports and exports might be price inelastic in the SR but in the LR are much more likely to respond. Inelastic imports increase the deficit in the short run but as substitutes are found, the deficit closes__*

Dealing with a Current Account Deficit.

18.   What is meant by expenditure reduction, when a country is facing a persistent current account deficit? Name two ways to accomplish this. *__reducing imports by reducing all spending: this can be done with monetary tightening or fiscal contraction; note raising interest rates can limit depreciation with inflow but does not reduce the Current Account deficit.__*

19.   What are the options for expenditure switching, when a country is facing a persistent current account deficit?   *__allowing the exchange rate to fall; applying tariffs on imports__*

20.   Under what macroeconomic conditions would expenditure reduction be particularly helpful?   *__when there is demand-pull inflation__*

21.   How might supply-side policy help solve a persistent current account deficit?   How long is that likely to take? Compare the speed of supply-side policy to expenditure switching and expenditure reduction.   *supply side policy such as infrastructure or flexible labour markets might increase competiveness of exports and import substitutes, but this will take many years*

22. *   What is the effect of inflation on the current account balance, if the exchange rate is fixed?   *since the exchange rate cannot fall to restore relative costs, there will be a deficit*

23 *h*.   Speculation refers to buying or selling in hopes of profiting by the movement in the price of an asset. For example a speculator might buy land if he or she expects its price to rise soon.

a)   Explain why speculators might sell the currency of a country facing a current account deficit.   *they expect it to fall in value soon*

b)   What effect would this have on the value of the currency?   *added S, depreciates the currency*

Fixed Exchange Rates

24.   Why might a fixed exchange rate allow investors to be more confident of the value of their future profits?   *often they are trying to make back an investment of funds from their own currency, and they care mainly about profits in that currency, so stable rates avoid loss of profit from foreign currency depreciation*

25.   Why might a fixed exchange rate signal that a country is not going to create high inflation?   *inflation discourages exports, making a fixed rate unsustainable, so a commitment to a fixed exchange rate is a commitment to avoid that pressure*

26.   Give three reasons a fixed exchange rate might increase the inflows of foreign investment.   *more stable expected profit; more stable macro policy; lower nominal interest rates; more stable cost of imported inputs such as materials*

27 *h*.   Explain how a common currency amounts to a fixed exchange rate. What is the exchange rate between the value of Florida's currency and the value of California's currency?   *Since the currency of one is the same as the other, they always remain 1 to 1*

28.**   If a region, sharing a common currency with many other regions, experiences a decline in demand for a major export of that region, such as movies from Mumbai ("Bollywood"), what is likely to happen to the value of factors of production such as land and labour in that region?   *labour and land become cheaper as demand declines, attracting new industry*

29.   When exports fall, what is the response if the country has its own currency, as Britain does, rather than sharing a currency with other regions, as Greece does? *depreciation in the first case; loss of demand for labour and land in the second*

30 *b*.   If a country with a flexible exchange rate experiences a fall in its exports, does the resulting fall in the exchange rate make its citizens better off or worse off? Explain. Why might it still prefer this to other outcomes which would be likely to occur instead if its exchange rate was fixed? *__cost-push inflation results, making the country worse off; however, conditions of falling wages and land prices cause unemployment and debt bankruptcies, so depreciation might be better*

EVALUATION   QUESTIONS (Balance of Payments)

31.   Evaluate the options (expenditure reduction and expenditure switching) for dealing with a current account deficit. To what extent does your answer depend on the cause of the deficit? What else might it depend on? *__Expenditure reduction: tight monetary or a contractionary fiscal policy to reduce Y which reduces M: slows economy, can cause unemployment and lost real income; expenditure switching: tariffs usually violate WTO treaty, distort resource allocation with welfare loss, but in times of unemployment may save jobs; depreciation raises import prices and may have to be severe and prolonged if imports and exports are price-inelastic, but may improve competitiveness and create employment. If the deficit is due to inflation expenditure switching by depreciation will probably be needed, but also expenditure reduction will be relatively painless, while if it is due to export loss then a painful adjustment would be made worse by expenditure reduction, so switching should be the option unless PEDm and PEDx are low in the long run. In a manufacturing economy depreciation is almost always the best option, while for commodity exports the depreciation would matter very little.*

32.   Evaluate the use of fixed exchange rates as opposed to flexible exchange rates. How might your evaluation depend on the types of exports the country depends on? The types of goods and services imported? *__Fixed exchange rates offer lower uncertainty and are a sign of stable policy, so foreign investment may be encouraged to enter. However they are subject to speculative attack if exports are shocked or inflation builds up, and they severely limit monetary policy freedom. Flexible exchange rates are usually less painful for adjustment to export shocks, but for commodity export economies they may not help adjustment. If imports are mostly unnecessary luxuries a flexible exchange rate amounts to belt tightening, but if they are necessities the added cost may be painful.*

33*.   Use the term "managed float" to mean that the central bank announces a range of acceptable exchange rates and only intervenes when the rate approaches one edge or the other of the range. It may announce future movement of the range.

a) Does a "managed float" produce any of the benefits associated with a fixed exchange rate? *Predictability and stable policy are still achieved, though to a lesser extent (but may avoid conditions for speculative attacks).*

b) Does a "managed float" produce any of the benefits associated with a floating exchange rate?

A managed float commonly anticipates the effects of changes in competitiveness and moves the exchange rate toward the forecasted level over time, and therefore also allows more freedom with monetary policy.

c) Evaluate the use of a managed float relative to the two un-mixed options.

A managed float probably provides the best of each, especially since fixed exchange rates are often subject to so much pressure they eventually have to change in large jumps.

25 ECONOMIC INTEGRATION

1.   Match these terms to their definitions at right.

_i_____Trading bloc   a. adoption of the same tariffs on each good by all members

_g_   Re-export   b. shift from importing from outside country to a member

_c_   Currency area   c. country group with a single common currency

_d_____Common market   d. FTA with free movement of finance and labour

_h_   Free Trade Area (FTA)   e. rules on how much of a product must be made in the bloc

_a_   Common external tariff   f. bloc with unified economic policies

_f_   Economic union   g. exporting a good which was first imported

_e_   Country-of-origin rules   h. country group with no barriers on imports from members

_j_   Customs union   i. group of countries encouraging trade within the group

_b_   Trade diversion   j. countries all using the same tariffs on imports

2 *h.*   The re-export problem involves shipping a product into a Free Trade Area member country with
low   tariffs, then further exporting it tariff free to another member with   _high_   tariffs.

3 *h.*   The re-export problem can be solved either by use of   _country-of-origin_ rules, so that
products made outside the area do not have zero tariffs, or by adopting a   _common external tariff_.

4.   Arrange the levels of integration (c, d, f, h, j) in order of increasing integration.

  h (FTA)

  j (customs union)

  d (common market)

  f (economic union)

  c (currency area)

5.   Besides the EU, free trade areas in the world today include all of these EXCEPT

   A.   *the Indian Ocean Free Trade Area*

   B.   the China-ASEAN Free Trade Area

   C.   Mercosur

   D.   the North American Free Trade Area

6 b.   Trade creation always (*increases*/decreases) economic welfare of a country because it removes some of the effect of a tariff, when reducing tariffs due to a customs union, for example.

7 b.   Trade diversion refers to a shift from importing from a lower-cost source outside the trading bloc, to a tariff-free but higher-cost source inside the group. This could happen, for example, when a country joins a customs union and must raise its tariff on the outside country to harmonize with the other members. For example, suppose the UK had no tariff on Brazilian shoes which cost €30 per pair, but then joins a customs union with Europe. Explain why this could cause it to buy from Italy at €40 per pair. How high would the new tariff need to be, to cause this to happen?   *A tariff above 33 percent on Brazilian would mean Italian shoes are cheaper*

8.   In the graph below, the example above is illustrated. The UK has put a tariff on Brazilian shoes, which cost €30 per pair without the tariff, and so begins to buy Italian shoes at the higher price of €40.

A.   Why is there no tariff revenue at the higher price?   *no tariff on Italian shoes*

B.   Compare the lost Consumer Surplus to the increased Producer Surplus. Which areas show the difference?   *-CS is CdEf, +PS is C, difference is dEf.*

C.   Why is there increased Producer Surplus in the UK shoe industry? *locals see P rise*

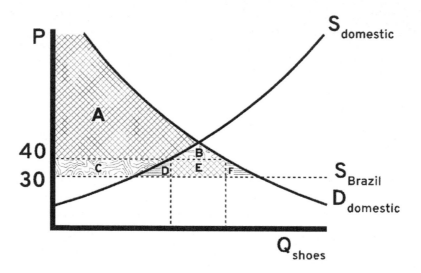

9 *b*.   Is the United States a currency area? Explain.   *no, a single country, but similar effects*

10.   Name two countries that are part of the EU but do not use the euro as their currency.   *the UK, Sweden, Poland, Czech Rep, Romania, etc*

11.   What is the WTO?   *the international organization to foster world trade: organizes negotiation to reduce barriers, administers disputes, and reviews policies of members*

12.   Which of the following is not among the guiding principles of the WTO?

    A.   Treatment of goods is to be the same regardless of what outside country they come from.

    B.   New agreements which modify the old commitments must be unanimous.

    C.   Enforcement of a treaty violation consists of an equivalent retaliatory tariff.

    D.   Countries must continue lowering their tariffs over time, when others lower theirs.

26 TERMS OF TRADE (higher only)

1. The terms of trade represent the value of **_exports_** relative to the value of **_imports_**. The actual calculation uses a **_price index_** for each, expressed in external (world) prices (so a small country cannot improve it by raising internal prices with a tariff, for example).

2. Which of the following gives the formula for the Terms of Trade?
   A. (PEDx/PEDm)
   B. **_Px/Pm_**
   C. Pm/Px
   D. PEDm-PEDx

3. A Terms of Trade value of 1.1 (approximation based on 115 and 104.5) would mean
   A. Exports prices are up about 10 percent more than import prices, since the base year.
   B. Export prices are higher, relative to import prices, since the base year.
   C. Exports will buy about 10 percent more imports per unit, on average, than in the base year.
   D. **_All of the above._**

4. A rise in the Terms of Trade means, all other things equal, the country
   A. Is worse off.
   B. **_Can afford more imports._**
   C. Is losing export sales to its competitors.
   D. All of the above.

5. Exporters of primary commodities generally experience a (rise _/ decline_) in their terms of trade, on average, over time.

6. The trend in primary commodity terms of trade is caused by all of the following except:
   A. Low Income Elasticity of Demand (YED) for primary commodities.
   B. **_A higher rate of growth in LEDC income than in MDC income_**
   C. The ability to use substitutes for commodities which get more expensive.
   D. Invention of alternatives to commodities which get more expensive.

7. Examples of primary commodities do NOT include:

   A.   Petroleum.

   B.   Coffee.

   C.   *Hydroelectric power.*

   D.   Animal hides.

8. Suppose a country imports significant amounts of oil. All other things equal, what is the effect of a fall in oil prices on the Terms of Trade? Use the definition to demonstrate.
   Better TOT. In Px/Pm, the import price index Pm would fall, increasing the ratio

9. Often, but not always, a country's Terms of Trade will change in the same direction as its exchange rate.

   a.   Show that a fall in demand for a country's exports will cause both measures (TOT and ER) to fall.   ***Px falls, so TOT fall, and PxQx falls, so exchange rate depreciates***

   b.   Explain how a rise in the Terms of Trade could result in a decline in quantity of exports. ***If Px rises due to world supply, Qx might fall***

   c.   How could such a decline cause a fall in the exchange rate?   ***if PxQx falls due to high PEDx, the demand for the currency will fall***

   d.   Does a high PED for exports make this more likely or less?   ***required***

10. ** The following PPC diagram is a typical illustration of a rise in the Terms of Trade of a country. Using examples, show that the change in the slope of its trade line (ability to trade its export, Apples, for its import, Bananas) illustrates a rise in the price of exports relative to imports. *A given trade of A (the triangles) buys more B after the rise. The P(A) increased from about 2/3 of the P(B) (3A trade for 2B) to about 2 P(B) (3A for 6B*

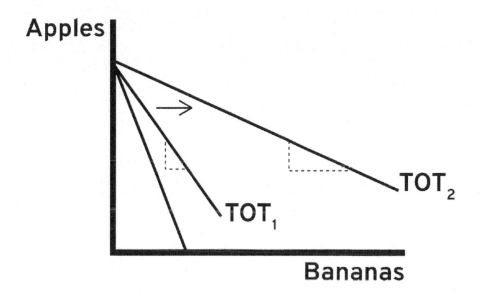

27 DEVELOPMENT

Cause and effects of development.

The meaning and measurement of economic development

1. The concept of standard of living most closely corresponds to which of the following?
A.   Happiness
B.   *Ability to get needs met*
C.   Productivity
D.   Amount of merit goods consumed
Explain **B**   *better captures overall consumption idea; A is next best*

2. The three dimensions of the Human Development Index (HDI) do NOT include:
A.   *level of technology*
B.   GNI per capita
C.   health of the population
D.   extent of education
Explain_A   *B, C and D are the main dimensions*

3. Which of these is included in the current HDI calculation?
A.   primary school enrolment rate
B.   share of population with internet access
C.   infant mortality rate
D.   *average years of finished schooling*
Explain **D**.

4. Many countries with a better ranking on the HDI than on per capita GDP are former communist countries. Explain why a communist country would tend to have a high HDI for its GDP per capita.
Explain   *Communism emphasizes meeting needs of all; system does not encourage innovation and efficiency of resource use, so GDP somewhat low.*

5. Many countries with a better per capita GDP ranking than HDI are oil exporters. Explain at least two reasons why a country exporting oil would have a high GDP per capita relative to its standard of living.
Explain   *inequality; corruption; GDP reflects resources of land rather than productivity of people*

6. Why does more unequal income usually mean more people will be in absolute poverty?
Explain   *More people further below the average (implied by inequality) will mean more whose income is below the poverty line*

7 . What reasons can you give why relative poverty is a problem, aside from possible impact on absolute poverty?
Explain   *People who feel much poorer than others around them feel alienated: mental illness or crime can result; low self-image reduces learning in school*

8. Explain why education both creates higher incomes and results from higher income.
Explain   *With more education the worker is more productive and probably earns more; higher earning parents hope for good education for their children*

9. Explain for health why it also both results from higher income and allows creation of more income.
Explain   *People prefer to be able to afford better health; Sick people have lower productivity*

10. Use a Production Possibility Curve diagram to illustrate the difference between development and economic growth (use Merit Goods on one axis and Consumer Goods on the other).

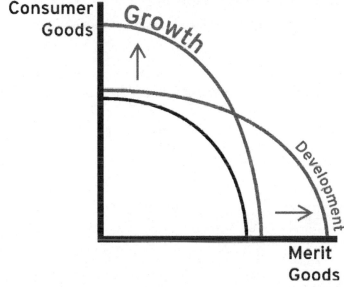

11. The Purchasing Power Parity (PPP) correction replaces _*exchange rates ("atlas method")*
as a method of converting from amounts in a given currency to amounts in dollars. It uses the ratio of local cost to U.S. cost for   *a basket of goods and services.*

12*. The PPP correction gives an improved picture of relative purchasing power because <u>***non-traded***</u> goods and services, such as electricity, haircuts and cement, can vary widely in cost between countries.

13. What happens to the mix of primary, secondary and tertiary sector production as industrialization occurs? Explain this in terms of the growth of productivity, as well as income elasticities of demand (YED).   *primary sector: smaller share, secondary sector: larger share as factories are built, agriculture more productive frees resources for 2d; tertiary a slowly rising share at first as people can afford more services, then dominates.*

Higher productivity comes mainly from machinery during industrialization, then mainly from education. YED for food and fibre (1st) is low, so higher incomes are spent first on cars and appliances (2d), then at higher levels, on school, medical care, travel, etc. (3rd) _

14.* Explain, with examples, the role of the secondary sector in making the primary sector more productive. *Tractors and chemicals are secondary sector output, these make farm yields higher*

15. Give some examples of countries with high Gini coefficients (and the approximate coefficient) and some with low Gini coefficients (with an approximate number*). Botswana (.60), Brazil (.50-.55), Denmark (.25-.30), Australia (.35) (source: World Bank)*

16. Which of the following policies would be least likely to make incomes more equal?

A.   *Shifting from direct taxes to indirect taxes*
B.   Land redistribution from landlords to tenant farmers
C.   Progressive income taxes
D.   Benefits such as education provided to all by the government

17. Why do policies to equalize income usually reduce incentives to produce more output? Evaluate to what extent this is true for the policy of providing sufficient nutrition and for providing basic health care to everyone in a society. *take from high earners, give to low earners = less incentive to achieve; providing food and health care may reduce desperation, so reduce incentive, but likely to make achievement more possible, (ending poverty traps) which is likely to matter more than incentives.*

Factors contributing to development

18. Show the effect of additions to the factors of production, such as more labour, education or physical capital, on a PPC and on a LRAS curve.

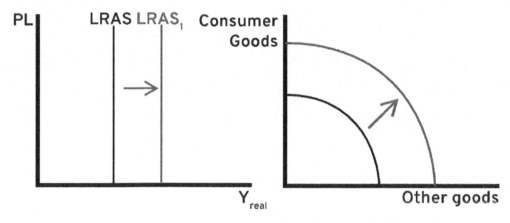

19. Give an example of an addition to physical capital which makes a country more productive.
    infrastructure such as railroad or port

20. Which of the following explains why education might be considered "human capital"?

   A   *Education takes current resources to produce, and can be used to produce other things*
   B   Education allows the student to earn more income in the future by getting better jobs
   C   Education is needed for proper direction of the society
   D   Education is provided by parents to help their children

Explain__A   *based on definition of capital*

21.* The raw material of education is student's time. Which has a lower opportunity cost: student's time in industrialized countries, or students' time in developed countries (measured in equivalent monetary value)?   *in LEDCs*

Explain   *students would earn less in LEDCs if they work instead of studying*

22. Which of the following is an example of "improving the quality of factors of production"?

   A.   Accumulating more physical capital per worker
   B.   Training more entrepreneurs in small business methods
   C.   Building infrastructure
   D.   *Adopting machinery with lower error rates than the machines it replaces*

Explain__**D**   *is clearest, but B could mean "more training" rather than "more entrepreneurs"*

23. Which of the following geographical factors is NOT generally considered an asset which contributes to development?

    A.   beautiful beaches
    B.   a temperate climate
    C.   *being an island*
    D.   a coastline

Explain_**C**   *islands can only trade by sea, but land trade is often very helpful*

24. Which of the following cultural factors is NOT generally considered an asset which contributes to development?

    A.   *cultural diversity within the country*
    B.   respect for authorities
    C.   a tradition of successful merchants
    D.   expectation that everyone will prosper

Explain_**A** *often leads to conflict and discrimination, (but recent research shows it can be beneficial if managed)*

25. Explain why experience with banking makes an economy more able to develop.

    Banks can better judge where to allocate scarce finance to create higher growth

26. Which of the following is likely to damage banking skills in an economy?

A.   speculation in the stock market
B.   a high rate of savings by the people
C.   a high rate of borrowing by the people
D.   *government requiring banks to lend to particular industries*

Explain D*:*   *this used to be common practice*

27. Explain why a strong court system makes an economy more able to develop. Give an example showing why business investment would benefit from enforceable contracts. Give an example showing why corruption might slow down business investment.   *transparent and consistent decisions allow better planning, which is crucial for investment; for example, a contract for a joint venture must be able to survive changes in prices, perceived risk, etc.,; contracts based on bribes or connections may lead to excess cost or poor quality for infrastructure, and businesses may feel that success will just draw more demands by officials to give bribes.*

28. Which of the following is NOT a part of a strong court system?

A.   honest law enforcement
B.   legal training of judges
C.   limits on government's ability to overrule property rights

D.   *different treatment for multinationals and local firms*
Explain_D__Arbitrary targeting of MNCs reduces direct investment.

29. Which of the following is an example of what is meant by "transparency" in government?

   A.   Copying of digital music and video is not allowed
   B.   The police treat all ethnic groups the same
   C.   ***Reasons for awarding a government contract are clear***
   D.   Government can be removed by election
Explain_C   *without verifiable reasons, bribes are likely to win the contract*

30. Explain why government transparency is likely to encourage business investment.

   businesses know rewards are more likely to follow strong performance, not connections

Barriers to development

31. Explain, using a simple diagram, the concept of a poverty trap or poverty cycle. Use the example of savings rate to explain the stages of the cycle.

When the effects of poverty create conditions which cause poverty, it is a cycle of poverty.   For example when people can't invest, e.g. in education or farm equipment, it holds down their earnings

32. Explain how child labour creates a poverty trap, ***child workers fail to get an education, so they earn less later, and may have to put their children to work***

33. Explain how large family size creates a poverty trap.   ***each child gets less attention, food, medicine, help with schoolwork, etc so they are less productive later***

34. Explain how poor health care can lead to poverty, which can lead to poor health care.

Poor health care leads to long-term damage, causing lower productivity, and can cause lost jobs and lost schooling. If health care is private, poorer families have trouble affording it.

35. Which of the following helps explain why a weak banking sector can contribute to a poverty trap?

    A.   There would be no rich people to save and provide funds
    B.   Foreign corporations would be unable to provide direct investment
    C.   ***Those with savings will find lending to companies too risky***
    D.   A strong banking sector provides microcredit

Explain **C**   *Average savers cannot diversify and have no technical skill to evaluate companies. D is generally false; A and B completely false as implications of weak banking sector.*

36. Explain how corruption holds back both the poor and the corporate sector, in each case contributing to a poverty trap. Explain how higher income in a country helps reduce corruption. *corruption may target the poor because they are vulnerable, pushes poor toward informal sector which loses government protection; corporations are singled out for corruption, esp. if successful, higher income countries can better afford enforcement of transparent methods, and officials have sufficient pay to afford a preference for professional approach.*

37. What is distinctive about informal sector work? How does this reduce income growth? *informal sector work lacks steady relationships and legal protections; both worker and employer are less likely to invest in training.*

38.* Which of the following is least likely to create a social barrier restricting women from full participation in the economy?

    A.   Parents who are unwilling to invest in girls' education
    B.   Social rules against women leaving home unescorted
    C.   Laws allowing only men to own property
    D.   ***Laws restricting reasons for which there may be a divorce***

Explain_D: *effect of easier divorce on women is mixed*

39. Explain several ways that barriers to women will contribute to poverty traps.

lower girls' education means lower capability and aspiration for their children's education; less income opportunity for women reduces opportunity cost of large family, leading to lower capital per worker, women's intelligence may fail to get market reward, women less able to make health and nutrition judgments for family.

40.** Evaluate whether barriers to women's participation matter most for poor families or matters most for those with high incomes, in the context of a developing country.

Hard to say: poor families suffer more from large families and high dependency ratios, and generally from poverty traps. But in rich families the lost productivity may be greater, as more of these women could achieve higher education and high productivity.

41. Which of the following does NOT help understand the reasons why a dual economy (modern sector enclave isolated from traditional or informal sector) reduces the effect of income growth on development?

A.   *The modern sector can hire labour from the traditional sector at low wages*
B.   The modern sector households typically spend on imports rather than buy from the traditional sector
C.   Workers in the traditional sector will have little reason to invest in skills since they will be unable to
    earn high wages working in the modern sector
D.   Traditional workers will not learn socially about practices and principles leading to higher incomes.

Explain   **A***:*   *the others do represent problems of growth in a dual economy*

42. Explain why barriers holding some of society back from development also contribute to income inequality. Apply this to discrimination or dual economies.

usually the ones held back are in lower income groups, so they end up further back.   For example, discrimination in hiring is usually against groups already disadvantaged, and dual economies provide more opportunities to those with education in English, etc.

43. Which of the following does NOT help to understand how limited physical infrastructure acts as a barrier to development?

    A.   Mobile phone service can be used instead of cash
    B.   *Fewer factories mean less employment*
    C.   Ports reduce the cost of a countries exports
    D.   Good roads reduce transport costs

Explain: B: *the others are examples of infrastructure, but not B*

44. Which of the following practices does NOT represent a barrier to development caused by trade practices of outside countries?

    A.   *WTO rules have required reductions in tariffs on one country to apply to all members*
    B.   Richer countries have usually maintained high tariffs on processing of raw materials
    C.   Richer countries often subsidise their agricultural sectors
    D.   WTO disciplines did not include agriculture or clothing, the easiest categories for LDCs to export,

    before clothing was included in 2005.

Explain: A   **A** *is neutral, the others have been barriers to growth*

28 DEVELOPMENT STRATEGY & ISSUES

Inward-looking vs. outward-looking

1. For each of the following policies, tell whether it would be favoured or opposed by an inward-orientated (import substituting industrialisation: ISI) or an outward-orientated strategy (OO), by ticking the appropriate columns. Multiple columns may be ticked for a policy, or even none.

		ISI		OSO	
		Pro	Anti	Pro	Anti
A	encouraging direct foreign investment to come to the country		×	×	
B	tariffs on most manufactured consumer goods.	×			×
C	assistance ("industrial policy") for industries expected to export	×		×	
D	taxes on industry to support basic human needs				
E	promotion of capital goods imports	×		×	

2. Which of the following would be examples of a country which followed ISI and a country which followed OO policies, before 1990?
   A Taiwan followed Import Substitution and Argentina followed Outward Orientation
   B India followed Import Substitution and Egypt followed Outward Orientation
   C *Brazil followed Import Substitution and South Korea followed Outward Orientation*
   D Malaysia followed Import Substitution and Pakistan followed Outward Orientation

3. Which of the following is essentially correct concerning the result of industrialisation strategy?
   A *Outward orientation has succeeded in leading to industrialisation, while import substitution has failed*
   B Outward orientation has failed to lead to industrialisation, while import substitution has succeeded
   C Both outward orientation and import substitution have generally succeeded in bringing industrialisation
   D Neither outward orientation nor import substitution has succeeded in bringing industrialisation

4. Explain why economies of scale in manufacturing helps OO (outward orientation) to succeed, but is likely to cause ISI to fail.   *since OO aims at exporting, the large world market offers potential economies of scale. ISI envisions the local market only for most industry.___*

5. Explain why the infant industry justification for protection might make ISI appealing, despite the contradicting comparative advantage in the near term. Explain why this logic frequently fails to translate into reality, even after many years. *An industry may have high costs initially, so comparative advantage would argue for importing. But experience makes costs fall. Unfortunately, they often did not fall by enough under ISI.*

6. A developing country should borrow money from abroad, in order to pay for an investment, under which of the following conditions?
   A It expects to run a balance of payments surplus due to the investment
   B It cannot attract direct investment by multinationals
   C *The expected growth from the investment is greater than the cost of borrowing*
   D The expected tax revenue from the investment is greater than the cost of borrowing

EVALUATION QUESTIONS   (development strategy & issues)

7. **Diversification:** *Evaluate the strategy of diversification by a Less Economically Developed Country*

Definition :

Diversification is an economic strategy of widening the range of goods and services produced in the economy. In the context of LEDC's this often means expanding into labour-intensive manufacturing rather than remaining dependent on commodity exports.

Reasons for diversification:

- *It avoids long-term decline in commodity terms of trade*
- *Diversification away from primary commodities reduces the impact of dramatic price fluctuations due to low PES and PED [consider using the inelastic S and D diagram]*
- *Strategic choice of industries may take advantage of potential comparative advantage*
- *Import substitution may avoid unnecessary imports*
- *Lack of diversification means risks to a few industries can seriously damage an economy*

Problems with diversification:

- *Specialization according to comparative advantage increases productive efficiency and the overall value of output produced*
- *Specialization according to comparative advantage improves the global allocation of resources*
- *Specialization allows countries to take advantage of economies of scale*
- *Specialization in agriculture may allow farmers to prosper when prices or productivity increase (but much of the profit goes instead to oligopolies processing primary commodities)*
- *The quickest route to diversification is by permitting Multi-National Corporations to invest (FDI). This has its own set of disadvantages, but may be very useful.*

Relevant Diagrams:

- *Diagram showing volatility of agricultural products and possibly buffer stocks*
- *Comparative Advantage diagrams [but these tend to take a lot of time to explain]*
- *Economies of scale*

Evaluation:

If it is not too costly, diversification may be the better option to avoid over-dependence on a single industry, like Finland on Nokia. Diversification from primary products into manufacturing is required to make education effective and bring higher productivity. Within manufacturing, some specialization is necessary in the modern, globalised economy. Tata, the Indian conglomerate is in the tea business as well as the truck and car business.

8. **Strength of Currency**: *Evaluate the possible consequences of the strengthening Euro on the countries which use the euro.*

Definition:

A country's currency is defined as strong or weak relative to another currency, or a basket of currencies. A stronger currency buys more units of other currencies.

Advantages of a strong currency:

- *Imports become cheaper, reducing inflation rates.*
- *Reduces need for high interest rates to support the currency, or contractionary macroeconomic policy in general.*

Problems of a strong currency:

- *EU firms become less competitive abroad and so exports suffer (note this is minor when strong exports caused the appreciation)*
- *Deterioration in the current account balance (again, not a problem if exports cause the rise)*
- *Increased unemployment (many countries have been trying to "export unemployment" with currency depreciation since the 2008 crisis).*

Relevant diagrams:

Currency diagrams: note main risk is if D rises due to financial inflow

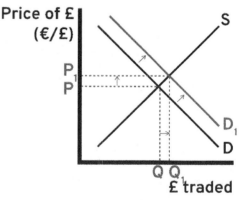

Evaluation: (Development Strategy & Issues)

Countries in the Euro area have had very different experiences in the crisis. Countries that lost many exports, such as Spain and Greece, or had borrowed heavily before the crisis, would have benefitted greatly from a depreciation. In general appreciation is good if it reflects greater competitiveness, and bad if unemployment is high. However, policy to reduce unemployment by depreciation for expenditure switching invites retaliation from other countries.

9.   **Outward orientation**:   *Evaluate the policy of outward orientation, seeking industrialisation by promotion of exports and encouragement of direct foreign investment into the country by multinational corporations.*

Definitions:

- An <u>outward-orientated strategy</u> *of industrialisation relies on exports, openness to the world economy, and promoting inward direct foreign investment to make the transition to widespread manufacturing. This is by contrast with the import-substitution approach which used trade barriers to promote manufacturing of goods which had formerly been imported from the MEDC's.*
- <u>Direct foreign investment</u> *is investment in a foreign country by a multinational company, with a controlling ownership share. By contrast, "portfolio investment" lends or buys shares for the returns, without taking a role in directing a company.*

Advantages of outward orientation:

- *Export industries are likely to be those in which the country has a comparative advantage, so the industrialization has a solid foundation.*
- *Infant industries are more likely to actually become competitive if they know they will lose their support otherwise.*
- *Multinationals (as well as market connections from exporting) bring technology and knowledge of consumer preferences, adding value to the manufacturing sector.*
- *Economies of scale are more likely if selling to the world market than just to the domestic market.*
- *Multinationals usually bring financial capital to invest without the burden of debt on the host country, overcoming a poverty cycle.*
- *Foreign direct investment by MNCs usually provides tax revenue and jobs, and may buy from local suppliers, creating growth in those sectors.*

Problems with outward orientation:

- *Comparative advantage in labour-intensive industries may offer little skill advancement.*
- *Multinationals are often reluctant to share technology or other sources of value.*
- *Multinationals may exploit lax regulation, bargain for tax reduction, or bribe host country officials. Key resources such as water may become unaffordable to the subsistence sector.*
- *Multinationals may drive smaller, less-specialized local producers out of business.*
- *Competing in the world market may require skills beyond those of LEDC entrepreneurs.*
- *Fallacy of composition: opportunity for one or a few exporters may, if too many try it, just reduce prices.*
- *Requirement of "picking winners" has proved difficult for many countries.*

Relevant Diagrams:

- *Comparative advantage.*
- *Economies of scale.*
- *LRAC falling due to experience (learning curve)*

Evaluation:

Countries trying import-substitution strategies ran into lack of economies of scale and isolation from world technological improvements. Trying to resist pressures of Comparative Advantage proved difficult, especially across a broad range of industries all at once. The world market sets a clear goal showing the requirements for being competitive and offering sources and incentives for further technological advancement. Likewise multinationals, despite their potential problems, have been part of rapid modernisation in a large number of countries. Countries need to be ready to manage the dangers if MNCs are encouraged.

10.   **Micro-credit:**   *Evaluate the role of micro-credit as an instrument of economic development .*

Definitions:

- <u>*micro-credit*</u>*: lending in amounts too small for the regular banking sector, usually to households or community groups.*
- <u>*economic development*</u>*: rise in the standard of living of an economy, including aspects of personal empowerment as measured by the HDI.*

Benefits of micro-credit programs

- *Breaking a poverty cycle. Households who are unable to save significant amounts may be unable to invest in small capital such as a sewing machine or carpentry tools which would allow higher productivity and entrepreneurship.*
- *Micro-credit often helps informal sector business which is otherwise excluded from access to modern sector customers.*
- *Many micro-credit programs target women due to irresponsible use of money by despairing husbands.*
- *Many micro-credit programs avoid the need for collateral against loans by using the group to monitor the use of funds and pressure borrowers to keep up their payments.*

Problems with micro-credit programs

- *May lead individuals into debt. Small businesses have a high failure rate and poor households are often one accident away from destitution.*
- *Borrowers use the money for consumption purposes instead of investment which generates a return.*
- *It may not help the extremely poor, who are too poor and unskilled to start a business.*
- *Informal sector businesses still face many barriers such as limited entrepreneurial skills and inability to afford really effective machinery, as well as excessive government regulations and corrupt practices from which they cannot afford legal protection.*
- *Lenders usually do not make a profit. Re-payment rates are significantly lower than for formal sector businesses (which have more of the owner's fortune depending on the success) and can be ruinously low in a recession. Most micro-credit programs have needed further funding from outside donors to continue. Profit is not the driving force in these programs.*

Diagram: *Poverty Cycle*

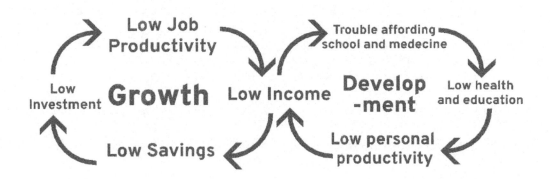

Evaluation:

Micro-credit seems to break poverty cycles which particularly affect the poor segments of LEDC's. The difficulties it faces are the same ones which prevent the markets from providing for opportunities. So, despite limitations, these programs appear to be a good use of outside funding, but require accountability to avoid being treated as "free money".

11.   **Debt:**   *Evaluate the wisdom of LEDC governments borrowing from abroad to finance investment in their economy.*

Definitions:

- *Debt refers to money owed due to past borrowing. If there is insufficient domestic savings, the alternative to borrowing may be direct investment by multinationals, for an LEDC.*
- *Debt service refers to payments needed per period of time to maintain good standing with the creditor. Often this is taken to be simply paying the interest due. (amortisation of the debt = interest + some portion of the principal)*

Advantages of borrowing:

- *If the investment is likely to be highly profitable, borrowing allows the investing country to keep most of these profits.*
- *Borrowing for very long terms is often available from, for example, the World Bank and other multilateral development banks.*
- *Since saving is difficult for the poor, borrowing from abroad is a way of providing finance for investment and growth.*

Problems of borrowing:

- *Risk falls on the borrower. If economic conditions deteriorate, or the market becomes too competitive in industries of the country's exports, it may become very difficult to make payments on the debt. If they cannot make payments some debt may be forgiven, but the cost of borrowing any further amounts may become very high. Also, "vulture" funds have specialized in "holding up" negotiations for forgiveness to extract higher repayment.*
- *A debt overhang, in which the country owes more than it can repay and the old debt therefore accumulates faster than the economy grows, will also discourage private investment. This is because future growth will go disproportionately to trying to meet debt obligations, through taxes, reduced infrastructure or reduced public services.*
- *Irresponsible leaders may be tempted to borrow for immediate political benefit without a basis for knowing the debt can be repaid.*
- *Unlike direct investment, debt brings finance without bringing expertise and proven skill.*

Diagrams: *possibly poverty cycle (borrowing can replace missing savings)*

Evaluation: **Borrowing from abroad has been used effectively by many LEDC's. It requires careful planning to avoid over-indebtedness and maintain some ability to respond to shocks, but offers the chance to keep the rewards from positive results of investment. In recent decades most countries have opted for direct investment if possible, since skills are included.**

12. **Aid vs. Trade.** *Compare and contrast the use of aid with the use of trade to bring development in LEDCs.*

Definitions:

- *Aid (development assistance): transferring resources to assist with the process of economic growth and development.*
- *Humanitarian aid: aid sent to deal with famine, refugees or other crises.*
- *Technical assistance: hiring expertise to train or solve problems of the LEDC.*
- *Bilateral assistance: from one country to another directly.*
- *Multilateral assistance: aid via the UN or development banks e.g. World Bank.*
- *Tied aid: aid which must be used to buy specific goods, such as earth-moving equipment, usually to benefit business in the assisting economy.*
- *Fair trade: systems to provide more favourable terms for LEDC suppliers, usually with verification of better prices, proper labour standards and environmental sustainability.*

Benefits of aid:

- *Resources are transferred, possibly overcoming a poverty cycle, often without debt.*
- *Multilateral assistance follows careful evaluation to be confident the investment will be helpful.*
- *Tied aid and other political abuses can be avoided using multilateral assistance.*
- *In recent decades aid has emphasized poverty reduction, increasing the chance of breaking poverty cycles. Aid can bypass social exclusion, such as due to caste or gender or ethnic barriers.*
- *NGO (non-governmental organisation) aid can tap private charity, develop specialized expertise, and address politically inconvenient issues such as the environment.*

Benefits of trade:

- *Overall efficiency of world resource use is improved when trade barriers are reduced.*
- *Reduced barriers give opportunities and incentive for the LEDC to become more skilful and competent.*
- *Integration into world trade reduces war, and WTO system fosters rule of law.*
- *Fair trade plans can limit exploitation by multinationals processing primary commodities.*
- *Until 1995, trade agreements emphasised reducing barriers against manufactures, but since 1995 the WTO has reduced barriers in clothing and agriculture, in which LEDC's often have comparative advantages.*
- *Reduced barriers to LEDC exports tend to increase demand for labour, since these tend to be labour-intensive industries. Wages have risen dramatically since 1995, and trade has lifted more than a billion people out of severe poverty.*

However:

- *Benefits of globalization tend to go disproportionately to capital-intensive industries, large corporations, and high-skilled workers, as rapid technological gains reduces competition.*
- *Social barriers (e.g. language, caste) can prevent benefits from reaching the very poor.*
- *Growth will not target the poor even though it may include them.*

Diagrams:

- *Subsidy effects on agriculture in MEDC's.*
- *Poverty cycle.*

Evaluation:

The two approaches can be complementary. Reducing trade barriers allows markets to benefit more people, while aid allows governments to target needs which may be neglected by markets (merit goods). Multilateral assistance avoids distorting the aid process for political goals. The debate has moved on from (Aid versus Trade) to (Aid and Trade) and now (Aid for trade) is the latest thinking in this area.

---

13. **Interventionism vs. Market-oriented Policy.** *Compare and contrast interventionist with market-oriented approaches to economic development.*

Definitions:

Economic development: increase in the well-being or standard of living as measured by the rise in the (HDI).

Interventionist Government Policies:

- *Providing education and access to basic health care.*
  Creating physical infrastructure.
- *Providing technical advice and public good information.*
- *Redistributing wealth, income or resources such as land.*

- *Targeting particular industries for protection from imports and subsidised credit, machinery or other resources.*

Market Oriented (similar to Supply Side) Policies:

- *Liberalisation: Remove distortions to the economy such as rationed foreign exchange (with over-valued currency, this can make imports of capital goods cheaper), directed lending (banks told which industries to lend to), and import-substitution tariffs or quotas. Prices allowed to reflect scarcity.*

- *Privatisation of State-Owned Enterprises including steel, telecommunications, rail, mining, and sometimes electric power and water.*
- *Remove costly subsidies on fuel, fertilizer, water, electric power and transport.*
- *Promote public-private partnerships, such as private-sector building of infrastructure to be paid for by user fees.*
- *Improve transparency and accountability in government, to reduce corruption.*
- *Deregulation: Reduce burdensome regulations, make it easy to start new businesses.*
- *Labour Market Reform: remove minimum wage regulations, dilute powers of unions and collective wage bargaining.*
- *Improve property rights, including land-ownership title and timely enforcement of contracts.*

Advantages of interventionist policies:

- *Poverty cycles may otherwise prevent development for a large segment of the population.*
- *Government may need to take the lead in reaching across social barriers to include all parts of the economy in development.*
- *Land reform often takes land from low-productivity absentee landlords to give to motivated farmers.*
- *Targeted industrial policy can overcome barriers to investment created by risks the private sector is reluctant to take, or by lack of key sectors such as fertilizer, steel or telecommunications.*

However:

- *Experience shows government is often no better than the private sector at finding industries worth developing.*
- *Even education and health care have to pay attention to cost, to allocate scarce resources effectively.*
- *Benefits to the poor are not a sufficient justification, and many subsidies have gone mainly to the urban residents who are comparatively well off.*

Advantages of market-oriented policies:

- *Market development now includes foreign technical expertise, which has been effective with public-private partnerships and privatisations, for example.*
- *Subsidies and pro-poor services are often poorly targeted or poorly administered, and private sector incentives can improve effectiveness dramatically.*
- *Many regulations serve no useful purpose but have been created or maintained to increase bribery income for public officials.*
- *Government transparency will improve the allocation of resources by focusing businesses on actual productivity rather than seeking favours and protection by the government.*

However:

- *Privatisation has also been a source of corruption, and awarding monopolies creates temptation.*
- *"Trickle down" approaches may benefit the modern sector without creating much benefit in the countryside or the urban informal sector.*

Relevant Diagrams:

- *Poverty Cycle Diagram*
- *Increase in LRAS or PPC,*
- *Difference between growth and development using PPC*

Evaluation:

The different approaches can be used together to some extent. Relative value and importance depends on conditions in the economy. If there are high social barriers between modern and traditional sectors, more government services and subsidies may be needed. If politics is relatively calm and stable, public-private partnerships are more likely to succeed and have terms favourable to users. If the private sector is neglecting obvious important opportunities, government may be in a position to intervene successfully with key infrastructure or targeted resources.

In general one of the most helpful things governments in LEDCs can do is manage themselves, limiting corruption and operating fairly. When the case for a type of intervention is weak, these governments should avoid it, allowing more effectiveness in pursuing the goals they have already.

14.   Evaluate China's export-oriented growth and development strategy:

Expanding on question: *China has used intervention in currency markets (primarily purchase of foreign currency reserves and lending to foreign governments with earnings from exports) to hold down the value of the Yuan, thus creating a very large trade surplus. (A regular diagram of market for the Yuan, with E below equilibrium or a capital outflow shifting S to the right). Its export expansion allowed it to move more than 100 million workers into the modern sector and raise wages by between 10 times and 50 times in 20 years. Besides holding down the Yuan, China encouraged vast amounts of foreign direct investment, especially from other East Asian countries, and negotiated entry into the WTO. Advocates argue the WTO accession has forced the ruling Communist Party to abide by the rule of law in dealing with foreign producers and multinational investors.*

Evaluation:

- *The Chinese export expansion has been unquestionably successful, leading to unprecedented rates of economic growth and wage increases. Since many of the workers came from unproductive jobs in the state heavy industry sector or the countryside, the opportunity cost of resources for expansion has been remarkably low.*
- *Inequality has grown dramatically, but this is entirely due to disproportionate growth in coastal and export-orientated regions, and absolute poverty has declined dramatically. (Lorenz diagram could be used).*
- *After the crisis of 2008, Western nations made it clear to China that it would have to turn to more growth of internal demand, as the scope for added exports was becoming limited. This was partly due to a sense that its policy of a weak Yuan represented unfair competition, but since labour and land have become much more expensive in Yuan terms, this "unfair competition" has clearly not been the major factor in its expansion. It has managed to change strategies rather effectively, although exports are still encouraged. (An AS/AD diagram showing a decline in X but an increase in C and G could be used).*
- *As growth rates have declined, capital investment has had to decline as well. Since Chinese economic data are politically distorted it is difficult to tell whether it is managing this reduction effectively.*

Printed in Great Britain
by Amazon